COMMAND HISTORY
SEVENTH AMPHIBIOUS FORCE

10 JANUARY 1943 -- 23 DECEMBER 1945

AUSTRALIA MOROTAI

NEW GUINEA PHILIPPINES

BISMARCK ARCHIPELAGO BORNEO

KOREA NORTH CHINA

Published by Books Express Publishing
Copyright © Books Express, 2011
ISBN 978-1-780391-94-6

Books Express publications are available from all good retail and online booksellers. For publishing proposals and direct ordering please contact us at: info@books-express.com

SEVENTH AMPHIBIOUS FORCE

COMMAND HISTORY

10 January 1943 - 23 December 1945

VICE ADMIRAL DANIEL E. BARBEY, U.S. Navy, Commander Amphibious Force, Southwest Pacific and Commander SEVENTH Amphibious Force from 10 January 1943 to 23 December 1945 which included the entire period of existence of these Commands.

COMMAND HISTORY

SEVENTH AMPHIBIOUS FORCE

CONTENTS

	Page
FOREWORD	
PART I - Narrative Summary	I - 1
PART II - Command, Staff Organization and Administration	
(a) Staff Organization and History	II - 1
(b) Amphibious Training of Ground Forces by SEVENTH Amphibious Force	II - 10
(c) Special Problems, Functions and Organizations	
1. Echelon Movement of Amphibious Shipping	II - 27
2. Beach Parties	II - 31
3. Engineer Special Brigades (Shore Parties)	II - 39
4. Landing Craft Control Officers - SEVENTH Amphibious Force Representatives	II - 46
5. Assignment of Australian and British Ships	II - 48
(d) Special Operations	
1. Minesweeping - Philippines and Borneo	II - 51
2. Movement of Service Units, Supplies and Equipment from Rear to Forward Bases	II - 57
(e) Medical Services and Casualty Care	II - 61
(f) Air Support Operations	II - 80
(g) Administrative Command	II - 86

ANNEXES (A) Chart of the Pacific Area showing operations by the SEVENTH Amphibious Force

           (B) Designation of Operation Plans and Operation Orders for Major Amphibious Operations

           (C) Charts of Task Organization of Forces

(D) List of Naval Commanders, Landing Force Commanders and Major Landing Units

(E) Table and Chart Showing Troops and Cargo Transported in Major Assault Operations

(F) Chart Showing Number and Displacement Tonnage of Amphibious and Supporting Ships Employed in Major Operations

(G) Miscellaneous Data

(H) List of Code Names used to designate Operations, Geographical Locations and Task Forces in the Southwest Pacific Area

ILLUSTRATIONS   Page

    Vice Admiral DANIEL E. BARBEY, USN   Frontispiece

    Rear Admiral WILLIAM M. FECHTELER, USN,
        Deputy Commander and first Commander
        Amphibious Group Eight   I - 18

    Vice Admiral BARBEY with Rear Admiral ARTHUR
        D. STRUBLE, USN, Commander Amphibious
        Group Nine and Rear Admiral WILLIAM M.
        FECHTELER, USN, Commander Amphibious
        Group Eight   II - 25

    Vice Admiral BARBEY with Rear Admiral FORREST
        B. ROYAL, USN, Commander Amphibious Group
        Six   II - 50

    Commodore RAY TARBUCK, Chief of Staff and Rear
        Admiral ALBERT G. NOBLE, USN, Former Chief
        of Staff and later Commander Amphibious Group
        Eight   II - 78

PART I

NARRATIVE HISTORY

SEVENTH AMPHIBIOUS FORCE

10 January 1943 - 23 December 1945

FOREWORD

For almost three years, the SEVENTH Amphibious Force trained its personnel, fought a determined enemy, and carried Allied troops forward with accelerating pace and swelling power. Its strength and its success derived from the qualities of the individuals who composed it--foresight, courage, indefatigable energy, resourceful "know-how", the will to endure danger and suffering and hardship.

I am tremendously proud of the performance of the officers and men of the SEVENTH Amphibious Force, and, that others may more fully share my pride in their accomplishments, I hope that a more complete history some day will be written.

We have collected here the material from which the future historian may frame an outline for a more finished and detailed work. Our purpose has been to record significant incidents and conditions, dates and statistics, methods and opinions of participants, while they are fresh in the minds of those who were a part of the SEVENTH Amphibious Force.

Supplements to this Command History will deal separately with the amphibious phases of the various campaigns in which the SEVENTH Amphibious Force took part.

DANIEL E. BARBEY,
Vice Admiral, U. S. Navy,
Commander Seventh Amphibious Force.

U.S.S. ESTES
SHANGHAI, CHINA
23 December 1945

COMMAND HISTORY OF THE SEVENTH AMPHIBIOUS FORCE

PART I

NARRATIVE SUMMARY

The SEVENTH Amphibious Force was in existence for less than three years. In that time it participated in every assault landing in the Southwest Pacific Area and took part in the occupation landings following the successful completion of the war. Allied troops were transported and landed in assault on NEW GUINEA, BISMARCK ARCHIPELAGO and the HALMAHERAS, in the major campaigns which regained the PHILIPPINE ISLANDS and the operations which secured control of the SULU ARCHIPELAGO and parts of BORNEO. Preparations were being made for participation in the amphibious assault on JAPAN when the abrupt capitulation of the Japanese changed all plans. The Force thereafter was employed in transporting Army troops to KOREA, Marines to NORTH CHINA, Chinese forces from SOUTH CHINA to ports in NORTH CHINA and in repatriation of the Japanese from KOREA and the CHINA COAST.

Initially the SEVENTH Amphibious Force was known as the Amphibious Force, Southwest Pacific. On 15 December 1942 Rear Admiral Daniel E. Barbey received orders from Commander in Chief, U.S. Fleet, to establish this force and he assumed command on 10 January 1943.

From January 1943 until September 1943, when assault operations commenced, Admiral Barbey was employed:

(1) In the organization of the Amphibious Force, Southwest Pacific.

(2) In the training of amphibious ships arriving from the United States.

(3) In the training of Army Units in amphibious operations.

(4) In the movement of Army, Marine, and Australian units to forward areas in anticipation of future operations.

Subsequent operations of the SEVENTH Amphibious Force to the time of the Japanese surrender can be divided into three general phases:

(1) September 1943 - September 1944 - Amphibious landings on the Eastern and Northern Coast of New Guinea, in New Britain, Admiralty Islands, and at Morotai in the Halmaheras.

(2) October 1944 - February 1945 - Amphibious landings at Leyte, Mindoro, Lingayen and supporting operations in Luzon culminating in the Bataan-Corregidor landings on 15-16 February 1945.

(3) February 1945 - July 1945 - Amphibious landings together with extensive minesweeping operations in the Central and Southern Philippines, Sulu Archipelago, and Borneo.

ORGANIZATION AND TRAINING

The entire strategic concept of the military campaign to drive the Japanese from their positions in the Southwest Pacific Area was predicated on amphibious operations. When he assumed command of the Amphibious Force, Southwest Pacific - a force in name only - in January 1943, Admiral Barbey had three immediate problems:

(1) Creation of an amphibious force
(2) Training of amphibious ships
(3) Training of army units

CREATION OF AN AMPHIBIOUS FORCE

LCTs and smaller craft began to arrive in the Southwest Pacific Area in December 1942 as part of a program to establish a large pool of LCTs, LCMs, and LCVs or LCPs primarily for use in training Army troops. The LCTs were shipped in three sections and assembled at Sydney, after which they were assigned with other landing craft to the amphibious training establishments at Port Sydney, New South Wales (about sixty miles below Sydney), and Toorbul, Queensland (about fifty miles north of Brisbane). Three flotillas of LCTs and landing craft for the units established at the various training centers were eventually obtained under the program.

The Commander in Chief, U.S. Fleet assigned LST Flotilla Seven to the Amphibious Force, Southwest Pacific and the ships, many carrying LCTs, arrived at intervals between April and July 1943. The flotilla consisted of two groups of LSTs built on the west coast, and one group, manned by Coast Guard personnel, which had participated in the North African campaign.

The ships of LCI Flotilla Seven, also assigned to the Southwest Pacific Force, commenced to arrive in April 1943.

No APAs or AKAs were originally assigned to the Amphibious Force, Southwest Pacific, because of the pressing need for transports in other war theatres. Because of the need for at least one ship of each type for troop training, the HENRY T. ALLEN (APA 15) and the ALGORAB (AKA 8) were assigned to the force in 1943, and reported at Sydney, the former in March and the latter in September. The TITANIA (AKA 13) replaced the ALGORAB in June 1944. Two other ships, the BLUE RIDGE (AGC 2) and CARTER HALL (LSD 3) reported for duty in December 1943.

To supplement the Amphibious Force, the Australian Government provided three passenger ships which had previously been used as merchant cruisers, to be converted into Landing Ships, Infantry (LSI), the British counterpart of APAs. The conversion of the MANOORA was completed in February 1943, the WESTRALIA in June and the KANIMBLA in September, and each immediately joined the force. These three LSIs plus the HENRY T. ALLEN and the TITANIA served with the SEVENTH Amphibious Force until the end of the war.

The RIGEL (AR 11) was assigned to the Seventh Amphibious Force, to provide repair and maintenance facilities for the ships of the force. Subsequently two LSTs, each with a Landing Craft Maintenance Unit embarked, augmented the maintenance facilities for a force that was constantly expanding and dispersed over a wide area. The facilities in these LSTs were increased until eventually they were reclassified as ARLs, and in December 1943 a third ARL joined the force. All these repair facilities remained under the operational control of Commander SEVENTH Amphibious Force until 30 June 1944 when Commander SEVENTH Fleet directed their transfer to Service Force, SEVENTH Fleet.

Except for a very short use of the HENRY T. ALLEN in March 1943, Commander SEVENTH Amphibious Force was without a flagship until June 1943 when he and part of his staff moved aboard the RIGEL. During the early assault operations, Commander SEVENTH Amphibious Force, with a small operational staff, used the CONYNGHAM (DD 371) as his flagship, while the rest of the staff remained in the RIGEL. When the BLUE RIDGE (AGC 2) arrived in the Southwest Pacific in December 1943, she became the force flagship and continued in that capacity until June 1945 when she returned to Pearl Harbor for overhaul and major alterations.

TRAINING OF AMPHIBIOUS SHIPS

In the early period of activity in the Southwest Pacific Area, no organized training program for ships and landing craft similar to those of the Atlantic and Pacific Training Commands could be adopted. Ships had to be constantly engaged in troop training or in moving Army units to forward areas in preparation for imminent amphibious operations. However, the operations for occupation of Woodlark and Kiriwina Islands in June 1943 revealed the definite need for ship training, and as a result, an intensive ship training program was carried out in the Townsville-Cairns area of Australia prior to the first assault landing at Lae in September 1943.

TRAINING OF ARMY UNITS

Commander SEVENTH Amphibious Force organized and established an Amphibious Training Command for troop training at Port Stephens on 1 March 1943. This command absorbed the existing facilities of the Joint Overseas Operation Training School (U.S. Army) and the amphibious training facilities of HMAS ASSAULT (Royal Australian Navy). In June 1943 the Amphibious Training Command was shifted to Toorbul and in an endeavor to maintain troop training in the vicinity of the staging areas, the Command was again moved forward to Milne Bay. However, the advance of our forces along the New Guinea coast was so rapid that three mobile training units had to be organized in order to train troops in forward areas. In March 1945, the Amphibious Training Command was transferred to Subic Bay, Luzon, to prepare for training troops for the prospective landings in the Japanese home islands.

The amphibious training curriculum was divided into two phases: intensive instruction of officers at the Training Center, followed by practice landings by Regimental Combat Teams under the direction of their own officers with mobile groups of instructors from the Amphibious Training Command serving as supervisors. A detailed account of the participation of Army, Marine and Australian Divisions in this training program is contained in a separate section of Part II.

ASSAULT OPERATIONS

NEW GUINEA: BISMARCK ARCHIPELAGO: MOROTAI
SEPTEMBER 1943 - SEPTEMBER 1944

The amphibious landing at LAE by the 9th Australian Division on 4 September 1943 was the first of a series of assault landings along the New Guinea coast, in the Bismarck Archipelago and in the

Halmaheras designed to provide staging areas, minor naval bases, and airfields to support the major assault on the Philippine Islands. From September 1943 to September 1944, the SEVENTH Amphibious Force made 14 major landings in these areas involving the movement of approximately 300,000 men and 350,000 tons of supplies and equipment.

The amphibious landing at LAE, in the Huon Gulf, on the northeast coast of New Guinea, was made by Australian troops of the Ninth Division, A.I.F., in conjunction with a parachute and airborne landing in the Markham Valley. The operation at LAE progressed so swiftly that it was evident that the same troops could begin amphibious landings at FINSCHHAFEN earlier than originally planned. FINSCHHAFEN landings were made on 22 September 1943 and the whole operation progressed smoothly. There was relatively little initial resistance by shore based forces at either LAE or FINSCHHAFEN but enemy air attacks in strength commenced in both areas about noon on D Day, followed by night attacks of small groups of enemy planes. Ships leaving the landing areas and resupply echelons were under persistent and determined air attacks until airfields were developed and aircraft brought forward to neutralize nearby Japanese air bases. This same general pattern of air resistance first adopted by the Japs at LAE and FINSCHHAFEN continued throughout the New Guinea campaign.

The 112th Cavalry Regimental Combat Team was landed at ARAWE, New Britain, on 15 December 1943 against strong enemy opposition. The plan called for two landings; an advance echelon of 300 men to land in rubber boats from APDs one hour before dawn, and the main force to land after sunrise in LVTs and landing craft from the CARTER HALL (LSD 3) and WESTRALIA (LSI). In the expectation of preserving the element of surprise, planners recommended that no naval gunfire be used to support the advance echelon. Surprise was largely unsuccessful, however, for two reasons: (a) the enemy had been forewarned by the landing of amphibious scouts on the same beach several days earlier, and (b) bright moonlight enabled the Japs to spot the movement. The advance echelon was repulsed with 50% casualties. The main landing, supported by excellent naval gunfire, was successful. As a result of this experience, the SEVENTH Amphibious Force never again omitted naval gunfire support in order to achieve surprise.

The splendid execution of the amphibious landing at CAPE GLOUCESTER, New Britain, on 26 December 1943 was a tribute to the professional skill of the 1st Marine Division. The navigational problems involved in the long overwater movement of a large number of landing craft and the skillful handling of these craft in the landing areas were particularly gratifying features of this operation. It was in this operation that Commander SEVENTH Amphibious Force inaugurated the employment of Landing Craft Control Officers who were responsible for guiding the landing craft through the reefs to the designated beaches. The direction of landing craft by a senior officer has since become standard practice in all assault operations.

The third amphibious landing by the SEVENTH Amphibious Force within 18 days was made at SAIDOR on 2 January 1944 as soon as landing craft could be released from the Cape Gloucester operation. The assault forces were the 126th Regimental Combat Team of the 32nd Division which were landed in order to establish advance bases from which aircraft and light naval forces could operate to secure control of the Vitiaz Straits Area.

The Amphibious landing in the ADMIRALTY ISLANDS on 29 February 1944 was intended as a reconnaissance-in-force to prepare for the main landing scheduled for 1 April 1944, to be executed in conjunction with simultaneous landings by the Central Pacific Forces in the vicinity of Kavieng, New Ireland. Negros Island was selected for the advance landing after air reconnaissance had revealed only a small enemy force there, but doubts arose as to the actual condition existing when amphibious scouts insisted there were large enemy troop concentrations on this island. To definitely determine the enemy strength, a squadron of the 1st U.S. Cavalry Division (dismounted) landed at NEGROS on 29 February 1944. Possibly because of the excellence of the supporting naval gunfire directed against defensive installations near the beach, the landing force met little resistance on the first day, and the situation was deemed sufficiently secure that the 40th Construction Battalion landed at once to develop the airfield at Mamote. However, the third day brought confirmation of the advance reports of the amphibious scouts, as Japanese resistance developed in great strength. The success of the entire operation was in danger until the arrival of reinforcements, especially artillery, which were rushed forward from New Guinea. During the engagement the "Sea Bees" assumed the role of combat troops, and served with such credit that the battalion was awarded the Presidential Unit Citation.

The AITAPE-HUMBOLDT BAY-TANAMERAH landings on 22 April 1944 represented the most ambitious amphibious undertaking to date in the Southwest Pacific. It was the largest overseas movement undertaken in that area and it effectively by-passed and cut off the strong enemy garrisons in the vicinity of Wewak. Excellent strategic surprise was effected. The Japanese had moved forward heavy reinforcements to the Wewak area in anticipation of attack, and as a result there was only nominal resistance where the landings were actually made. Carrier based planes were used for the first time for landing support, and APAs and AKAs assisted in transporting 25,000 troops for the three simultaneous landings. Fast carriers from the Pacific Fleet furnished support.

Experience in amphibious warfare has taught that: (a) assault echelons should carry a minimum of supplies, sufficient only for immediate needs, and (b) preliminary reconnaissance and photo-interpretation can be very misleading unless skillfully evaluated and analyzed. These lessons were learned again during this operation. At Hollandia, a large amount of supplies were brought in to beach dumps and insufficiently dispersed. On the evening of D Day, a lone enemy plane dropped a single bomb in the concentrated supply area and the resulting fire destroyed all the supplies landed that day, the equivalent of 11 LST loads. In the Tanamerah Bay area, photo intelligence had reported a road behind the beach. During the landing it was discovered that the "road" was an unfordable swamp which made it necessary to unload supplies at Humboldt Bay, forty miles distant. The results could have been disastrous for the Tanamerah Attack Force had the enemy opposition been stronger. Fortunately, these mishaps did not seriously affect the success of the landings.

The next amphibious operation was at WAKDE ISLAND on 17 May 1944 followed on 27 May 1944 by the landing on BIAK ISLAND. The Biak operation was not originally contemplated but was quickly conceived and planned when it became evident that the air strips at Hollandia would not be ready to support heavy bombers for some months. Several calculated risks were accepted in the execution of the Biak landing in order to meet the early date set. However, the landing and unloading were conducted with unanticipated success although the troops met considerable resistance. A minor reversal was successfully recouped two days after the initial landings when LCTs evacuated an Army battalion which had been cut off at one point by a large enemy force. Naval gunfire was effectively employed for several days to support the troops in their advance against the strong enemy positions.

On 2 July 1944 an assault landing was made at NOEMFOOR ISLAND and on 30 July 1944, the final landing of the New Guinea campaign was made at SANSAPOR.

Rear Admiral W. M. Fechteler, USN, Deputy Commander SEVENTH Amphibious Force, directed the amphibious operations at WAKDE, BIAK, NOEMFOOR and SANSAPOR while Rear Admiral D. E. Barbey, USN, was on temporary duty in the United States. Ships that participated in these four landings and in the resupply echelons that followed were under constant threat of attack by a strong Japanese surface force concentrated in the Philippine-Borneo-Netherlands East Indies Area. During this period, the Pacific Fleet was concentrated far to the north in the Marshalls-Marianas Area, and the combatant units of the SEVENTH Fleet would have been entirely inadequate at the time to withstand an attack of enemy heavy units. The failure of the Japanese Navy to attempt to capitalize on this opportunity to retard the advance and prevent the consolidation of our ground force positions is an unexplained aspect of the enemy's strategy.

The amphibious landings at MOROTAI in the Halmahera Islands took place on 15 September 1944, when over 50,000 troops disembarked in record time without opposition but under very difficult landing conditions. There was one other operation, relatively small, in the same area in November 1944. Under the direction of Commander SEVENTH Amphibious Force and under the immediate command of Captain Lord Ashbourne, RN, in the British minelayer ARIADNE, United States troops transported in LSMs and LCIs landed unopposed to establish radar and loran stations on ASIA and MAPIA ISLANDS as aids to future naval operations.

CAPTURE OF THE PHILIPPINES

October 1944 - February 1945

The projected increase of the SEVENTH Amphibious Force began to be realized in August 1944. Between then and November the Force was increased threefold by the addition of three LST Flotillas, four LCI Flotillas, three LCT Flotillas, and one LCS(L) Flotilla. Also many transports from the Pacific Fleet joined the force under the temporary operation control of Commander SEVENTH Amphibious Force.

Original plans for the capture of the Philippines provided for an amphibious landing at Sarangani Bay, Mindanao, but on 15 September

1944, Commander SEVENTH Amphibious Force was advised that the initial assault would be made at Leyte, and plans were revised accordingly. The changes were the result of the new strategic concepts, arrived at in early September, which stepped up the tempo of the whole program of war against Japan.

The amphibious landings at LEYTE, Philippine Islands, were made on A day, 20 October 1944, proceded by minor landings on Dinagat and Homonhon Islands at the entrance to Leyte Gulf on A-3 and A-2 days respectively. Commander SEVENTH Fleet was in overall command of the ships engaged in the Leyte Operation; Commander SEVENTH Amphibious Force was responsible for landing the XXIV Army Corps on the Southern Beaches in the vicinity of Dulag; and Lieutenant General Walter Kreuger, Commanding General SIXTH Army was responsible for securing LEYTE and the adjacent island of SAMAR.

In this operation the fire support ships did not operate directly under the amphibious force commanders, but under Commander Battleships (Rear Admiral Oldendorf) temporarily operating with part of his force under the SEVENTH Fleet, who served as Commander Support Force during the Leyte Operation. He conducted the preliminary bombardments prior to the landings and thereafter covered the amphibious forces during the Battles of Surigao Straits and Samar.

The amphibious landings were eminently successful, but the supporting ships suffered from suicide air attacks, effectively employed against our naval forces for the first time. Fortunately ships of the SEVENTH Amphibious Force in the assault echelon were lightly loaded and were able to unload and depart on the first day, with the result that the large transports were out of the landing area before the suicide attacks commenced.

When Commander SEVENTH Amphibious Force left Leyte for Hollandia to begin preparations for the Lingayen Operation (which was originally scheduled for 20 December 1944), Commander Amphibious Group 8 (Rear Admiral Fechteler) was designated to remain at Leyte. He was relieved as SOPA, LEYTE on 16 November 1944 by Commander Amphibious Group Nine (Rear Admiral Struble) who directed subsequent amphibious operations in the area.

The advance of the ground forces on Leyte was seriously threatened by the arrival of substantial Japanese reinforcements landing at Ormoc on the west coast. On short notice, Commander Amphibious Group 9 skillfully planned and directed an amphibious landing at ORMOC on 7 December 1944. One week later, on 15 December 1944, he made another successful landing on MINDORO and conducted the resupply echelons in support of this landing as long as the Japanese air threat existed. His flagship was hit by a suicide plane while enroute to Mindoro, and his Chief of Staff, several other members of his staff, and several members of the staff of the Landing Force Commander were killed. Ships of the SEVENTH Amphibious Force suffered high personnel casualties and heavy material losses from suicide air attacks during the ORMOC and MINDORO operations. However, these two landings contributed materially to the final capture of Leyte and to the success of the impending operations on Luzon.

The amphibious landing at LINGAYEN on 9 January 1945 followed the same general organization plan used at Leyte. Commander SEVENTH Fleet was in overall command of the landing; Commander SEVENTH Amphibious Force landed the I Corps on the northern beaches; and Commander THIRD Amphibious Force landed the XIV Corps on the southern beaches. Initial opposition to the landing was not strong but it stiffened as the troops moved from the beachhead to the hills just beyond, and naval gunfire support was used for several weeks. Fire support ships and minesweepers suffered substantial losses during the preliminary minesweeping and preassault bombardment. If the enemy had concentrated air attacks on transports with the same effectiveness achieved against supporting ships, the Lingayen operation might not have succeeded.

After the Lingayen Landings, matters of first importance were the immediate reinforcement of the Philippines, and the exploitation of the rapid advance of the SIXTH Army down the Luzon plain. The SEVENTH Amphibious Force assumed the task of transporting troops to accomplish these ends. A major portion of those amphibious ships from the Pacific Fleet which had participated in the Leyte and Lingayen operations were made available to Commander-in-Chief Southwest Pacific Area until 15 February 1945, and under the operational control of Commander SEVENTH Amphibious Force, they were immediately employed in a rapid turnaround which brought six divisions from Leyte and New Guinea to Luzon within a month.

After LINGAYEN, the amphibious operations of the SEVENTH Amphibious Force assumed a new pattern to meet the need for simultaneous operations for the earliest control of the entire Philippine Archipelago. Vice Admiral Barbey during this phase acted as the Attack Force Commander and assumed overall control of operations assisted by three Rear Admirals as Group Commanders. These were Commanders Amphibious Groups 8 and 9, regularly assigned to the Southwest Pacific Area, and Commander Amphibious Group 6 (Rear Admiral Royal), assigned temporarily from the Pacific Fleet. Individual operations were under the command of these group commanders or, in some cases, under command of subordinate officers of the Force.

The first of the consolidating operations took place on 29 January 1945, when one division and regimental combat team were landed near Subic, Zambales Province, followed on 31 January 1945 by the 11th Airborne Division landing at NASUGBU, South of Manila Bay, which assisted materially in the capture of the Capital. During the same period, three more divisions were landed at Lingayen, and a fourth at Mindoro.

The BATAAN-CORREGIDOR operation on 15 February 1945, was a combined air bombardment-naval bombardment-airborne-amphibious attack. The intensity of the air bombardment, the excellent timing of airborne and amphibious operations, and the accuracy of the naval gunfire support by cruisers and destroyers reduced what might have been a long and costly campaign to one successfully concluded in a few days. The amphibious phase of the operation was commanded by Commander Amphibious Group 9, Rear Admiral Struble.

CONSOLIDATING AND MINESWEEPING OPERATIONS THROUGHOUT THE PHILIPPINES AND BORNEO

February 1945 - July 1945

In February 1945, Commander SEVENTH Amphibious Force was charged with the clearance of minefields and reopening of ports and sea routes in the Philippine Area. The opening of Manila Bay to shipping was given first priority. Though a relatively small number of minesweepers were available for this difficult task, Manila was open as a port before 1 March 1945, not quite two months after the first troops had landed in Luzon. The clearance of Philippine water was by far the largest minesweeping operation of the war up to that time. Including the Borneo operations, over 1300 mines (both Allied and Japanese) were destroyed in more than 8,000 square miles swept during continuous operations which lasted five months. Six AMs and approximately 25 YMS did the job.

While fighting on Luzon was still in progress, the campaign for the recapture of the remaining islands in the Philippines and for the control of Borneo and the Netherlands East Indies was begun. Between February and May 1945 more than sixteen landing operations were conducted in the central and Southern Philippines, and three major operations on the east and west coast of Borneo.

The first in the series was the landing of a regimental combat team of the 40th Infantry Division at PUERTA PRINCESSA, PALAWAN ISLAND by Commander Amphibious Group 8, Rear Admiral Fechteler, on 28 February 1945. In this operation there were no losses by either Army or Navy. When PUERTA PRINCESSA was secured, air bases were established which enabled the air force to gain control over the China Sea.

On 10 March 1945 in another amphibious operation under Rear Admiral Royal, Commander Amphibious Group 6, two regimental combat teams also of the 40th Infantry Division, were landed at ZAMBOANGA. In April, landings at JOLO, TAWI-TAWI, and on SANGA-SANGA ISLAND conducted by the same troops achieved control of the Sulu Archipelago.

The next series started on 18 March 1945 when two regimental combat teams landed in the vicinity of ILOILO, PANAY under Commander Amphibious Group 9. This was followed on 26 March 1945 by landing two regimental combat teams on CEBU with Acting Commander Amphibious Group 8 (Captain A. T. Sprague) in command. Over a two months period Commander Amphibious Group 9 conducted landings on NEGROS ISLAND: BOHOL ISLAND, and additional landings on CEBU and PANAY.

During March and April, amphibious landings were also made on LUBANG ISLAND, TICAO-BURIAS ISLANDS, MASBATE ISLAND, CABALLO ISLAND, CARABAO ISLAND, EL FRAILE ISLAND, and at LEGASPI, LUZON. These operations were all commanded by subordinate officers of the SEVENTH Amphibious Force, usually flotilla or group commanders. In one of these operations, the landing of one Regimental combat team at LEGASPI on 1 April 1945, low-level bombardment prior to D Day supplanted naval gunfire with very effective results.

I - 12

On 17 April 1945, Rear Admiral Noble who had succeeded Rear Admiral Fechteler as Commander Amphibious Group 8 directed a two division landing by the X Corps at PARANG and MALABANG in the Cotabato area of Mindanao. The landing areas had previously been secured by guerrillas, and troops moved quickly overland and captured DAVAO. Meanwhile, naval support forces moved into DAVAO GULF and destroyed suicide boats, midget submarines, and their bases. Elements of the X Corps moved northward from Davao and met increasing Japanese resistance in the mountainous part of Central Mindanao. To assist in enveloping the remaining Japanese, Commander Amphibious Group 9 landed a regimental combat team at MACAJALAR BAY and on 1 June 1945 he assumed responsibility for support of the entire Mindanao Operation while Commander Amphibious Group 8 withdrew to prepare for the Balikpapan operation.

Owing to the importance of preparation for the invasion of Japan, plans for control of the Netherlands East Indies were restricted to the capture of strategic areas in Dutch and British Borneo. The first operation took place on 1 May 1945 when a brigade group of the 9th Australian Division, equivalent in size to a regimental combat team, landed at TARAKAN, Dutch Borneo. Commander Amphibious Group 6 conducted this landing which was unopposed, following effective air strikes, naval bombardment, and minesweeping operations. An unusual feature of the TARAKAN operation was the extreme tidal range encountered and the fact that LSTs beached in mud instead of sand. Seven LSTs were stranded in mud for 11 days. Another was the iron rails set upright in the mud to form beach obstacles. Such obstacles had not been encountered previously and no Underwater Demolition Team had been assigned to remove them. However, the Royal Australian Engineer Unit undertook and successfully accomplished the job on D-1 Day.

Commander Amphibious Group 6 conducted the second landing in Borneo on 10 June 1945 at BRUNEI BAY; (The orignial date of 22 May was extended to permit the arrival of support units and supplies from Austraila). This was an extensive operation involving the simultaneous landings of one brigade group of the 9th Australian Division on LABUAN ISLAND and another on the mainland adjacent to BRUNEI BAY. Subsequent operations resulted in the capture of the rich oil area of MIRI-LUTONG .

The untimely death of Rear Admiral Royal occurred at sea while his flagship was enroute to Leyte following the Brunei Bay operation.

The final amphibious assault landing in Borneo was made on 1 July 1945 at BALIKPAPAN. Vice Admiral Barbey was in overall command of this operation with Commander Amphibious Group 8 directly responsible for landing the 7th Australian Division. Many elements of this division had been transported the entire distance from Australia in LSTs of the SEVENTH Amphibious Force. The following factors made BALIKPAPAN an extremely difficult amphibious operation:

(a) A very shallow beach gradient which did not permit fire support ships nearer than five miles out from the beach.

(b) Shallow waters thickly sown with magnetic mines.

(c) Landbased air support operating from bases more than 400 miles away.

These difficulties were overcome by the excellent work of the minesweepers, intensive naval bombardment, and three Escort Carriers of the Pacific Fleet which contributed air support.

The Borneo operations were unique in the respect that serious difficulty was encountered with previously sown allied magnetic mines. The Fifth Air Force and RAAF had planted numerous magnetic mines, many incapable of self-sterilization, in the shallow waters of TARAKAN, BRUNEI BAY, and BALIKPAPAN, and pre-assault sweeping was conducted for several days in each of these three areas. At BALIKPAPAN where the threat of magnetic mines was especially great, minesweeping continued for two weeks before the landing. No serious difficulty was encountered in clearing Japanese mines, However, off LUTONG, the sweeping groups swept one enemy field of 600 mines all more than 80 feet deep. The field had obviously been designed as a defensive measure against Allied submarines. Because of the slight gradient of the ocean bottom near LUTONG, Japanese tankers were obliged to anchor three miles from the beach and load oil through long pipe lines, thus being particularly exposed to submarine attack.

Throughout the BORNEO operations, the small minesweeping group attached to the SEVENTH Amphibious Force did an outstanding job in spite of heavy losses--about one ship damaged or lost for every two magnetic mines destroyed.

POST WAR OPERATIONS

Although it was not realized at the time, the BALIKPAPAN operation was the last for the SEVENTH Amphibious Force which completed a two-year combat record of 56 amphibious assault landings involving overwater movement of a total of more than a million men.

During July and August 1945, ships of the SEVENTH Amphibious Force were engaged in the roll-up of men and material from New Guinea, the Solomons, and Admiralty Islands. Many of the same ships had carried the same troops to those ports in assault landings a year or two before. During this period, the SEVENTH Amphibious Force also was engaged in redistributing Army Units, and preparing plans for the final assault on the Japanese homeland.

15 August 1945 had been set for the transfer of the SEVENTH Amphibious Force from the SEVENTH Fleet to the Amphibious Forces, Pacific Fleet, where it was to have a status comparable to the THIRD and FIFTH Amphibious Forces. Administrative and training functions of the force were to be transferred to the Administrative Command, Amphibious Forces, Pacific Fleet, and the ships to various commands, primarily the Philippine Sea Frontier.

When the Japanese surrendered on the very day the transfer was to take place, plans were quickly revised, and the SEVENTH Amphibious Force continued under the operational control of the SEVENTH Fleet. The movement of the XXIV Corps for occupation in KOREA and movement of the III Marine Amphibious Corps for similar duties in NORTH CHINA were begun immediately. Upon completion of these lifts, the SEVENTH Amphibious Force transported the 8th, 13th and 52nd Chinese Armies from South to North China ports and simultaneously began the repatriation of Japanese from Korea and North China. Commanders Amphibious Groups 7, 8 and 13 were in immediate command of these various phases.

On 19 November 1945, Vice Admiral Barbey assumed command of the SEVENTH Fleet, and simultaneously delegated the responsibility for continuation of the repatriation program to Commander Amphibious Group 8. The same date marks the end of the operations of the SEVENTH Amphibious Force, for while it continued as a command, and Vice Admiral Barbey retained his title as Commander, the flagship with the staff embarked, proceeded to the Atlantic. On 23 December 1945, the SEVENTH Amphibious Force was finally disestablished. The organization, which Vice Admiral D. E. Barbey created, trained, and led, had completed its task.

PART II

COMMAND, STAFF ORGANIZATION

AND ADMINISTRATION

SEVENTH AMPHIBIOUS FORCE

PART II (a)

STAFF ORGANIZATION AND HISTORY

Rear Admiral DANIEL E. BARBEY, USN, assumed command of the Southwest Pacific Amphibious Force on 10 January 1943. By 1 February 1943 the Staff was complete, and established in headquarters ashore at BRISBANE, AUSTRALIA. The Staff of Commander Southwest Pacific Amphibious Force was initially organized as shown in Appendix 1, Sheet 1.

The first concern of the Commander Southwest Pacific Amphibious Force was the establishment of base facilities for landing craft and the initiation of amphibious training for all branches of the armed forces in preparation for forthcoming operations. By 13 March 1943, the following had been activated under his jurisdiction and control:

(1) Headquarters, Southwest Pacific Amphibious Force, BRISBANE.

(2) Amphibious Training Command, PORT STEPHENS, NEW SOUTH WALES.

(3) Landing Force Equipment Depot, PORT STEPHENS.

(4) Naval Landing Craft Depot, TOORBUL POINT, QUEENSLAND.

(5) Naval Landing Craft Depot, MACKAY, QUEENSLAND.

On 15 March, 1943 Commander Southwest Pacific Amphibious Force became Commander Amphibious Force, Seventh Fleet.

The U.S.S. HENRY T. ALLEN reported for duty as flagship, and on 17 March, 1943 the staff moved aboard. However, the ship was in poor material condition and also was needed urgently for use in amphibious training and transportation of troops. As a consequence the Staff remained aboard only a short time.

For the WOODLARK-KIRIWINA Islands Operation, the Commander Amphibious Force SEVENTH Fleet, took forward an advance echelon of his staff to serve as an operating group. This echelon, which embarked in the USS RIGEL on 22 June, 1943, consisted of the following officers: Operations, Assistant Operations,

Aviation, Aerology, Medical and Communications plus the necessary communication watch officers and enlisted personnel. The rest of the staff under the Chief of Staff remained at the BRISBANE headquarters.

During the conduct of actual operations, commencing with Woodlark-Kiriwina and concluding with AITAPE-HUMBOLDT BAY-TANAMERAH operation Admiral Barbey used a destroyer as a flagship. At these times three or four watch officers and necessary communication personnel accompanied him. The remainder of the forward echelon, usually engaged in operational planning, remained in the RIGEL.

For the purpose of controlling the movements of the large number of landing craft employed in widespread Southwest Pacific Areas, certain officers of the staff of Commander Seventh Amphibious Force, known as Landing Craft Control Officers, were established in various New Guinea ports. In assault operations Landing Craft Control Officers directed the movement of landing craft to the beach. After the assault phase ended and the attack force commander left the area, they assumed entire control of shipping for the immediate support of the landing force. In the rear areas, the LCCO in each port controlled the movement of amphibious ships, primarily the echelons scheduled for resupply.

On 15 August 1943, when the Amphibious Forces throughout the Pacific were reorganized, Commander Amphibious Force, Seventh Fleet became Commander Seventh Amphibious Force.

In December 1943, the U.S.S. BLUE RIDGE (AGC 2) reported as flagship, and on 18 December the rear echelon embarked in the Blue Ridge and moved forward to Buna, New Guinea, where the forward echelon transferred from the Rigel. A Progress Section for material and supply remained at Brisbane.

On 27 January 1944, Rear Admiral W.M. FECHTELER, USN, reported as Deputy Commander Seventh Amphibious Force. He served in this capacity, acting as Attack Group Commander in several operations, until 1 October 1944, when Amphibious Groups were established in the U.S. Fleet and he was ordered as Commander Amphibious Group Eight.

The frequency of operations and the rapid movement forward during the period 30 June 1943 to 1 May 1944 resulted in a need for

more staff personnel. The requirements fell generally into two
categories: Officers to command attack operations and the various
phases thereof, and officers to control the movements and logistics
of amphibious shipping at numerous points. On 7 May 1944 it was
proposed to reorganize the Staff as shown in Appendix 1, Sheet 2,
but this proposal was not approved, and the Staff organization continued to function without attack group commanders.

With the approach of the Leyte Operation, it was considered
desirable to again divide the staff, since the Blue Ridge was to
take part in the operation. The Staff had grown considerably as
the size of the force increased, and it was difficult to maintain
the entire staff in one ship. On 7 October 1944, the "Administrative Group of the Staff of Commander Seventh Amphibious Force"
was established in the U.S.S. Henry T. Allen with Captain H. J.
NELSON, USN, as Commander Administrative Command, Seventh
Amphibious Force. The mission of the Administrative Command
was defined:

"(1) To provide the necessary personnel, training, and
logistic requirements and to maintain in a satisfactory
condition the ships assigned to this force in order to
enable Commander Seventh Amphibious Force to provide transportation and close support for amphibious
operations against enemy held positions.

(2) To carry out all the administrative functions and to take
over any other duties that can be delegated to it in order
that Commander Seventh Amphibious Force may have
the minimum amount of details and influence distracting
him from his combat missions."

The administrative Command was organized as shown in Appendix 1,
Sheet 3. The operating Staff was organized as shown in Appendix 1,
Sheet 4.

On 22 November 1944 the Progress Section (in Australia) was
discontinued and its personnel returned to the Administrative Command.

On 17 February 1945 the Administrative Command was augmented
by a logistics officer, whose duty was to coordinate all sections
having to do with logistics of any type (see Appendix 1, Sheet 5).

Beginning in early February 1945, the Blue Ridge based in the

Manila-Subic Area and the Henry T. Allen in Leyte. With the progressive occupation of the Philippines, it became necessary to provide representatives in many ports to control amphibious shipping. By 1 May 1945 the Staff had representatives in Manila, Lingayen, Subic, Mindoro, Palawan, Leyte, Hollandia, Zamboanga, Malaban, Tarakan, and Morotai.

On 7 June 1945 the operating staff moved aboard the U.S.S. Ancon (AGC 4) and the Blue Ridge returned to Pearl for overhaul.

On 13 August 1945 the Ancon departed for service in connection with the occupation of Japan, and the operating staff was temporarily housed in the U.S.S. St. Croix (APA 228) until it moved aboard the U.S.S. Catoctin (AGC 5) on 28 August.

On 15 August 1945 the Seventh Fleet became a unit of the Pacific Fleet, and Commander Seventh Amphibious Force reported to Commander Amphibious Forces, Pacific Fleet. The Administrative Command Seventh Amphibious Force also reported to Commander, Amphibious Forces, Pacific Fleet and became the Administrative Command, Amphibious Forces Pacific Fleet, Philippine. Since Commander Amphibious Forces, Pacific Fleet became the type commander, it was not necessary for the operating Staff to absorb a major portion of the function previously performed by the Administrative Command. However, a logistics sub section was added to the operations section. The staff has since performed with a gradual reduction in personnel due to demobilization, but with no essential change in organization.

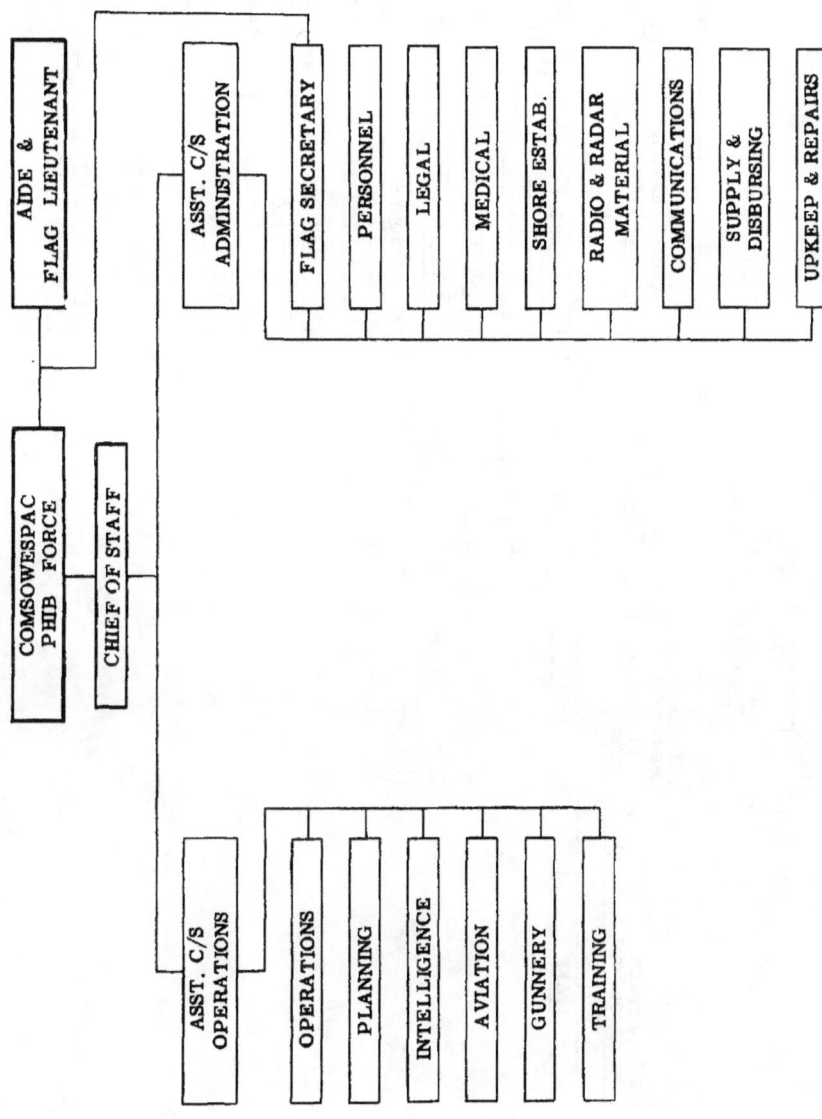

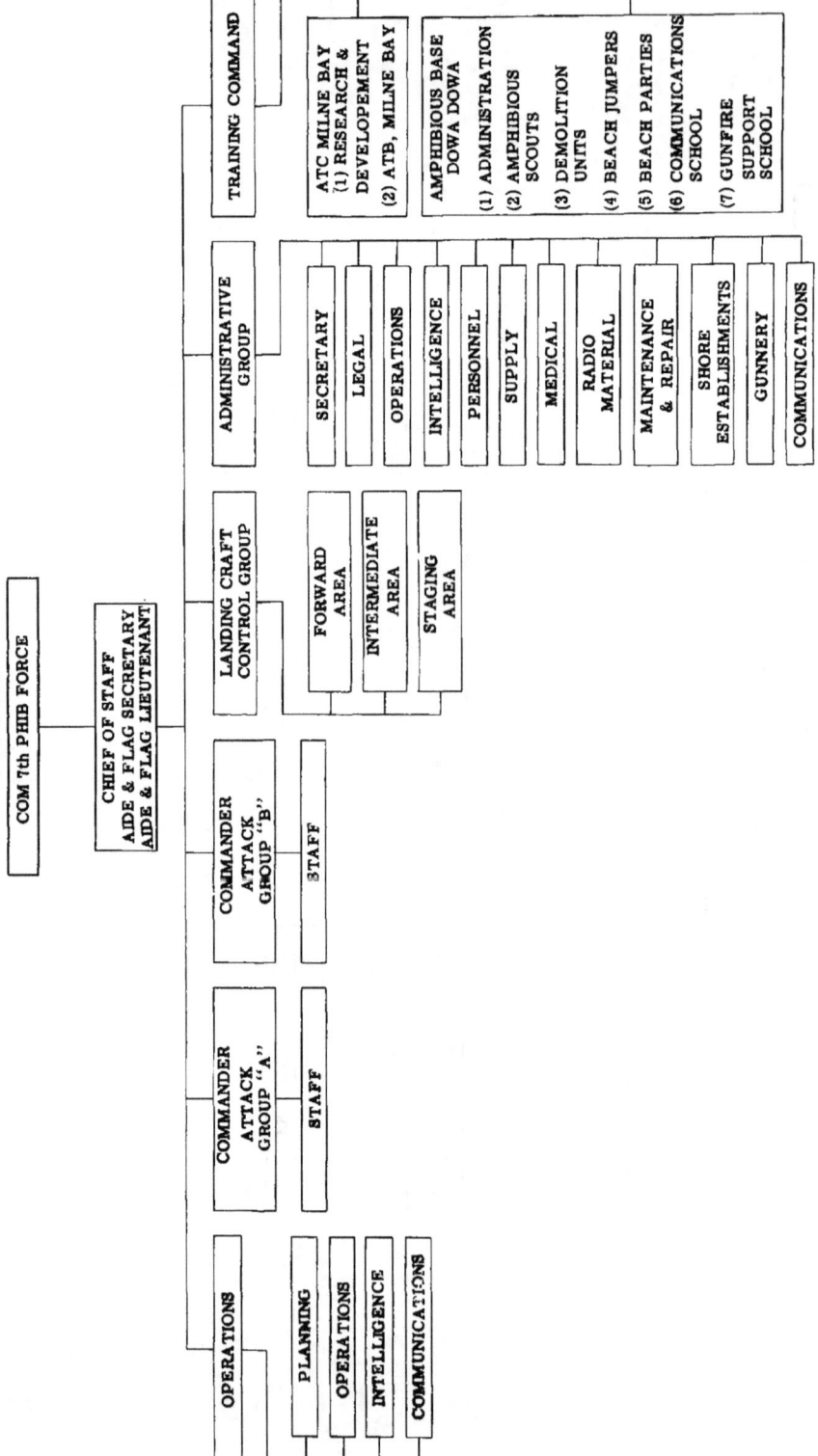

Appendix 1
Sheet 2

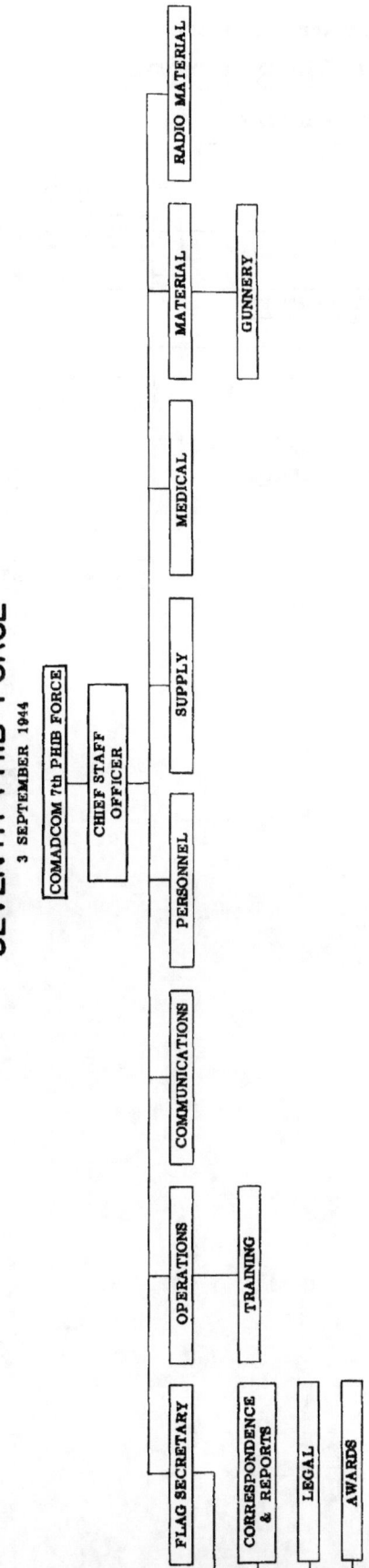

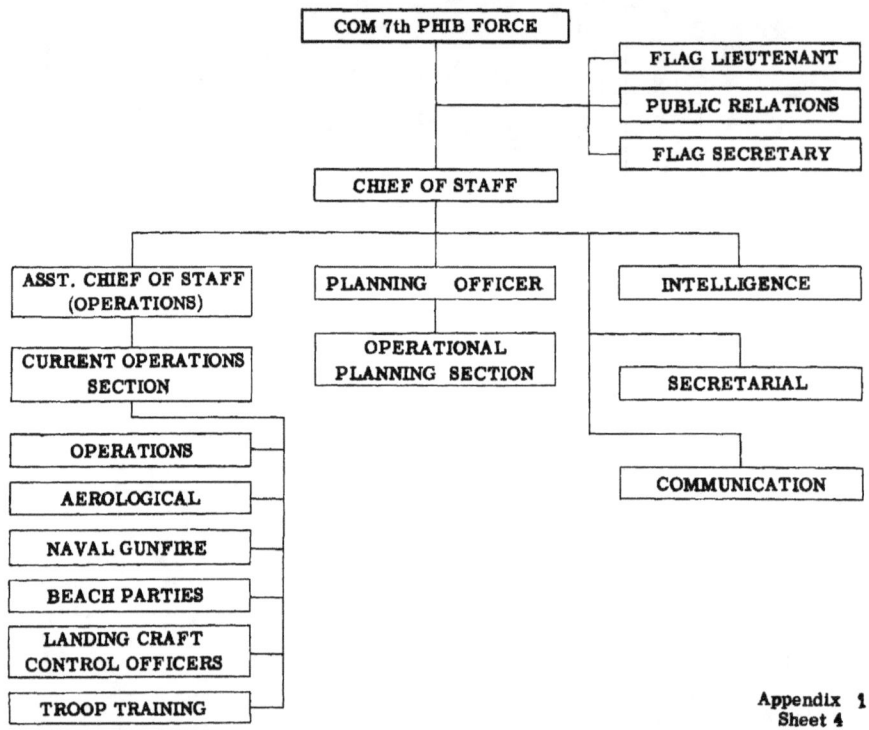

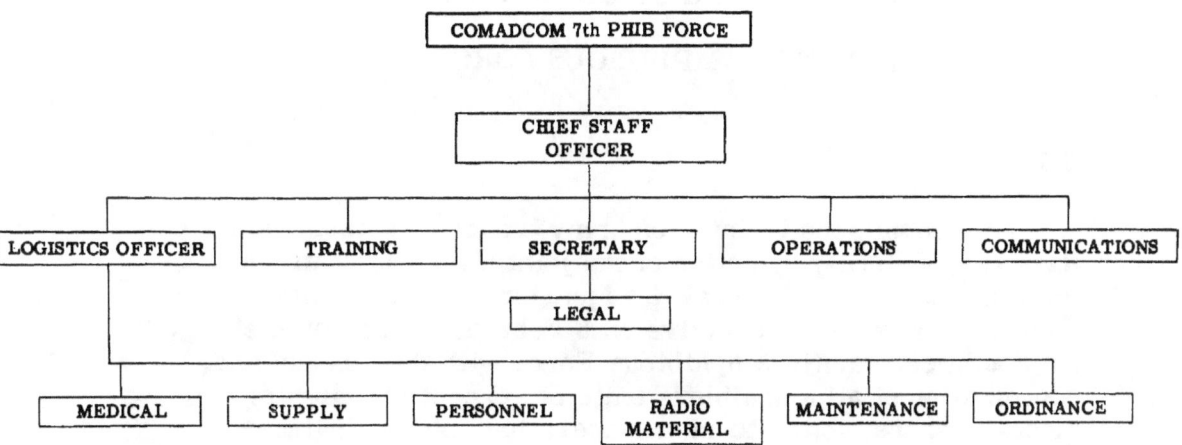

Appendix 1
Sheet 5

PART II (b)

AMPHIBIOUS TRAINING OF GROUND FORCES BY SEVENTH AMPHIBIOUS FORCE

INTRODUCTION

The amphibious training of Army troops was assigned as a Navy responsibility by action of the Joint Chiefs of Staff. In conformance with this, General Headquarters of the Southwest Pacific Area issued a directive on 8 February 1943 which charged the Southwest Pacific Amphibious Force with the conduct and coordination of all amphibious training, except training for close-in-shore, shore-to-shore-operations of the Engineer Special Brigades. It will be noted that in this particular function only, that of amphibious training of army troops, Rear Admiral BARBEY was to be directly responsible to General Headquarters and not through the Commander Southwest Pacific Force as he was in all other matters.

All amphibious training activities then functioning were placed under his command. These were:

(a) Joint Overseas Operational Training School at Port Stephens, New South Wales. This activity had been operating directly under General Headquarters and was engaged in a program of basic amphibious training for officers of the United States and Australian Armies. An Australian infantry battalion with a battery of artillery served as school troops and gave landing demonstrations on the battalion landing team scale. A naval advanced base unit of 3 officers and 40 enlisted men with 40 landing craft of the 36' LCP type was attached to this school. This advanced base unit was also engaged in instructing Royal Australian navy personnel in the operation of the U.S. type of landing craft.

(b) At Toorbul, Queensland, another naval unit of 3 officers and 60 enlisted men with 10 landing craft of the 36' LCP type were also engaged in elementary training of Royal Australian Navy personnel in the handling of landing craft.

(c) At Camp DOOMBEN, Queensland, in the vicinity of Brisbane were 21 officers and 250 enlisted men who had been trained in the operation of landing craft and who were awaiting the arrival of landing craft from the United States. These personnel were later transferred to the Amphibious Training Command at Port Stephens when that Command was established.

(d) The Royal Australian Navy had an amphibious training base at Port Stephens, known as HMAS Assault. On 25 February 1943 the Australian Commonwealth Naval Board directed that the HMAS Assault and also the Australian Landing Ship Infantry HMAS MANOORA be placed under the operational control of Commander Southwest Pacific Amphibious Force. The HMAS KANIMBLA and WESTRALIA, two additional LSIs were to be similarly assigned as soon as their conversions had been completed.

AMPHIBIOUS TRAINING IN AUSTRALIA

INITIAL OPERATIONS

On 1 March 1943, the Joint Operational Overseas Training School, HMAS Assault and U.S. Advanced Base Unit were all combined to form the Amphibious Training Command under temporary command of Captain K. J. CHRISTOPH, USN. He was relieved the following month by Captain J. W. JAMISON, USN who had had considerable experience in amphibious training in the Atlantic and who had served as Beachmaster during the North African Landings.

The Seventh Division, Australian Imperial Forces were the first troops scheduled for amphibious training. In preparation for the large scale training, special training was conducted for selected officers of the division. Subjects covered were shore and beach parties, communications, naval gunfire support, air support, amphibious scouting and the duties of transport quartermasters. Sixty four officers attended these courses.

The Seventh Division was unable to meet its date for troop training because of difficulties in organization, lack of replacements, and the large number of personnel down with recurrent malaria. It was estimated that the division would not be ready to commence training until the end of April.

The Commander Southwest Pacific Amphibious Force recommended that the First Marine Division, then in the vicinity of Melbourne, be made available for training. This was approved and training of this division was conducted in the Dromana Beach Area, Port Phillip, Victoria, from 28 March until 15 May. During this period officers of the Seventh Australian Division observed the training of the Marines but no troop training was given this division.

The HMAS MANOORA and USS HENRY T. ALLEN were initially used for amphibious training of the First Marine Division. The H.T. Allen had arrived in the area on 13 March from the South Pacific. The material condition of this ship was such that it had to be withdrawn from training on 10 April for a five weeks overhaul availability at Sydney. It was planned that LSTs, LCIs and LCTs as they became available in the area would take part in this training, commencing about 15 April. Such craft however were required for the movement forward of troops as soon as they arrived. Only the Manoora remained available for training, embarking one battalion landing team at a time.

PATTERN OF TRAINING

While refresher training of First Marine Division was proceeding at Port Phillip, preparations were made for training troops at Port Stephens. Standard operating procedures were developed for Shore Parties, Naval Gunfire Support and Air Support, Landing Force Communications, Transport Quartermasters, and Combat Loading, Conduct of Troops aboard Amphibious Ships and Craft, Technique of the Soldier in Debarking from Amphibious Ships and Craft.

The 32nd Infantry Division was the first unit to attend the Amphibious Training Center. The method of instruction was found to be successful and was adopted as a pattern for all future training. A staff and command course, specialist course and course for troop instructors was given prior to training of troop units.

Officers attending staff and command courses were; Division or Assistant Division Commander; Intelligence, Operations, and Logistic Officers; Division, Regimental and Battalion Staffs; Division Engineer; Division and Regimental Surgeons; Regimental and Battalion Commanders.

The first week of the staff and command course consisted of

lectures, discussions and demonstrations covering all phases of amphibious operations. The second week was devoted to a school problem which required students to prepare plans, field orders, and administrative orders for a Regimental Combat Team landing. RCT and BLT Staffs worked as groups in solving this problem.

The Specialists School was divided into sections. Communications attended by division, regimental and battalion communication officers; Naval Gunfire Support by forward observers, liaison officers and S-3s of Field Artillery Battalions; Shore Party by selected officers of Engineer Battalion, Pioneer Platoons and Infantry units; Transport Quartermaster section which was attended by two officers from each Battalion; Medical by Division, Regimental and Battalion Surgeons.

Students in the Specialists School attended those first week lectures and discussions of the Command and Staff Course which were of general interest to all. The balance of the two week period was spent on the particular specialty with lectures, discussions, school problems, and practical work.

The assistant troop-instructor school was held for each RCT one week before scheduled troop training for that unit. It was attended by one officer and one half of the non-commissioned officers from each company, battery, or similar unit. The purpose of this course was to provide personnel qualified to instruct and correct the individual soldier during troop training and therefore stressed technique of embarkation, debarkation, individual procedure aboard transports, wearing of equipment, etc.

Officers attended the Staff and Command and Specialist Schools on a temporary duty status. During troop training, all Commanding Officers retained command of their units. The Amphibious Training Center published the schedule of training and the Troop Commanders executed it. Instructors acted as supervisors of training and advisors to the Commanding Officers of units undergoing training.

In May 1943, the Combined Operations Training School at Toorbul, Queensland was turned over to Commander Seventh Amphibious Force. This school had been operated by the 1st Australian Army and had been training separate Infantry Battalions, Anti-Aircraft Groups, and Armoured Brigades.

The Amphibious Training Center, Cairns, Queensland was

established on 25 June 1943. Captain P. A. STEVENS, USN, former Commanding Officer of the USS Henry T. Allen, was assigned as Commanding Officer. The 2nd Engineer Special Brigade consisting of amphibious trained Army Troops, was located at Cairns and was placed under the operational control of Commander Seventh Amphibious Force for use in training the 6th and 9th Australian Divisions.

UNITS TRAINED

Following is the training accomplished by amphibious training centers in Australia during 1943:

UNIT	ATC	Inclusive Dates
32nd U.S. Inf. Div		
Staff & Command & Specialists School	Port Stephens	31 May - 14 June
Troop Training	Port Stephens	16 June - 28 August
1st U.S. Cav. Div		
Staff & Command & Specialist Schools	Port Stephens	2 - 16 August
Troop Training		
1st Brigade	Port Stephens	13 Sept - 4 October
2nd Brigade	Toorbul	13 Sept - 4 October
9th Australian Div.		
Troop Training	Cairns	1 July - 10 August
6th Australian Div.		
Troop Training	Cairns	16 August - 18 Sept.
24th U.S. Inf. Div.		
Staff & Command & Specialist School	Port Stephens	15 - 30 September
Troop Training	Toorbul	5 Oct. - 11 Dec.

II - 14

UNIT	ATC	Inclusive Dates
41st U.S. Inf. Div.		
Staff & Command & Specialist School	Toorbul	6 - 18 Dec.
Troop Training	Toorbul	20 Dec. - 29 Jan.

SHIPS & CRAFT AVAILABLE

Throughout this entire period training was severely handicapped by the lack of equipment and particularly by the lack of necessary number of ships and landing craft. No more than four transports (1 APA and 3 LSIs) were available at any one time. While training was in progress at Port Stephens, Toorbul, and Cairns, simultaneously, only two transports were available; the other two (Henry T. Allen and Westralia) were lifting troops from Australia to New Guinea in preparation for forthcoming operations. An average of one LST, four LCIs, 3 LCTs, 40 LCVs, and 8 LCMs was available at each of the Centers during the period of training. Because of this shortage of equipment, improvisation had to be made. At times LSTs were rigged with debarkation nets and used as transports, carrying as much as a battalion landing team aboard. Ships sides were built over the water and troops debarked over these into landing craft, simulating debarkation from transports.

SHORE PARTIES

Although Engineer Special Brigades were arriving in this theater, they were required for immediate operational use and were not available as Shore Parties during training of the several divisions. As a result, General Headquarters directed that the divisions concerned organize Shore Parties for use in training. This situation was not desirable but it did make some units cognizant of the Shore Party problem. On the other hand most troops did not take the Shore Party training seriously, since it was generally believed that Engineer Special Brigade units would be provided for operations against the enemy. Also most divisions were unable to obtain adequate and sufficient mechanical equipment for proper Shore Party; i.e., bull-dozers, cranes, trucks, trailers, etc.

NAVAL GUNFIRE SUPPORT

Because of the dearth of combatant ships during this period, officers who were being instructed in naval gunfire support had little opportunity for practical exercises with such ships.

SICKNESS

During their training periods the 1st Marine Division, the 32nd U.S. Infantry Division and the 6th and 9th Australian Divisions were as much as 30% below strength because of recurrent malaria among the troops.

AMPHIBIOUS TRAINING, NEW GUINEA AREA

GENERAL

General Headquarters, Southwest Pacific Area on 11 January 1944 directed that training at ATC TOORBUL be discontinued by 5 February 1944 after completion of training of the 41st Infantry Division and that personnel, equipment and records be moved to ATC, MILNE BAY, NEW GUINEA. This directive was complied with; the ATC at MILNE BAY was comissioned on 26 January 1944 and the remaining facilities at TOORBUL were turned over to the Asutralian Army.

The Amphibious Training Center, Milne Bay, established on the shore of Stringer Bay, consisted of a boat pool, repair shops, quarters for assigned personnel, one large lecture hall (40' X 100' quonset hut) and seven small classrooms (20' X 40' quonset hut) with a mock-up ship's side build out over the water and rigged with debarkation nets. This was the same type installation used at the Centers in Australia except that quarters or mess facilities were not available for students since it was anticipated that units trained at this center would be staged in the Milne Bay area and would be able to commute to ATC from their camp.

COURSE OF TRAINING

The course of training at ATC Milne Bay followed the same pattern as used at the Centers in Australia; Staff and Command and Specialists School, Assistant Troop Instructors Course, and finally, Troop Training.

The 6th U.S. Infantry Division entered the training period on 28 February 1944. In addition to the customary officers' schools during the first two weeks, each RCT was to have three weeks training using transports, LCIs, and LSTs. However, on 8 April training had to be suspended because all available transports and larger type landing craft were required for the forthcoming Aitape-Humboldt Bay-Tanamerah Operation.

As training would be at a halt until completion of the initial phases of this operation, ATC instructors were detailed as observers with the various elements of the Task Force and Landing Force. This move was particularly valuable to instructors because it afforded them an opportunity to observe two divisions, the 24th and 41st, in their first amphibious operation since completing training at the ATC Toorbul.

ATC Milne Bay resumed training of the 6th U.S. Infantry Division on 1 May and completed work with that division on 5 June 1944.

MOBILE TRAINING UNITS

As a result of the Aitape-Hollandia-Tanamerah Bay landings, Milne Bay became a rear area location and it was apparent that no other combat troops would stage from there. Transportation difficulties prevented movement of troops to Milne Bay for training. It was decided therefore to organize Mobile Training Units which figuratively would take the Training Center to the troops. Three such units were formed, each one capable of training one division. These units were composed of officers, transports and landing craft available to the Center. Since the 33rd U.S. Infantry Division was the only one on the training program which had had no previous amphibious work, officers of this organization attended the last Staff and Command and Specialists Course held at Milne Bay during the period 5 - 17 June 1944. Troop training for the 33rd was carried out at its staging area, Finschhafen.

The remaining divisions on the program were given refresher training only, since they had all had basic amphibious work and had been in at least one amphibious operation. The following chart shows organization of the Amphibious Training Group based on the use of Mobile Training Units:

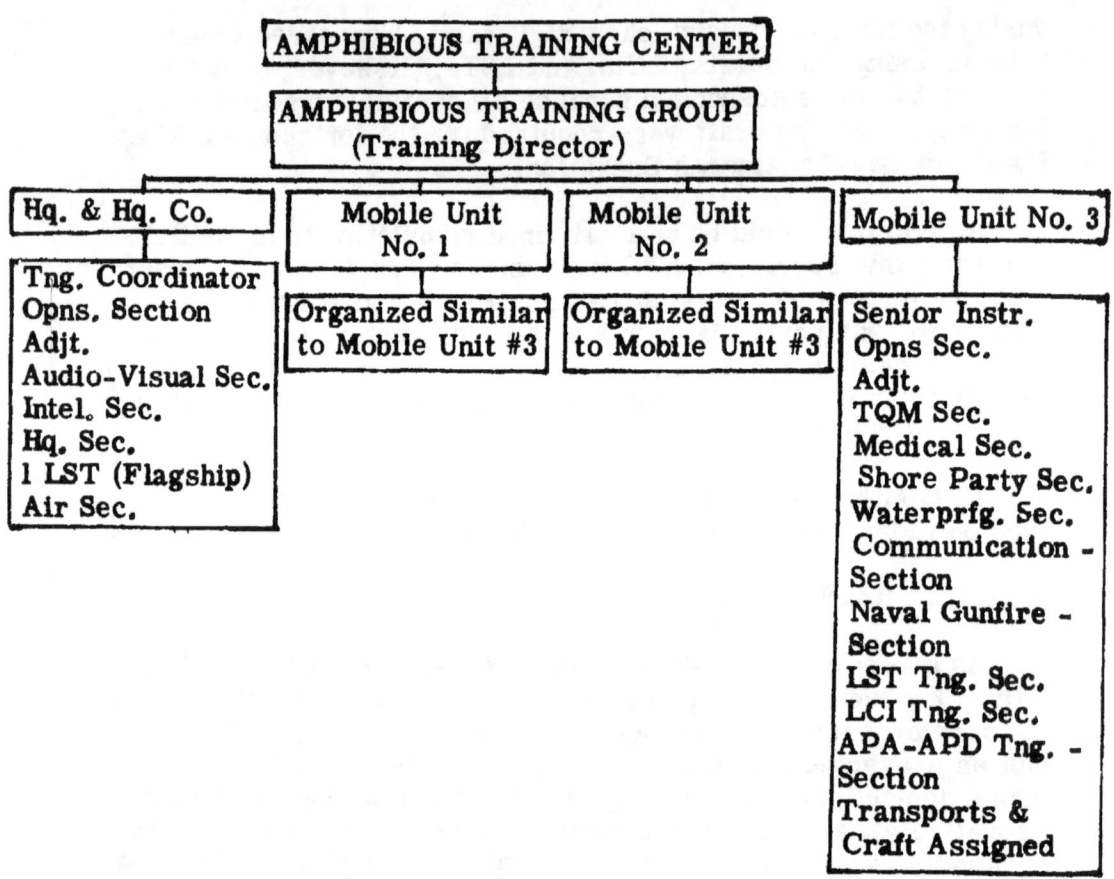

UNITS TRAINED.

Following is a list of the units trained by the Amphibious Training Group, Seventh Amphibious Force, during the New Guinea Phase:

UNITS	PLACE	INCLUSIVE DATES
6th U.S. Inf. Div.		
Staff & Specialist School	Milne Bay	28 Feb - 11 Mar. 1944
Troop Training	Milne Bay	13 Mar. - 8 Apr. & 1 May - 5 June
33rd U. S. Inf. Div.		
Staff & Specialist School	Milne Bay	5 - 17 June 1944
Troop Training	Finschhafen	26 June - 29 July 1944

II - 18

UNITS	PLACE	INCLUSIVE DATES
6th U.S. Ranger Bn.		
Troop Training	Finschhafen	17 - 29 July 1944
37th U.S. Inf. Div.		
Troop Training	Bougainville	13 July - 24 Aug 1944
43rd U.S. Inf. Div		
Troop Training	Aitape	28 Aug - 26 Sept 1944
31st, 33rd, 43rd Divs' Arty. 120th, 126th, 129th F.A. Bns.		
Naval Gunfire Support	Aitape	12 - 20 August 1944
112th U.S. Cav. RCT	Aitape	28 Sept - 12 Oct 1944
25th U.S. Inf. Div		
Troop Training	New Caledonia	8 Sept. - 13 Oct 1944
7th Australian Div.		
Troop Training	Cairns, Aust.	14 Oct. - 14 Nov. 1944
40th U.S. Inf. Div.		
Troop Training	Cape Gloucester	15 Oct. - 18 Nov. 1944
9th Australian Div.		
Troop Training	Cairns, Aust.	17 Nov. - 2 Dec. 1944

SHIPS AND CRAFT USED

An average of 2 APA (LSI), 2 LST, 4 LCIs were available to each training unit during this period.

On 2 October 1944, six British LSIs reported to Commander

Seventh Amphibious Force and were assigned to the Amphibious Training Group for duty. These were HMS Clan LaMont, Glen Earn, Empire Mace, Empire Spearhead, Empire Arquebus, Empire Battleaxe. These ships were not satisfactory, but no other were available since other transports under control of Commander Seventh Amphibious Force were engaged in combat operations.

The LSIs carried only the British LCA (landing craft assault) which were personnel boats only, similar to the LCP(R). Davits could not take the LCVP without extensive conversion. The Amphibious Training Group issued two LCM(3)s to each ship. In addition, these ships had limited troop and cargo capacity-- about 800 troops, eight 2 1/2 ton trucks and 20 1/4 ton trucks. Cleanliness and sanitation were not up to the standards maintained by ships of the United States Navy.

All LVTs and DUKWs in the Southwest Pacific Area were either in use on operations or being assembled in staging areas for future operations. None were available for training.

SHORE PARTIES

As in previous training, the units involved were required to form Shore Parties from organic elements of the division. Again, the lack of mechanical equipment and sufficient engineer troops hampered complete and efficient Shore Party training. The most common source of Shore Party personnel was from one of the regiments not in training. This assignment was rotated among the three regiments of the division.

NAVAL GUNFIRE TRAINING

During the period 12-20 August, 1944, forward observers of the 31st, 33rd, and 43rd U.S. Infantry Divisions and 120th, 126th, and 129th Field Artillery Battalions received training at Aitape with a destroyer division furnishing gunfire. Training was coordinated with combat missions of the 43rd Infantry Division operating in the Aitape sector. In this manner forward observers not only gained experience in working with firing ships, but found "live" targets and performed under combat conditions.

PHILIPPINE PHASE

ESTABLISHMENT OF ATC SUBIC

During the period of the Leyte and Lingayen operations, troop training was at a standstill since nearly all combat units were being employed in the Philippine Campaign. However, it was deemed essential to commence refresher amphibious training as early as practicable in preparation for the eventual invasion of Japan. Several areas along the Coast of Luzon, Philippine Islands, were reconnoitered and Subic Bay, Zambales Province was finally selected as the site for an Amphibious Training Center in the Philippines.

In early March 1945, General Headquarters directed that the ATC, Milne Bay, be transferred to Subic Bay and that preparations be made to train three Divisions simultaneously. Because most Army units would have a considerable number of officer replacements since their last amphibious operation, it was directed that a Staff and Command Course and Specialists School for officers be conducted prior to troop training of each division. The organization for this training was to be along the same lines as that used during the training in New Guinea--officer schools at the Center and troop training in the staging areas conducted by Mobile Training Units.

In early April 1945 the Amphibious Training Center, Subic Bay, was placed high on the construction priority list so that the first course could start by 12 June 1945. The completed installations at Subic Bay included facilities for the Amphibious Training Base, Headquarters Amphibious Training Group, lecture halls and class rooms for the Staff and Command and Specialists Schools, and quarters and mess for 300 officers.

STAFF AND COMMAND AND SPECIALISTS COURSES

In accordance with General Headquarters' directive, a two-weeks Staff and Command and Specialists School proceeded all troop training. Increased emphasis was placed on such subjects as air support, naval gunfire support, and communications. As soon as it was known that JASCOs (Joint Assault Signal Company) would be assigned certain divisions for training, a Specialists School for the Air Liaison and Shore Fire Control Sections of these units was initiated. The JASCO Shore Party Communications Sections were to receive instruction and training with the Shore Parties.

Since the Seventh Amphibious Force was to be transferred

to the control of Amphibious Forces Pacific on 15 August 1945, "Transport Doctrine, Amphibious Force Pacific Fleet" was used as a basis for all instruction. While this required some changes in technique, the basic doctrine was the same as previously taught in the Southwest Pacific Area.

TROOP TRAINING

Troop training was accomplished by sending Mobile Training Units to the divisions concerned rather than attempting to transport all divisions to Subic Bay. Training Units were organized in the same manner as those used in New Guinea and had in addition one transport division of four APAs and one AKA. The transport division commander was also the commanding officer of the Mobile Training Unit.

Because of the limited time for training, it was necessary to handle up to three divisions at once. Again the transports and landing craft had to be split three ways. The shipping allocated each training unit was only sufficient to lift one RCT. Thus exercises involving the embarkation and landing of an entire Army division could not be accomplished.

UNITS TO BE TRAINED

Following is a list of the units scheduled for training, including dates and location of training:

UNIT	PLACE	INCLUSIVE DATES
81st and Americal U.S. Inf. Divs.		
Command & Staff & Specialists Troop Training	Subic. Leyte; Cebu.	15 - 24 June 1 - 23 July
1st U.S. Cav, 40th, 33rd, Inf. Divs.		
Command & Staff & Specialists Troop Training	Subic. Lucena, Luzon; Iloilo, Panay; Launion, Luzon.	13 - 22 July 30 July - 21 Aug.

II - 22

UNIT	PLACE	INCLUSIVE DATES
24th, 41st, 43rd U.S. Inf. Divs.		
Command & Staff & Specialists Troop Training	Subic. Lingayen, Luzon; Zamboanga, Mindanao.	11 - 20 Aug. 28 Aug. - 19 Sept.

ATC ORGANIZATION

On 10 June 1945, Rear Admiral J. L. HALL, Jr., USN, Commander Amphibious Group 12, reported to Commander Seventh Amphibious Force for duty as Commander Amphibious Training Group. He succeeded Captain R. E. HANSON, USN, who had commanded the group since July 1944. Captain Hanson then became Commanding Officer of the Amphibious Training Center, Subic Bay and Commodore J. B. McGovern, USN, who had reported with Transport Squadron 16, was placed in charge of troop training.

The following diagram illustrates the Amphibious Training Group Organization:

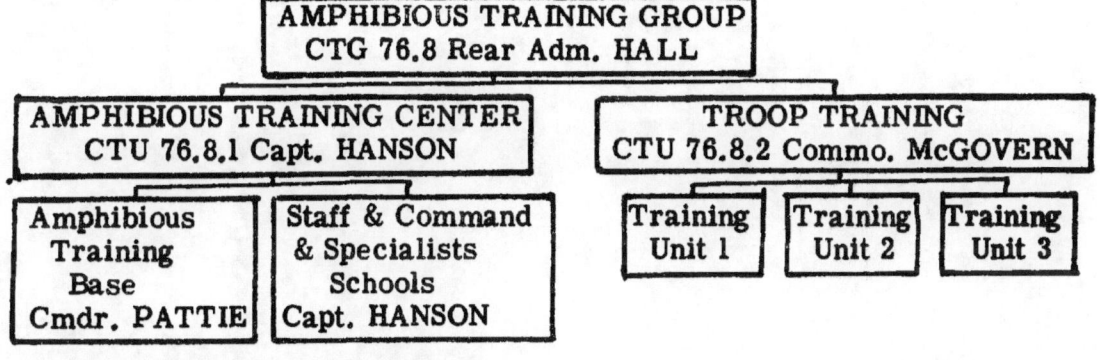

CANCELLATION OF TRAINING

The cessation of hostilities brought about the cancellation of all amphibious training since the troop units concerned were required for the occupation of Japan and Korea. At this time the 81st and Americal Divisions had completed their course of training; the 1st Cavalry, 40th and 33rd Infantry Divisions had finished the Command and Staff and Specialists Schools and were midway in their troop training, and officers of the 25th, 41st, and 43rd divisions had started the Command and Staff and Specialists School.

At its end the Amphibious Training Group was embarked on one of the most extensive amphibious training programs of the war; initially the training of eight army divisions for the assault on Kyushu and later the same program for ten divisions for operations against Honshu.

Vice Admiral BARBEY with Rear Admiral ARTHUR D. STRUBLE, U. S. Navy (left), Commander Amphibious Group Nine and Rear Admiral WILLIAM M. FECHTELER, U. S. Navy (right), Commander Amphibious Group Eight.

PART II (c)

SPECIAL PROBLEMS, FUNCTIONS AND ORGANIZATION WITHIN SEVENTH AMPHIBIOUS FORCE

PART II (c) (1)

ECHELON MOVEMENT OF AMPHIBIOUS SHIPPING

GENERAL

During the New Guinea Phase of operations in the Southwest Pacific Area, Commander SEVENTH Amphibious Force had the responsibility of not only establishing the landing force in the assault area, but also of supporting it for a considerable period after the initial assault. This support consisted of bringing forward both reinforcements and resupply, and generally continued until the landing force had captured and developed an air field from which fighters and medium bombers could operate. Thereafter the responsibility for support of the operation would be assumed by U.S. Army Service of Supply (USASOS).

Movements of amphibious shipping in the Southwest Pacific were not by large convoys as was the practice elsewhere, but rather by small groups, sailed in frequent echelons. There were several reasons for employing such a system:

(a) Distances were relatively short, and fast turn-around of shipping was not only feasible but essential due to the small number of ships available.

(b) Japanese air threat, usually from the west, was always present.

(c) The jungles offered few exits from beaches, and disposal and dump areas were few and difficult to find.

(d) Satisfactory beaching areas for landing craft were limited by coral, shoals and other offshore navigational hazards.

UNLOADING AND DISPERSAL OF SUPPLIES

The jungle vegetation along the New Guinea coast offered few landing beaches with satisfactory exits and disposal areas. Swamps often were located back of the beaches and clear areas and roads were almost non-existent. In addition the heavy jungle limited intelligence which could be derived from air photographs. Employment of scouts and periscope photographs from submarines also produced insufficient information. There were few white men with a knowledge of the area and these had no appreciation of the military problems involved. Their reports were usually too optimistic. As an example, what they would describe as a "good road" was never able to support our heavy equipment. Consequently, one of the assumptions in every plan had to be that poor unloading conditions would prevail.

Under such handicaps, the movement of supplies in the assault and early echelons exposed both the supplies and ships carrying them to serious danger of attack and destruction. This fact was strikingly demonstrated in the destruction of 11 LST loads of supplies by one bomb dropped from a single plane on the night of D day at HOLLANDIA, and in the successful air attack on the USS ETAMIN, an AK loaded with 5000 tons of cargo, which then had been unloading for six days at AITAPE during the same campaign. Nevertheless, there was always a tendency for Army planners to demand too large a proportion of equipment and supplies in the assault and early echelons. This was a natural tendency brought on by (a) a desire to be able to exploit any initial success and (b) fear that supply lines would be interrupted. Such concern was never warranted by experience. Echelons always arrived as scheduled and delivered supplies and equipment when needed.

JAPANESE AIR AND SUBMARINE THREATS

Japanese aircraft presented a constant threat to supply lines into the combat areas. Except at HOLLANDIA and MOROTAI all air protection was provided by land based aircraft and in these latter campaigns, carrier based air was only available for the early echelons. In the early campaigns, Japanese air bases practically surrounded, not only the objective areas but in some cases, as in the LAE and FINSCHHAFEN campaigns, also the staging areas. Later along the north coast of New Guinea the Japanese air bases were to the westward, whereas our fighters had to come from the east. This meant that the Japanese were free to launch late afternoon attacks practically free from the danger of fighter interception.

It was therefore necessary that amphibious shipping and their escorting ships be exposed to this constant threat in as small numbers as possible and for as short of time as possible. During the LAE and FINSCHHAFEN campaigns, night unloading of reinforcement and resupply echelons was resorted to. Subsequent practice was to proceed to the objective area during darkness, unload in the early hours of daylight and move out of the objective area by 1000. This allowed more expeditious and efficient operations while substantially reducing the threat of enemy air attack.

SCHEDULE OF RESUPPLY ECHELONS

The echelon system of reinforcement and resupply with its fast unloading, frequent turn-arounds and the relatively few ships employed required close timing and attention to detail by staff personnel planning these operations and exact execution by the operating personnel. It was necessary that loading time be limited and much mobile loading be done to obtain maximum use of few ships. Ships were scheduled to depart from the staging area at times and by routes best calculated to avoid enemy aircraft and to obtain maximum protection from our own land based cover. Plans were carefully made for ships to arrive in the objective area at the most propitious time, to be unloaded quickly and to depart before the Japanese reconnaissance discovered their presence. It was seldom that an LST remained more than 6 hours in the objective area. Sometimes when unloading did not progress satisfactorily, ships even departed with cargo still on board rather than to expose ship and cargo to danger of loss by air attack.

The usual practice in New Guinea was to sail LSTs and LCIs in echelons of about six, the LSTs normally being escorted by three destroyers and the LCIs by a similar number of SCs with one or more destroyers. In the earlier campaigns, from WOODLARK to FINSCHHAFEN, LCTs were also used for resupply and sailed in echelons, accompanied by an APc for navigational escort and some SCs. Later with increasing distances LCTs were generally towed to the objective areas and left there for use in unloading LSTs, APAs, AKs and merchant ships under control of USASOS.

RESUPPLY IN PHILIPPINES AND BORNEO CAMPAIGNS

The system of using small echelons of amphibious craft for resupply was employed until the MOROTAI campaign. The long distance involved in the LEYTE and LINGAYEN campaigns made it necessary to supplement amphibious craft with heavy merchant shipping sailed in convoy. In the later Philippine and Borneo campaigns the majority of amphibious ships were required for the numerous operations scheduled and therefore were not available for resupply functions. The reduction of the Japanese air threat in the Philippines made early use of merchant shipping for resupply feasible and it was successfully employed.

Amphibious shipping was normally used for assault and for one turn-around. Commander Amphibious Force, however, retained the responsibility for the protection of amphibious, Navy Auxiliary, and USASOS merchant ships in the objective areas until relieved by Commander Philippine Sea Frontier.

PART II (c) (2)

BEACH PARTIES

HISTORY

When Amphibious Operations by the SEVENTH Amphibious Force commenced in June 1943, no established or organized beach parties were available. Some personnel had been temporarily assigned to beach party duties. These assisted in the loading operations of amphibious craft at MILNE BAY during June 1943 and in beaching at WOODLARK and KIRIWINA ISLANDS on 30 June. The landing at WOODLARK ISLAND was smooth and satisfactory due to previous experience in loading at MILNE BAY. The landing at KIRIWINA ISLAND was confused and unsatisfactory. The difficulites in the latter case were caused by lack of prior training, poor beaches and insufficient equipment.

During the LAE and FINSCHHAFEN Operations in September 1943 the beaches were operated by the Military Landing Officer (Army). Soundings were taken by Engineer Shore Brigade boats and landing craft direction was under Army supervision. At FINSCHHAFEN an Australian beach party of two officers and six men was designated to assist the Army but their effectiveness was limited by lack of equipment, and by the loss of their senior officer (Lt. Comdr. J. M. BAND, RANR) who was mortally wounded while landing. Beaching control was unsatisfactory during the assault and also for the resupply landings. Beaches were not adequately marked, communications were poor, and liaison between ships and shore activities was practically non-existent.

The unsatisfactory conditions on the beaches in the early landings indicated the need for trained beach parties to perform purely naval duties on the beach and to act as direct liaison between Army Units and the Naval Commanders. In organizing such parties it was evident that some variations from FTP 167 and 211 was required. No APAs were available in the Southwest Pacific Area to furnish standard beach parties. Beach parties would be needed primarily in connection with the beaching and retracting of LSTs, LCIs, LCTs, and LSMs. The Commander SEVENTH Amphibious Force therefore directed the organization of independent beach parties, to operate directly under him or under the Attack Group Commander. Such parties were to be especially trained to meet the conditions expected to be found in amphibious landings in the Southwest Pacific Area.

Beach Party No. 1 was organized about 1 October 1943, and Beach Party No. 2 about a month later. Both based and trained at Amphibious Training Command, MILNE BAY, NEW GUINEA. Organized Parties were employed at ARAWE and in all subsequent operations.

Beach Party No. 1 (Lt. Comdr. FLIPPIN with 16 men) assisted in the landing at ARAWE. Inexperience and personnel shortage in the Beach Party, an untrained shore party, and the inexperience of Army Boat Control Officers caused this first beach operation to be poorly conducted. Beach Party No. 1 again too part in the CAPE GLOUCESTER operation. With the experience gained at ARAWE, it performed well, and the beach operations, despite a difficult landing, were good. The performance of Beach Party No. 2 in its first operation, SAIDOR, was also satisfactory.

On 6 January 1944, the Australian LSIs were directed to form beach parties on board similar to the American APA type beach parties. These beach parties were trained by the ships themselves independent of the other beach parties.

In April 1944 three additional beach parties were formed and these were used in the AITAPE-HUMBOLDT-TANAMERAH Landings. In these operations the beach parties performed well with a Navy beachmaster in full charge of beaching ships and craft at each beach.

Between operations all parties reorganized and retrained at the Amphibious Training Center, MILNE BAY, NEW GUINEA. By 1 September the number of beach parties was increased to eight and in late September their home base was changed to HOLLANDIA, NEW GUINEA. Single parties took part in the WADKE, BIAK and SANSAPOR Operations, while two parties were used at both NOEMFOOR and MOROTAI. The personnel in these parties were all selected volunteers and as an incentive it was planned to grant leave in Australia after every third operation.

Beach parties 1, 3, 7 and 8 engaged in the LEYTE Operation. For the first time they operated with APA beach parties and with a large number of small craft. The situation was handled by assigning certain beaches to APA landing boats and other beaches to large amphibious craft. The APA beach parties handled their own boats while the SEVENTH Amphibious Force beach parties (who remained in some cases for as long as seven weeks) supervised all beaches. This system was used because of the rapid turnover of transport beach parties. With sufficient equipment and a workable procedure between the two types of beach parties in effect, the beach operation was well conducted.

In December 1944 the Naval Beach Parties were commissioned as a unit under command of Lt. Comdr. E. R. HALLORAN, USNR. This unit was based at HOLLANDIA. New beach parties were formed from B4D (Port Director) units arriving from the United States until by 1 January there were eleven in all.

Amphibious Scouts acted as beachmasters for the Mapia-Asia landing.

Beach Party operation was satisfactory in the MINDORO landing.

Beach parties 2, 4, 5 and 6 took part in the LINGAYEN GULF Operation. They worked again in conjunction with APA beach parties with good results.

Beach parties engaged in the SUBIC, the NASUGBU and the PALAWAN Operations with continued success.

On 9 March 1945 the Beach Party Headquarters was lifted from HOLLANDIA, NEW GUINEA and later established in SUBIC BAY, LUZON, adjacent to but independent to the Amphibious Training Command.

Beach parties engaged in ZAMBOANGA, PANAY, CEBU, NEGROS, LEGASPI, SANGA SANGA, JOLO, PARANG, and DAVAO GULF Landings.

One beach party was assigned for each of the BORNEO operations. However actual beach party functions in these operations were performed by a RAN Commando Unit, organized and trained for such and attached to the FIRST Australian Corps. The SEVENTH Amphibious Force Beach Party performed liaison and standby communication functions only. The RAN units performed their duties with proficiency and enthusiasm.

During June and July 1945, the SEVENTH Amphibious Force Beach Parties and the Beach Party Camp at SUBIC were absorbed into the beach party organization of the Amphibious Forces, U.S. Pacific Fleet. This was done in anticipation of the transfer of the SEVENTH Amphibious Force to the Amphibious Forces, Pacific. A new type of beach party known as the Beach Party Transfer Team consisting of 2 officers and 10 men was to be organized in the Amphibious Forces Pacific. These teams were to perform overall beach party functions beyond capabilities of APA Beach Parties and to provide for continued beach party responsibility which was not possible with constant turnover of APA beach party personnel. These beach transfer teams were composed primarily of former SEVENTH Amphibious Force personnel.

In addition Force Beachmaster staff was organized, to assist that officer in controlling the beaches over which a full Corps would be landed from an Amphibious Force. The staff consisted of one LST officer, one LSM officer, one LCT officer, all with experience in previous operations, two experienced beachmasters and one or more Civil Engineer Corps officers experienced in pontoon causeway and barge management.

Training of the Force Beachmaster staffs and the Beach Party Transfer Teams of the THIRD and SEVENTH Amphibious Forces was conducted at the former SEVENTH Amphibious Force Beach Party Headquarters. This training was in charge of Commodore M. O. CARLSON, USN, Commander Transport Squadron THIRTEEN. The training was terminated with the end of the war and personnel transferred to the various Amphibious Forces for employment in the JAPAN and KOREA occupations.

Six Transfer Teams, with 2 medical officers and 4 corpsmen, and 10 communication personnel were assigned to the SEVENTH Amphibious Force, and organized into one company of 3 platoons. Each platoon had sufficient equipment to care for one assault beach. This trained personnel with the Force Beachmaster staff, all under Captain C. W. GRAY, USN, SEVENTH Amphibious Force Beachmaster, formed the beach parties used in the KOREAN and NORTH CHINA occupations. They performed the new and unusual beach party tasks required in these landings with much credit. (A Garrison Beach Party was assigned by Commander Amphibious Forces Pacific to the SEVENTH Amphibious Force for the occupation landings. It was not required and never left MANILA, P.I.).

Upon completion of their tasks in NORTH CHINA, beach party personnel not due for release embarked in the U.S.S. CATOCTIN to form a nucleous of a beach party organization of Amphibious Force, U.S. Atlantic Fleet.

BEACH PARTY ORGANIZATION

As already noted Beach Parties in the Southwest Pacific Area have varied both in organization and procedure from the standard set forth in FTP 167 and FTP 211. This variation was designed to meet the geographical and operational conditions existing in this area and to service the type of shipping used.

The personnel normally assigned were:

1 Beachmaster (Lt. or Lt. Comdr.)
1 Asst. Beachmaster (Lt. or Lt.(jg))
1 Medical Officer (Lt. or Lt.(jg)) and 3 Pharmacist's Mates
8 Men in Hydrographic section
7 Men in Communication section
3 Men in repair section
9 Men in Boat crews
Special equipment assigned included:
2 LCV(P)
1 Weapon carrier with 1/2 ton trailer.

The Beachmaster normally operated directly under the command of the Naval Attack Force Commander. He was responsible for a hydrographic reconnaissance of the beach; for small craft salvage; for issuing instructions to landing craft and landing ships with regard to beaching, unloading, evacuation of wounded and retracting, and for liaison with the Army Shore Party.

This type of organization worked well because most of the operations were primarily shore-to-shore and the shipping used principally amphibious, (LSM, LCT, LCI, LST). In the few large operations were APAs from other areas were used, the beaches were divided and the APA beach parties handled their own boats on their assigned beaches while the SEVENTH Amphibious Force Beach Parties handled the large amphibious craft on their assigned beaches.

After the assault the prime function of the Beach Party was

to maintain liaison between the ships and the shore party. This liaison was extremely important as the shore party furnished bull dozers for building sand ramps, trucks and working parties for unloading cargo and it was the function of the beach party to relay Army requests for priorities.

During the assault phase of an operation all naval boats and amphibious craft on leaving the line of departure came under the control of the senior beachmaster at the designated beach and followed his instruction concerning beaching, unloading, evacuation of wounded and retracting. This control continued as long as Navy ships were unloading in the objective area. It applied however, to the Engineer Special Brigade boats only during the assault unloading and when these boats were assigned to unload amphibious craft in resupply echelons.

SEVENTH AMPHIBIOUS FORCE BEACH PARTIES
(Southwest Pacific Area Operations)

Organized	No.	Original Beachmasters	Later Beachmasters
1 Oct 1943	1	Lt.Comdr. R. N. FLIPPIN	Lt. R. G. WALTER
1 Nov 1943	2	Lt. R. G. CONGDON	Lt. R. H. LUNDIN
1 Apr 1944	3	Lt.Comdr. E. T. HALLORAN	Lt. W. M. DOX
1 April 1944	4	Lt. E. ZINZER	Lt.(jg) J. H. LEE
1 April 1944	5	Lt. M. M. WILLIAMS	Lt. E. R. JOHNSON
1 Sep 1944	7	Lt. Comdr. J. R. AVERY	
1 Sep 1944	8	Lt. T. NORDYKE	
1 Jan 1945	9	Lt. J. T. RATYOWSKI	
1 Jan 1945	10	Lt. D. F. MYERS	
1 Jan 1945	11	Lt. B. W. JONES	

SEVENTH AMPHIBIOUS FORCE BEACHMASTER AND STAFF
(Olympic Operation and Occupation of Korea and North China)

Captain C. W. GRAY - Force Beachmaster

Commander D. M. BAKER - (Former LST Group Commander)

Commander SCHEPHERS - (CEC) - Pontoon Specialist

Lt. Comdr. W. A. BURGETT - (Former LSM Group Commander)

Lt. Comdr. T. NORDYKE - (Former Beachmaster)

Lt. A. S. KAMINSKI - (Former LCT Group Commander)

Lt. E. R. JOHNSON - (Former Beachmaster)

Lt.(jg) R. E. STILGENBAUER (CEC) - Pontoon Specialist

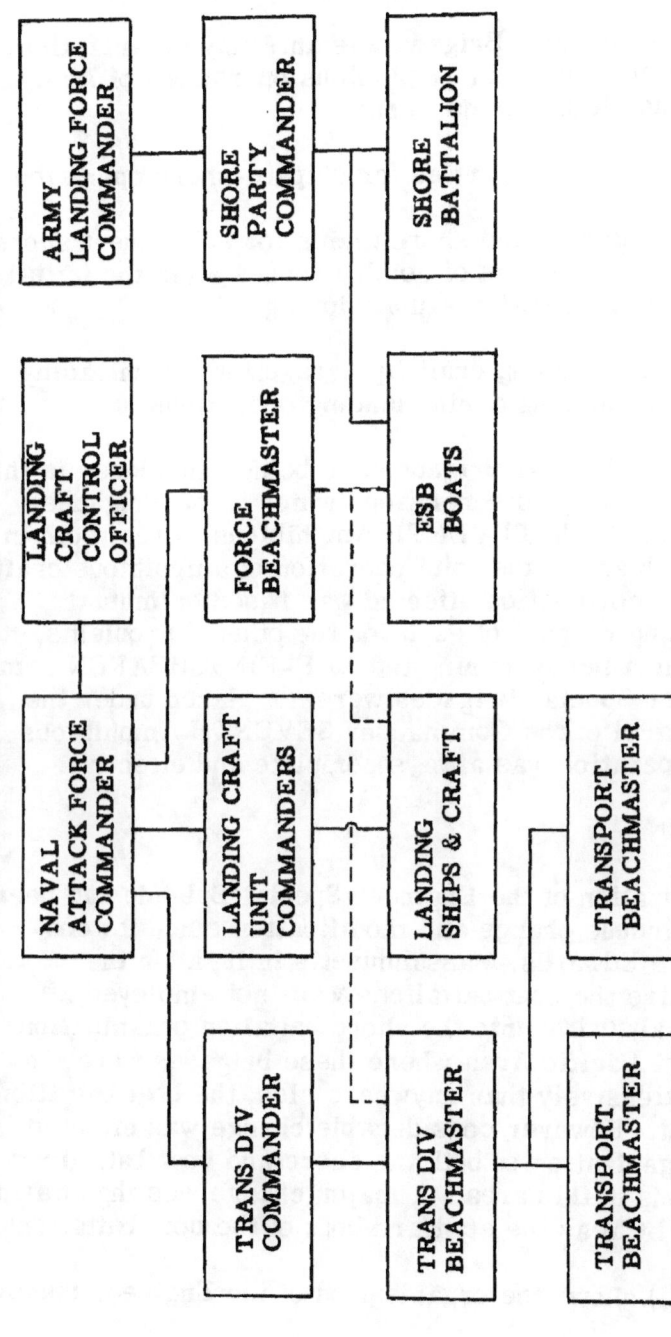

PART II (c) (3)

ENGINEER SPECIAL BRIGADES (SHORE PARTIES)

GENERAL

The Engineer Special Brigade was an Army organization, especially created to support amphibious operations of Army troops. Its principle missions were:

(1) To provide shore parties for ship-to-shore operations.

(2) To provide boat and shore teams for subsequent shore-to-shore operations of combat forces after the initial landing from naval assault shipping.

(3) To provide landing craft lighterage for the unloading of heavy shipping during landing operations.

The Engineer Special Brigades are being considered in this history because of the close relations which these Brigades necessarily had with the SEVENTH Amphibious Force, both in shore party work and in the joint operation of amphibious craft. The successful coordination effected was based on mutual understanding and respect of each for the others' problems. Except for a short period during the LAE-FINSCHHAFEN campaigns, Engineer Special Brigades were not placed under the operational control of the Commander SEVENTH Amphibious Force, but cooperation was always complete and effective.

ORGANIZATION

The organization of the Engineer Special Brigade had been subject to continuous change and modification since its conception at Camp Edwards, Massachusetts in 1941. In the European Theatre the boat battalions were not employed as such, but were absorbed into the shore battalion organization. In the Southwest Pacific Area where these brigades were employed more extensively than anywhere else, the boat battalions remained intact. However, considerable change was effected in the internal organization of both the shore and boat battalions, to suit conditions in this area. A major change was the shifting from LCVP to LCM as the standard boat of the boat battalions.

Appendix (1) shows the organization of the Engineer Special

Brigade as used in the Southwest Pacific. Appendix (2) indicates the composition of Engineer Special Brigade Task Groups which were formed to operate with the various sizes of landing forces.

The Engineer Special Brigade units were only the nucleous of the shore party organization and were augmented by labor and service troops. The number of additional troops required depended entirely upon the size of the landing force and the mission, but included any or all of the following type units: Engineer Combat Battalion, Quartermaster Service Companies, Port Companies, Truck Companies, Amphibian Truck Companies, Military Police, and Ordnance Ammunition Companies.

FUNCTIONS

During planning and assault phase the Commanding General of an ESB or the Commanding Officer of the ESB Task Group served as a special staff officer and advisor to the Landing Force Commander. When the Landing Force command post moved forward, control of the service command area (the immediate beachhead area) was then vested in the Brigade or Task Group Commander. When a higher echelon of command, such as an Army Service Command, assumed control of the beaches; the ESB Task Group passed to the control of this higher command.

The Engineer Boat and Shore Regiment was the basic element of the Engineer Special Brigade. The Boat Battalion transported and landed troops, supplies and equipment, evacuated prisoners and wounded, and effected resupply. These functions were performed either as a ship-to-shore or a shore-to-shore operation. The Shore Battalion facilitated the movement of troops, supplies and equipment across the beach and into bivouac and dump areas, assisted in the evacuation of wounded and prisoners, and provided a perimeter defense for the immediate beach area. These Battalions were especially trained in the organization and development of beachheads and the handling of cargo and had the necessary equipment to perform these duties. The personnel were mostly machinery operators, mechanics, checkers and supervisors. Semi and unskilled labor came from the attached labor and service units. Appendix (3) illustrates the layout of an Engineer Boat and Shore Regiment for beach operations.

COMMAND RELATIONSHIP

The Engineer Special Brigade Shore Battalions with attached

service troops performed all shore party functions under control and direction of the Landing Force Commander or his designated subordinates.

In all ship-to-shore operations, boats and personnel of the Boat Battalions were lifted to the target area in transports, LSDs, and LSTs which left their regularly assigned boats temporarily in the rear area. Commander SEVENTH Amphibious Force or his designated Amphibious Group Commanders retained control of these Boat Battalions until all assault shipping had been unloaded - usually a period of four or five days. Control was effected in the same manner as though the boats were navy-manned, through the Beachmasters, Landing Craft Control Officers, Transport Division and Squadron Commanders. Usually Commanding Officers of ships carrying these boats placed a coxswain aboard each army manned boat to interpret signals and to ensure that boats reported to the control ships and returned to the correct ship for subsequent loads.

When assault shipping was unloaded, ESB boats were released to the control of the Boat and Shore Regiment Commander concerned. A portion of these boats were then available for shore-to-shore movements, supply of outposts along the coast and various administrative duties. The balance of the boats remained in a pool to be used for lighterage to unload heavy shipping of subsequent echelons.

The Engineer Special Brigade LCVPs and LCMs could not meet all lighterage requirements, and a navy lighterage pool of LCTs was usually provided. Control of the navy craft was maintained through the Landing Craft Control Officer. Some Army Commanders believed that this Navy lighterage should have been under ESB control after the assault phase, but it was believed that ESB personnel did not have sufficient understanding of hydrographic conditions, seamanship, handling and maintainence of these larger craft to warrant such a transfer of control. Therefore, after the assault phase, lighterage requirements were jointly determined and agreed upon by the ESB unit commander concerned and the Landing Craft Control Officer in that area.

These Landing Craft Control Officers were not always designated as such. In the later stages of an operation when only heavy shipping under army control was being unloaded, liaison was maintained directly between ESB personnel and the LCT Flotilla or Group Commander. In the Philippines and Borneo operations, the SEVENTH Amphibious Force representatives assumed the duties formerly performed by the Landing Craft Control Officers.

SUMMARY

The Engineer Special Brigade or the Shore Battalion of the Engineer Boat and Shore Regiment is believed to be the best solution developed for the still unsolved shore party problem in amphibious operations. Throughout the New Guinea and Philippines campaigns these units performed their missions well. With sufficient service troops attached, they have always been capable of accomplishing the main task of a shore party - the expeditious movement of supplies across the beaches.

SHORE PARTY

ENGR. SPECIAL BRIGADE

- BRIG. Hq. — 26-0, 1-WO

Hq. Co. & Med. Det. — 19-0, 210 EM
- Hq. Co. 4 MED. DET. — 5-0; 112 EM
- Hq. DET. & SP. PTS. PLAT. — 8-0, 72 EM

BOAT MAINT. BN. — 32-0; 797 EM
- BN. Hq. — 3-0
  - QM. Hq. — 3-0
    - Hq. Co. — 1-0; 61 EM
    - HV. SHOP CO. — 6-0, 165 EM
  - MAINT. Co. — 6-0, 185 EM
  - MAINT. Co. — 6-0, 185 EM
  - MAINT. Co. — 6-0, 185 EM

BOAT & SHORE REGT. — 95-0; 2-WO, 1864 EM (×3)
- REGT. Hq. — 7-0
- Hq. DET. — 3-0, 40 EM
- MEDICAL BN. — 31-0, 389 EM
  - BN. Hq. — 4-0
  - Co. A — 8-0, 117 EM
  - Co. B — 8-0, 117 EM
  - Co. C — 8-0, 117 EM
- SIG. CO. — 6-0, 1-WO, 117 EM
- ORDNANCE CO. — 5-0, 1-WO, 87 EM

BOAT BN. — 44-0, 990 EM
- BN. Hq. — 3-0
- Hq. Co. — 5-0, 75 EM
- Co. A — 12-0, 305 EM
- Co. B — 12-0, 305 EM
- Co. C — 12-0, 305 EM
- 42 LCM, 9 LCVP

SHORE BN. — 25-0, 664 EM
- BN. Hq. — 3-0
- Hq. Co. — 4-0, 142 EM
- Co. D — 6-0, 174 EM
- Co. E — 6-0, 174 EM
- Co. F — 5-0, 174 EM
- 4 DUKW

Seventh Amphibious
Force History
Shore Party - Engineer
Brigade
Sheet 1

ENGINEER SPECIAL BRIGADE TASK GROUPS

(1) BRIGADE TASK GROUP; to support a Corps.

    Engineer Special Brigade

    Total Strength;   403 Officers   7155 enlisted men
    Total vehicles;   1258 vehicles of 7783 DWT
    DWT bulk cargo;   4400 DWT
        (DWT cargo does not include class I-V supplies)

(2) REGIMENTAL TASK GROUP; to support an Infantry Division.

    1 Engineer Boat and Shore Regiment
    1 Engineer Boat Maintenance Company
    1 Medical Company
    Detachment Ordnance Maintenance Company

    Total Strength;   119 Officers   2265 enlisted men
    Total vehicles;   341 vehicles of 2295 DWT
    DWT bulk cargo;   900 DWT

(3) REGIMENTAL TASK GROUP, REDUCED, (less 1 Bn Task Group) to support an Infantry Division (less 1 RCT)

    1 Engineer Boat and Shore Regt (less 1 Boat Co, 1 Shore Co.)
    1 Engineer Boat Maintenance Co. (less 1 Plat.)
    1 Medical Co. (less detachments)

    Total strength;   80 Officers   1500 enlisted men
    Total vehicles;   247 vehicles of 1530 DWT
    DWT bulk cargo;   600 DWT

(4) BATTALION TASK GROUP; to support an Infantry RCT.

    Detachment Regt'l Headquarters Company
    1 Engineer Boat Company
    1 Engineer Shore Company
    1 Platoon, Engineer Boat Maintenance Company
    Detachment Medical Company

    Total strength;   40 Officers   755 enlisted men
    Total vehicles;   94 vehicles of 765 DWT
    DWT bulk cargo;   300 DWT

NOTE: All Task Groups to have attached labor and service units as required for the particular operation.

APPENDIX (2)

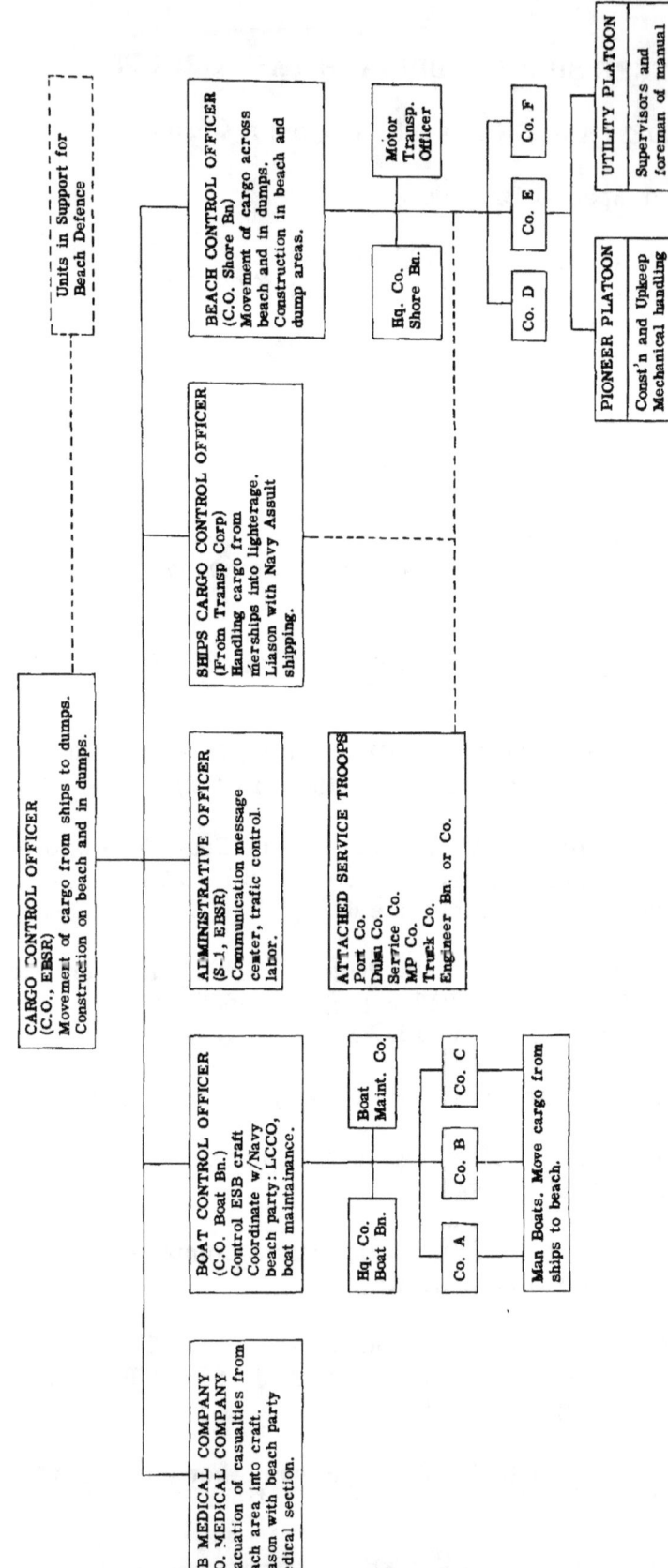

Seventh Amphibious Force History
Shore Party, Eng Special Brigade
Sheet 2

PART II (c) (4)

LANDING CRAFT CONTROL OFFICERS -

SEVENTH AMPHIBIOUS FORCE REPRESENTATIVES

The successful completion of each Amphibious assault meant the immediate establishment and development of a new base of operations. At these new bases Commander SEVENTH Amphibious Force would assume the responsibility for the operation of the port and to a certain extent for the naval facilities. He retained this responsibility until other naval agencies, usually Service Force or the various Sea Frontier Commands had their equipment brought forward and were in a position to relieve him. In the early stages of the New Guinea Campaigns, this period lasted for several months. As Sea Frontier Commands became better organized, they were able to assume these duties within a shorter period of time after the completion of a landing, and did so in later campaigns within a month of the initial landings. This was the usual period required for one turn-around of amphibious shipping.

It was generally necessary for Commander SEVENTH Amphibious Force or the Attack Group Commander to leave the assault area soon after the landing force was firmly established in order to plan and prepare for subsequent operations. To effect control of these ports and to control the amphibious shipping which continued to operate therein, Commander SEVENTH Amphibious Force would appoint an officer to directly represent him there. The officer designated was usually one who had had a part in the assault operation. During the New Guinea campaign, these officers were termed Landing Craft Control Officers. Later, during the Philippine and Borneo campaigns, they became known as SEVENTH Amphibious Force Representatives. Their duties consisted in the operation of the port so long as Commander SEVENTH Amphibious Force had this responsibility, and in addition, providing services for amphibious vessels and maintaining liaison with the local Army authorities.

An important duty of the landing craft control officer during the New Guinea campaign was the direction of landing craft in the assault landings. At Cape Gloucester the LCCO was made responsible for the safe passage of the landing craft through the navigational dangers in the assault area and for guiding the craft

to beaches. The outstanding success of this landing attested
to the merits of this system which was used thereafter throughout the Southwest Pacific Area and became standard doctrine in
all amphibious operations, i.e., using a senior and experienced
officer with suitable navigational aids to direct the landing craft
to their assigned beaches.

Several Captains and Commanders were attached to the Staff
as Landing Craft Control Officers. Other officers on the staff
also performed this duty in addition to their regular duties. Later
during the Philippines and Borneo Campaigns when the size of
the force had materially increased, it was sometimes practicable
to assign flotilla or group commanders to the duty as SEVENTH
Amphibious Force Representatives in various ports for short
periods.

Landing Craft Control Officers and SEVENTH Amphibious
Force Representatives not only routed amphibious ships but also
performed such administrative duties for them as was necessary,
especially in connection with maintenance and supplies.

A large proportion of the SEVENTH Amphibious Force operated
from Leyte during the Philippine and Borneo campaigns and the
task of Representative at Leyte was of major importance. From
the date of the initial landing until February 1945, either Commander
SEVENTH Amphibious Force or one of his Group Commanders was
present at Leyte. In February, when Commander SEVENTH Amphibious Force moved in his flagship to Subic Bay, he directed
the SEVENTH Amphibious Force Representative at Leyte to
control the loading, unloading, and movement of the large number
of ships that were in that area and to coordinate his work
with the Administrative Command SEVENTH Amphibious
Force and the Service Force, SEVENTH Fleet, in providing
for their upkeep. In July 1945 the operation of all Amphibious
Craft in the Philippines was assigned to Commander Amphibious
Group NINE.

PART II (c) (5)

ASSIGNMENT OF AUSTRALIAN AND BRITISH SHIPS TO SEVENTH AMPHIBIOUS FORCE

During the period that the SEVENTH Amphibious Force operated in the Southwest Pacific Area, certain Australian and British naval vessels were assigned to the operational control of Commander SEVENTH Amphibious Force.

AUSTRALIAN SHIPS

The first such ships to be assigned were three Royal Australian Navy Landing Ships Infantry (LSI) -- HMAS MANOORA, WESTRALIA and KANIMBLA. Before conversion into LSIs, these ships had been used as Armed Merchant Cruisers. MANOORA was the first ship converted and conformed to the British plan of mess decks and hammocks for troops aboard. Troop capacity was limited to about 850 and the hammocks did not prove to be satisfactory. Upon recommendation of Commander SEVENTH Amphibious Force, the two remaining ships were converted on the pattern of U.S. type APAs with installed standee bunks and a cafeteria system for messes. Troop capacity was thereby increased to 1250, and results were so satisfactory that MANOORA was then returned to the Navy Yard at Sydney where similar alterations were made. These ships carried U.S. landing craft, 20-22 LCVPs and 2-3 LCM(3)s. Landing craft were furnished by the SEVENTH Amphibious Force.

From the middle of 1943 until the AITAPE-HUMBOLDT BAY-TANAMERAH BAY operations in April 1944, these three LSIs, with the USS HENRY T. ALLEN, were the only transports available to the SEVENTH Amphibious Force. They continued to operate with this force through the NEW GUINEA, PHILIPPINES, and BORNEO Operations and accomplished all missions assigned them in a most creditable manner.

The AUSTRALIAN frigates HMAS BURDEKIN, BARCOO, HAWKSBURY, and GASCOYNE were assigned to the SEVENTH Amphibious Force for escort duty in several of the NEW GUINEA Operations and for the landings in BORNEO.

HMAS LACHLAN and WARREGO formed the hydrographic

and survey unit in the NEW GUINEA, PHILIPPINES, and BORNEO Operations and their invaluable service contributed materially to the success of these campaigns.

BRITISH SHIPS

HMS ARIADNE, a cruiser type minelayer of the Royal Navy, was assigned to the SEVENTH Amphibious Force from October 1944 to January 1945, and was temporarily converted to carry troops while working with APDs in the landings on DINAGAT and HOMONHAN ISLANDS in the LEYTE Operation. Later, Captain Lord ASHBOURNE, Commanding Officer of the ARIADNE, was the Task Group Commander for the landings on ASIA and MAPIA ISLANDS off the Coast of DUTCH NEW GUINEA. These missions were accomplished with credit to the ship and its commanding officer.

In September 1944, seven British LSIs under command of Rear Admiral TALBOT, RN, reported to Commander SEVENTH Amphibious Force for duty. These ships were:

HMS LOTHIAN (Headquarters Ship)
HMS EMPIRE MACE   HMS EMPIRE SPEARHEAD
HMS GLENEARN   HMS EMPIRE BATTLEAXE
HMS CLAN LAMONT   HMS EMPIRE ARQUEBUS

The design and material condition of the British LSIs made them unsuitable for use in assault operations and they were assigned to the Amphibious Training Group for duty. These ships carried the British type LCA and it was not practicable to alter them to accomodate the U.S. type LCVP. Capacity was limited to about 800 troops and cargo space was extremely limited.

Upon completion of troop training in the NEW GUINEA area, the British LSIs made a lift of service troops from NEW GUINEA to the PHILIPPINES and at the end of February 1945, were released to the British Pacific Fleet.

Vice Admiral BARBEY with Rear Admiral FORREST B. ROYAL, U.S. Navy, Commander Amphibious Group SIX.

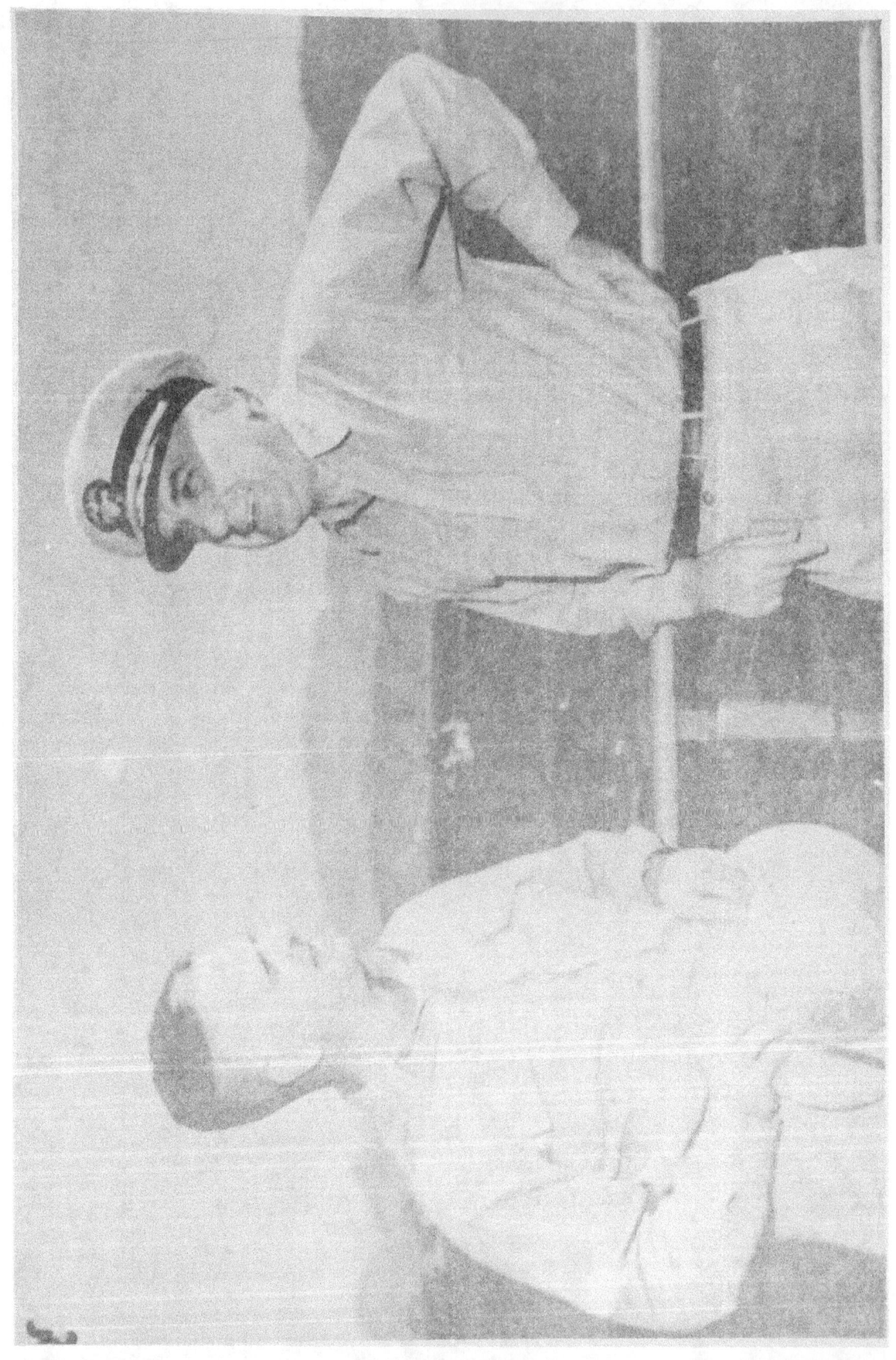

PART II (d)

SPECIAL OPERATIONS

SEVENTH AMPHIBIOUS FORCE

DURING PHILIPPINES - BORNEO

CAMPAIGNS

PART II (d) (1)

MINESWEEPING OPERATIONS - PHILIPPINES AND BORNEO

PHILIPPINE MINESWEEPING OPERATIONS

Minesweeping operations in the Philippines began on 17 October 1944 in preparation for the assault landing on LEYTE which took place three days later. The minesweeping group, which was part of the Fire Support and Bombardment Force under Rear Admiral Oldendorf, consisted of 17 DMSs, 10 AMs, 2 DMs, 22 YMSs, and one APD with small boat sweeping gear. In sweeping the entrances to Leyte Gulf between HOMOHAN and DINAGAT Islands, the transport and fire support areas, and the approach to the assault beaches, the group discovered a large mine field and cut 306 mines. Typhoon weather rendered the work more difficult and so seriously damaged the YMS 70 that she was later abandoned and sunk. In order to complete the operation within the scheduled time, a narrower channel was swept than had originally been planned, but all ships of the two amphibious forces engaged in the landing passed through without loss. One destroyer of the support force was damaged by a mine but managed to make port.

Minesweepers were employed to prepare the way for the assault landings at ORMOC and MINDORO on 7 December and 15 December respectively, but no mines were encountered. Minesweepers in both operations were under air attack but none were hit.

For the assault on LINGAYEN, the minesweeping group again served under Vice Admiral Oldendorf. The group consisting of 10 DMSs, 10 AMs, 2 DMs, 42 YMSs and 1 APD, proceeded to Lingayen

Gulf with Fire Support and Bombardment Group, and began sweeping on 6 January. In three days only two mines were cut in sweeping 490 square miles of the Gulf of Lingayen despite advance intelligence that a large mine field was located there. The explanation was supplied later by a report that Filipinos, acting independently, had cut 350 mines in the Gulf during a six-weeks period before the sweeping commenced. The ships conducting the pre-assault bombardment and minesweeping at Lingayen were subjected to the full strength of the enemy air forces of the Philippines and Formosa, including suicide attacks, and sustained heavy losses. In the minesweeping group, the DMSs HOVEY, LONG and PALMER were sunk, and the HOPKINS, SOUTHARD and YMS 53 were damaged.

Upon completion of the assault landings on 9 January, Commander LINGAYEN ATTACK FORCE, Vice Admiral Kincaid, directed the minesweeping group to report for operational control to Commander Task Force 78 who was the Commander SEVENTH Amphibious Force, Vice Admiral Barbey. From that time until the completion of the BALIKPAPAN Operation in July 1945 all but a few of the Seventh Fleet minecraft operated under his command.

After assuming operational control of the minesweeping group, the Commander Seventh Amphibious Force moved damaged vessels to the rear for repairs, and begun the gradual release of the large number of vessels temporarily assigned from the PACIFIC Fleet. In the meantime minesweepers were clearing approaches for supporting operations on LUZON. Approach and transport areas were swept for the assault landings at SAN FELIPE, ZAMBALES PROVINCE and at NASUGBU, south of Manila Bay. No mines were discovered in these operations, but one mine was cut in a sweep of SUBIC BAY.

After Subic Bay had been secured, six AMs and 16 YMSs were assigned as minesweepers to clear approaches for the assault landing to be made at MARIVELES on 15 February and on CORREGIDOR on 16 February. Although protected by fire support of cruisers and destroyers, several minesweepers were hit by gunfire from shore. One AM and two destroyers were damaged by mine explosions but reached port. The approach to MARI-VELES BAY, the fire support and transport areas, and the south channel between CORREGIDOR, and FORT DRUM (EL FRAILE) were swept before the assault landings.

While Army forces were still fighting on CORREGIDOR, and in the city of MANILA, one AM and 15 YMSs commenced the clearing of Manila Bay for shipping. This was a large and difficult task, which began on 24 February and continued until the middle of April. Numerous sunken hulks interfered with sweeping and in the inner harbor LCVPs fitted with small boat sweeping gear worked around the sunken hulks. 615 square miles were swept in Manila Bay and 561 mines destroyed.

During the remaining period in which the minecraft operated in the Seventh Amphibious Force, minesweeping operations were of two general types: (1) Sweeping in advance of amphibious operations and (2) Clearing Philippine waters for shipping in areas already secured. Operations of the second type had not been completed when the Seventh Amphibious Force relinquished minesweeping responsibility to Commander Philippine Sea Frontier on 15 July 1945.

Until the BORNEO Operations, where influence mines were encountered for the first time, minesweeping in support of amphibious landings was not difficult of accomplishment, and only one minesweeper (YMS 71 at Tawi-Tawi in the Sulu Archipelago) was sunk by mine explosion. However the large number of landings added to other minesweeping committments placed a heavy burden on the ships engaged. The personnel were subjected to long operations without respite and there was insufficient time for complete overhaul of vessels.

While some of the minesweepers were sweeping as part of amphibious operations, others began the work of clearing the way for shipping in the SAN BERNADINO STRAITS - VERDE ISLAND Passage approach to Manila Bay: CASIGURAN SOUND on the east coast of Luzon; BATANGAS, BALAYAN, and TAYABAS BAYS on the south coast of Luzon, and the BALABAC Straits, between Palawan and Borneo. The Sentry, Salute, Scrimmage, Scout and Scuffle, five AMs of Mine Division 34, temporarily assigned to the Seventh Fleet from the Pacific Fleet, did most of this sweeping. CASIGURAN SOUND was swept without finding any mines but a field was discovered to the south at BALER BAY where 95 mines were cut. A later exploratory sweep was made of the area to assure that this field was cleared.

On 22 April, 4 AMs, accompanied by 2 LCIs serving as mine disposal vessels and with DEs for support, began sweeps in BALABAC Straits which resulted in 57 mines being cut.

BORNEO MINESWEEPING OPERATIONS

Minesweeping for the Borneo Campaign was more extensive and difficult than any undertaken in the Philippines subsequent to the Manila Bay Operation. The four landing areas selected, TARAKAN, BRUNEI BAY, MIRI-LUTONG and BALIKPAPAN, were all of considerable strategic importance, and the Japanese had mined them all. In addition, many magnetic mines had been planted by the Allied Air Force and RAAF. About 30 of these mines were dropped at TARAKAN, 10 at BRUNEI BAY and almost 100 at BALIKPAPAN.

Twelve YMSs began sweeping operations at TARAKAN on 28 April, in preparation for the assault landings on 1 May 1945. Both magnetic and moored sweeping was conducted in the approach to the harbor and for fire support areas outside the harbor. The landings were to be made inside the harbor and that whole area as well as the entrance around the north end of the island were swept, and 89 mines cut. A mine damaged the YMS 329, while YMS 481 was sunk, and YMS 334 and YMS 364 were damaged by fire from enemy shore batteries. One destroyer was mined but succeeded in making port.

Operations in the BRUNEI BAY area commenced on 7 June in anticipation of the first assault landings on 10 June. 5 AMs, 12 YMSs and one APD carrying small boat minesweeping gear were assigned for the operation. Sweeping was conducted off the approaches to BRUNEI BAY, then inside the BAY itself, and finally off MIRI-LUTONG, the rich oil area about 120 miles south of BRUNEI BAY where an assault landing was to follow about 10 days after the initial landings at BRUNEI. In the BRUNEI BAY area 94 mines were swept. The AM, SALUTE, was mined and sunk during these operations. In conducting exploratory sweeps off MIRI-LUTONG a deep mine field was found; more than 600 mines were cut at depths greater than 80 feet. This field evidently had been placed to catch Allied submarines which might approach to sink tankers loading off LUTONG. Surface ships could have passed over this minefield with safety.

At BALIKPAPAN the minesweeping operations were the most difficult in the Southwest Pacific Area and perhaps in the whole war. There were almost 100 Allied magnetic mines, the water was shallow and filled with navigational hazards, and strong enemy shore batteries threatened the mine sweepers. The area in which Allied mines had been sown extended for about seven miles along the beach and five miles out. In addition, enemy moored mines in the entrance channels were reported.

Minesweeping operations commenced sixteen days before the assault date of 1 July 1945. It was not planned to complete the clearing of all danger areas before the assault, but only those required to be safe for the operations. Magnetic sweeping consumed most of the time since each ship could sweep a path of only about 100 yards.

To reduce the danger of loss, the wooden hulled YMSs were selected to do the magnetic minesweeping, and were carefully readied by a degaussing officer. Moored mine sweeping was started by 16 YMSs on 15 June 1945, a day in advance of the commencement of magnetic sweeps. No mines were uncovered until 18 June when YMS 50 was sunk by exploding a magnetic mine. On 19 June shore batteries opened upon the minesweepers, and, because of the continuing danger of mines, fire support vessels did not dare approach near enough to counter the fire. On three successive days commencing 20 June, YMS 368 was damaged by mine explosion, and YMS 335 and YMS 10 were hit by enemy shell fire. The continued harassment by shore batteries obliged the minesweepers to take evasive action, and many jettisoned their magnetic tails in order to escape the zone of fire. Loss of gear, and frequent engine and mechanical break-downs severely handicapped the ships which were serviced by only one minesweeper tender, an LSM, carrying limited spare parts and equipment. Some extra gear was flown in from MANUS and even from the UNITED STATES, but nevertheless there were times during the sweeping when not more than three YMSs were in operable condition for magnetic sweeping.

However, by 23 June there was reason to believe that the magnetic mines did not constitute as great a menace as had been feared. A more optimistic note appeared in reports of the commanders. That day several more minesweepers arrived to join in the task, while two destroyers and the Dutch Cruiser TROMP moved into the swept area to render much needed fire support to the harried minesweepers. The supporting fire dealt effectively with the shore batteries, and was a major factor in the successful completion of the minesweeping operations.

On 25 June one moored and three magnetic mines were swept.

At 2030 that night the minesweeping group was attacked with torpedoes launched by four enemy aircraft, but no hits were sustained. Three enemy planes were shot down. The following day a total of 11 moored and 6 magnetic mines were destroyed, but YMS 39 and YMS 365 struck mines and were lost during the course of the work. On 27 June one influence mine was swept and several of the jettisoned cables and magnetic tails were recovered.

On 28 June, two magnetic mines were swept, one of which exploded and badly damaged YMS 47, but the minesweeping commander was able to report that by F Day, 1 July, a channel would be cleared to the assault beaches reasonably safe for large ships. One more magnetic mine was swept on 30 June.

After the assault on 1 July, minesweepers transferred their activities to BALIKPAPAN Harbor, and completed the clearing of a channel by 7 July. 20 Japanese chemical horn type mines were disposed of.

SUMMARY OF MINESWEEPING OPERATIONS AT BALIKPAPAN

	Moored	Magnetic
Mines swept	34	16
YMSs sunk by mines	0	3
YMSs damaged by mines	0	1
YMSs damaged by gunfire	3	
Sets of Magnetic gear lost	15	
Personnel killed in action	7	
Personnel wounded in action	43	
Personnel missing in action	None reported	
Mental cases transferred from YMSs	10	
Other types of ships damaged by mines	0	

The BALIKPAPAN operation was the only instance in which the extremely effective ALLIED magnetic mines were swept under difficult combat conditions. The method by which the Japanese had previously disposed of a large number of these mines is not known.

Throughout the Philippines and Borneo operations Commander SEVENTH Amphibious Force was handicapped not only by the limited number of minecraft available but also by a lack of experienced senior minesweeping officers to direct and command YMS type ships. In several operations the senior YMS commanding officer doubled as commander of the minesweeping unit. For extensive operations, experienced officers from AMs or from the staff of Commander SEVENTH Amphibious Force had to be ordered to command task units.

During the Philippines and Borneo operations it is estimated that the Seventh Fleet minecraft swept 7500 miles of sea area. Approximately 1300 mines were cut or otherwise destroyed. About 400 mines were cut by native divers.

PART II (d) (2)

MOVEMENT OF SERVICE UNIT, SUPPLIES AND EQUIPMENT

FROM REAR TO FORWARD BASES

The advance of the forces of the Southwest Pacific along the North Coast of New Guinea and thence into the PHILIPPINES resulted in a chain of bases extending from AUSTRALIA to MANILA. These bases were established as rapidly as possible in order to provide the logistic support for Army and Navy elements involved in amphibious operations. The speed of advance was such that many so-called forward area bases were far in the rear before they could become either established or operative. Nevertheless these bases, as concentration areas from which troops and supplies could be staged forward, were vital to the success of the strategy of the campaign. However, each base established required a complement of service personnel for its operation, and due to the fact that strong forces of enemy troops were by-passed in the advance of our forces, each base also required the assignment of combat units for its protection. As a result of these factors, thousands of combat and service troops and tons of military supplies were scattered along the line of advance when MANILA was finally occupied and the task begun to make it a major base for further operations against Japan.

With the fall of MANILA to our forces, bases along the North coast of NEW GUINEA and elsewhere in the Southwest Pacific Area outside the Philippines were no longer essential. It was most important that the troops and their equipment be moved forward as rapidly as possible to the Philippine area, especially to LUZON. The critical problem was to get sufficient shipping not engaged with other committments, to make these important troop movements.

Forward movements of supporting troops, including Army Service units for air and ground forces, and Naval base units continued from the time of the capture of Manila until the end of the war. These troops should not be confused with those sent forward as part of operations to develop a new base. Their primary functions were to increase the capacity of already established bases. The movement of such troops was customarily by ships other than amphibious. But because of the accelerated tempo of operations, some amphibious shipping, with quick turn-around capability, was used for these movements.

In so far as naval amphibious shipping is concerned, these movements may be grouped into two general classes:

(a) Movement of critical support personnel from Leyte, Mindoro and New Guinea to Luzon.

(b) "Roll-up" or the moving forward of men and equipment from and the deactivation of rear area bases especially in New Guinea and the Solomon Islands.

Movement of Troops for Developing Luzon as a Base

In February 1945, General Headquarters, Southwest Pacific Area, ordered the expeditious movement of Service troops, both ground and air into the Luzon area. The movement was considered of sufficient importance that all possible amphibious shipping was made available, even to the extent of curtailing ship assignments to scheduled operations. About 125 LST loads of personnel and equipment, most of it of a heavy type, were moved, 25 LST loads from New Guinea, the remainder from Leyte and Mindoro. To do this job, Commander SEVENTH Amphibious Force, organized a Task Group 76.19 under Captain Manees, Commander LST Flotilla 15. 21 LSTs were originally assigned to this group. Additional LSTs and LSMs and LCIs were assigned from time to time as they were temporarily available for lifts in this operation, but the basic number was maintained until the operation neared its completion. Close liaison was established between GHQ, the units to be moved, and Commander Task Group 76.19, in order that time lost in loading and unloading could be reduced to a minimum. The operation was completed about 1 June 1945.

"Roll-Up" of Rear Areas

This operation constituted the bringing forward of all the

troops and equipment which were at bases no longer essential to the effort against Japan. Some were taken directly from New Guinea to Okinawa, but the majority were transported to the Philippines. The period between the completion of operations in Okinawa, Philippines and Borneo and the commencement of active preparations for the planned campaign against Kyushu was to be used for this movement. All shipping that could be made available was to be employed.

The SEVENTH Amphibious Force was concerned only with the movement to the Philippines and such movements as were necessary within the Philippines. LSTs released from active operations were overhauled and assigned to roll-up duties. APAs and AKAs from the Pacific Fleet in numbers equivalent to two transport squadrons were also assigned. These ships made one or two lifts, depending on the time they were made available. LSMs were employed for redistribution of troops between Philippine bases, especially divisions which required concentration for training in preparation for the invasion of Japan.

Commander Task Force 78 was given the task of operating all the naval shipping in "roll-up" movements within the Southwest Pacific Area. The loading and sailing of merchant shipping so employed was the function of the Chief Regulating Officer of the SWPA. This officer was also designated as the loading agency for naval ships. In order to effect the closest possible coordination, a liaison officer from the Chief Regulating Officer's Staff was assigned to the Staff of Commander Task Force 78.

The limiting date on "roll-up" operations was set at 15 September 1945. It had been planned that Commander Philippine Sea Frontier relieve Commander SEVENTH Amphibious Force of all duties in connection with "roll-up" operations on 15 August 1945 so that the latter might concentrate on preparations for the proposed Olympic operations. However, with the ending of the war all "roll-up" operations were canceled. As fast as the movements then underway could be completed, shipping was assigned to the "Campus" operation which was the movement of occupation forces to Japan.

SUMMARY

It is to be noted that during the period that naval shipping was used to transport troops, equipment and supplies from rear areas, amphibious assault operations were also being conducted. The concentration of operational control of all amphibious shipping under Commander Task Force 78 furnished the only means by which the often conflicting requirements could be satisfactorily met. These operations also furnished many examples of the splendid results that can be accomplished in amphibious operations by close coordination and effective liaison between Army and Navy Commands.

PART II (e)

MEDICAL SERVICES AND CASUALTY CARE IN THE SEVENTH AMPHIBIOUS FORCE

INTRODUCTION

Two major problems confront military medical services--the first, treatment of wounded men and their return to duty - the second, illness. Since seasoned and well-trained soldiers and sailors are of inestimably greater value than raw recruits, and since manpower is always limited, it is imperative that the medical services shorten the healing process and return to duty, and effect hygienic, preventive and epidemiologic measures to reduce casualties from disease.

Warfare in the Southwest Pacific involving island to island moves presented difficult problems in addition to the task of caring for combat casualties. The area abounded with hazards to the health of combatant and non-combatant personnel alike, the most prominent being malaria, scrub typhus, enteric diseases and tropical skin afflictions. In addition to these objective hazards, there existed the subjective danger of mental breakdown precipitated by combat, close restraint and confinement incident to long months at sea, lack of recreational facilities, and other environmental factors.

Medical services furnished by the SEVENTH Amphibious Force were based on the foregoing concepts-treatment of casualties, and prevention of illness. In that phase in which it was principally concerned, care and transportation of the wounded, combat experience exerted a progressive influence. The concentrated experience and the accelerated activity that accompany war permit a more rapid evaluation of methods and procedures. Measures which prove ineffectual can be discarded, and those found efficacious can be just as quickly expanded. The present day health standards of troops and the survivor rate among the wounded is unequalled in the history of warfare. Perhaps one of the most important factors contributing to this highly gratifying record has been the cooperation of military commanders with the medical department. The majority of commanders early recognized the inadequacy of certain preformed concepts in management of the wounded. With this flexibility of mind and with elastic organizations they used an investigative approach and drew on battle experience to sanction methods that evolved increasingly rational and effective care of the wounded.

1. PREVENTIVE MEDICAL ASPECTS

Preventive medicine was practiced from the beginning in diseased areas, even though the majority of personnel were afloat. Directives from higher authority concerning preventive measures were disseminated and passed by despatch or letter to all units for compliance. The Force Surgeon and the SEVENTH Fleet Medical Officer prescribed measures which were put into effect.

Preventive inoculations were kept up-to-date for all personnel and health records of individuals newly arrived in the area were carefully examined to insure that all received appropriate inoculations. Malaria discipline was recognized to be of the greatest importance, although it was not always effectively maintained. The high incidence of malaria in many small craft in frequent touch with the beach in the early days of the war can be attributed to the lack of proper precautionary measures. In one case of an LST which beached overnight in a New Guinea port, 25 of the crew contracted malaria.

There were no serious epidemics in the ships of the force, nor were there any serious outbreaks of food-poisoning. Respiratory infections were not a problem, at least among personnel afloat, although on one occasion a destroyer escort had 6 cases of virus pneumonia among her officers and was unable to get underway for one week. The hot, humid environemnt caused prickly heat of varying degree in practically all persons, and it became necessary to return a few individuals to a temperate zone when they failed to respond to treatment over a long period of time.

The incidence of venereal disease was very low throughout the history of the force. There were only rare opportunities for exposure in the New Guinea Area and practically no cases developed there. After the Philippines were invaded, and opportunities for infection were abundant, the case rate was lower than had been anticipated. Information concerning the high incidence of venereal diseases in the islands was disseminated to all units, and medical personnel were directed to observe strict prophylaxis in returning liberty parties. Action taken by the Army to prevent the spread of these diseases, particularly in Manila, also benefited naval personnel.

The hygiene and sanitation of all types of ships was consistent and of remarkably high standard, considering the youth and inexperience of ships' personnel, and the fact that ships were almost constantly at sea. Adequate supply of fresh water presented the greatest problem in the hundreds of small craft because of the low evaporator capacity. Opportunities for bathing were limited and it was necessary to use minimum amounts in sculleries and washing machines. Despite these limitations, there was no illnesses directly attributably to a lack of water.

The imminence of mental breakdown is not always forewarned by recognizable symptons and the problem of taking timely anticipatory measures has not been wholly solved. The majority of the cases of mental breakdown in this force appeared to be due to environmental factors rather than to combat, and were related to the close confinement and necessary restraint contingent on many months of sea duty in an area affording little in the way of recreation and entertainment. It is surprising that there were not more cases of operational fatigue and mental disease under the monotonous conditions of living in small amphibious craft.

2. CASUALTY CARE AND EVACUATION FOR ASSAULT LANDINGS

It became apparent very early that due to the number and type of landings which were to be made on enemy-held islands a smoothly functioning system of casualty care and evacuation must be divised. As distances to rear area bases lengthened, increased casualties could be anticipated enroute to landing beaches and the treatment and transportation of early casualties in the assault phase would be a constantly expanding task. The medical plan was based on the assumption that the forces afloat would be responsible for treatment and transportation of casualties until such time as Army hospitals were operative ashore, a variable time influenced by resistance encountered, terrain, weather, and cargo unloading conditions. Close liaison was maintained with the Army medical department at all times and the resultant teamwork left nothing to be desired.

In assault landings, maximum medical facilities were made available for casualty care in every ship. Because of the unpredictable nature of the Japanese, and the frequent lack of accurate intelligence concerning the capacity of enemy resistance, preparations always were made to care for heavy casualties. Advance estimates of killed, wounded and sick were found to be very unreliable in the theatre.

The SEVENTH Amphibious Force was the only such force composed almost entirely of amphibious type craft. There were no APA types permanently assigned. For almost a year after the Southwest Pacific Campaign began it was necessary to transport casualties in LSTs, LCIs, and even LCTs. While these types are not desirable for long hauls, they were suitable for short distances in quiet tropical waters encountered in the first operations. Hospital ships became available by the time the overwater distances materially increased.

(a) <u>WOODLARK-KIRIWINA ISLANDS - 30 June 1943</u>

This was the first landing in which the force participated. It entailed transporting about 16,800 men a distance of 180 miles through dangerous waters. Medical facilities included 4 LSTs, 8 LCIs, 2 APcs, each with a medical officer and corpsmen on board.

The landing was unopposed and there were no casualties to evacuate during the initial stages. Those incurred were due to enemy air action several days after the island was secured, and they were sent to Milne Bay via LSTs in resupply echelons.

(b) <u>LAE, NEW GUINEA - 4 September 1943</u>

This operation involved the landing of 16,600 Australian troops in an area firmly held by the Japs. Transports consisted of 13 LSTs, 20 LCIs, and 4 APDs. Each of the LSTs carried one medical officer who was equipped to do emergency surgery. One of the LCIs had a doctor aboard and the others a corpsman each.

Rear area facilities included two Army General Hospitals at Buna and Army casualty clearing stations at Milne Bay and Morobe, with a total number of about 3,000 beds. The USS RIGEL and the LST 464 were at Milne Bay to receive Navy casualties. This was the first appearance of the LST 464, which had been converted to a hospital facility. This ship will be mentioned in a subsequent paragraph. Evacuation from the beach was a responsibility of the Engineer Special Brigade and a Regimental Medical Detachment.

The landing was initally unopposed and casualties were few. However, air attacks on the convoy while enroute resulted in 37 naval personnel killed and 40 wounded, while among the embarked troops there were 36 killed and 51 woulded. The wounded were cared for aboard DDs, APDs and LSTs and returned as soon as possible to the rear. This experience was not forgotten. Obviously, if air attacks were to be a feature of the approach to the landing beach, then it was logical that a ship be designated and equipped with facilities to care for casualties sustained while enroute.

(c) <u>FINSCHHAFEN, NEW GUINEA - 22 September 1943.</u>

The 20th Australian Infantry Brigade was landed from 6 LSTs, 16 LCTs, and 4 APDs. Again, medical officers were aboard the LSTs and APDs, and plans were made to evacuate wounded to Buna and Milne Bay. The landing was unopposed and there were only 10 men wounded initially. The number of Australians later killed in action is not known, but it is not believed to be large. One week following the landing only 134 casualties had been returned to the rear areas.

This operation demonstrated the need for a Naval Medical officer to be attached to the Naval Beach Party in order to move casualties more expeditiously. Such an officer would be familiar with the capacities of ships, the medical specialties available in them, and able to classify and move the wounded quickly. In addition, he would be available to treat injuries sustained by the Beach Party. Accordingly a medical component was included in the new Naval Beach Parties being formed. It consisted of a medical officer and three hospital corpsmen, responsible for the supervision of casualty evacuation from the beach.

(d) <u>ARAWE, NEW BRITAIN - 15 December 1943</u>

The landing force in this operation consisted of the 112th Cavalry Regimental Combat Team, about 4,000 men, later reinforced by the 158th Regimental Combat Team. By the time this assault was made, the Force Surgeon had organized several surgical teams. These teams were composed of 2 surgeons and 10 hospital corpsmen and constituted a mobile unit which could be shifted from ship to ship on short notice. For the Arawe landing, since no LSTs were used, the teams then available were placed in LCTs two teams to each LCT designated.

The majority of casualties were suffered on D-Day in an

attempted pre-dawn landing via rubber boats and there were about 60 men killed and wounded. The wounded were treated by the surgical teams and evacuated via APDs.

The use of the surgical teams in LCT was a makeshift for this particular operation since it was not planned to use LCTs for care of casualties in later operations. Conversion of LSTs for casualty care had been approved and alterations in them were being carried out by their own personnel. This alteration consisted of installing a water-tight hatch in the tank deck bulkhead affording access to the forward troop compartments on both port and starboard sides. Certain troop spaces were converted into a receiving room, sterilizer and scrub-up room, and operating room, and additional plumbing installed. Thus, wounded could be brought in over the ramp onto the tank deck, passed into the receiving room through the hatch, and treatment begun. The ships' medical officer and corpsmen were responsible for classifying casualties. Those requiring surgery were prepared for the surgical team, and those with minor injuries were treated on the spot. The flow of patients was from forward to aft, from the receiving room to the troops sleeping spaces.

These surgical LSTs, as they came to be called, obviously were of limited capacity and it was not desirable to use them for transporting wounded for long distances. But the lack of Geneva-protected hospital ships, and the nature of the warfare waged in this area, made their use imperative if the wounded were to receive early definitive treatment. Their conversion did not interfere with their capacity to carry troops and cargo.

(e) CAPE GLOUCESTER, NEW BRITAIN - 26 December 1943

The FIRST Marine Division with 24,000 men was landed at Cape Gloucester.

This operation marked the first use of Surgical Teams in LSTs converted for casualty care, and the first time that a Naval Beach Party functioned. The Beach Party Medical Officer worked in conjunction with the medical elements of the FIRST Marine Division in the evacuation of casualties. In addition to the surgical teams, each LST carried one medical officer.

The LST 464 was stationed at Cape Sudest to receive

casualties. Naval Base Hospital #13 was by this time in commission at Milne Bay with a capacity of 400 beds. Other rear area reception centers consisted of Army hospital facilities at Buna, Finschhafen, Goodenough Island, and Milne Bay.

The casualties suffered in the initial phases of this assault were, for the most part, due to enemy air attack. An 86 plane attack on the destroyers and LSTs sank one destroyer and damaged several other ships. Casualties were 6 killed, 37 wounded, and 124 missing. After initial treatment by APD and LST, the wounded were transferred to the LST 464 at Cape Sudest, and later to Base Hospital 13 at Milne Bay.

The value of the surgical teams was clearly demonstrated at this landing and all future plans for casualty care were to be based on their presence at the assault beach.

Because of the poor condition of the few available roads, a number of casualties were evacuated from the vicinity of the front lines to the main landing beaches by small landing craft.

Evacuation from the area by LST proved entirely satisfactory. 1146 Marine casualties were evacuated by these ships during the month following the initial assault landings.

(f) SAIDOR, NEW GUINEA - 2 January 1944

This landing of 7200 troops was only lightly opposed and by midafternoon of the first day only two men had been wounded. Again, LSTs with surgical teams were in the first echelon of ships. The LST 464 had returned from Milne Bay, where she evacuated her casualties, and was stationed at Cape Sudest, but she was not needed for this operation.

By this time, the pattern for the overall care and evacuation of casualties had been formed. To recapitulate--Beach Party medical sections would receive the wounded on the beach and be responsible for their evacuation. LSTs with surgical teams embarked would be distributed in initial and suceeding echelons of ships and some of them would be designated to remain on the beach or to lie off the beach as long as necessary. As their facilities became overtaxed, they would unload into ships departing the area. Only the organization of more surgical teams as personnel became available, and the conversion of more LTSs for casualty remained to be done.

(g) ADMIRALTIES; AITAPE-HUMBOLDT-TANAMERAH; WADKE; BIAK; NOEMFOOR; SANSAPOR; MOROTAI OPERATIONS - 29 February to 30 July 1944

Throughout the Spring and Summer of 1944 assault landings continued at the rate of about one a month. The Admiralty Islands were seized, the leap-frog landings along the north coast of New Guinea were carried out, and with the capture of Morotai a series of bases was established extending from the Coral Sea to the eastern edge of the Celebes Sea.

81,000 troops were landed in these operations. As lines of communications lengthened with each new landing, the transporting of casualties in amphibious craft was avoided when possible. Early and adequate surgical treatment at the far beach was stressed, each assault echelon was accompanied by surgical teams, and the wounded were transferred to large, fast ships for return to the rear. An APH and one AH were available for the first time at the Aitape-Humboldt-Tanamerah landings. At Wadke, two Australian LSIs were held for evacuation.

A total of 5447 sick and wounded were evacuated to the rear from this series of assaults.

While these operations were in progress, rear bases were being consolidated in preparation for future campaigns. Both Army and Navy medical facilities were brought forward. Naval Base Hospital #15 with 1,000 beds, was commissioned at Manus in the Admiralties. Additional dispensaries made available another 1,000 beds there. Base Hospital #17 was moved into Humboldt Bay and Base Hospital #16 into Woendi. These facilities permitted hospitalization in the forward areas and obviated the necessity for the long trip to Milne Bay, Brisbane and Sydney.

Additional medical personnel were constantly arriving. A total of 23 surgical teams were organized and assigned to LSTs. Most of the LSTs with no surgical team aboard carried a medical officer. There were no APAs or APHs attached permanently, as in other amphibious forces, and medical facilities for small craft were provided by LSTs or other ships. The LSTs were constantly on the move, either in assault or resupply echelon, usually in company with LCIs, LSMs and LCTs to whom they provided medical service.

A Blood Bank was established in the LST 464 at this time.

Its function was to prepare and furnish whole blood for the surgical teams prior to their departure for assault landings. The Army 24th General Hospital at Hollandia also established a Blood Bank and very generously provided blood to naval facilities when needed. Donors for these banks were obtained from service personnel exclusively.

(h) **LEYTE - 20 October 1944**

The invasion of the Philippines at Leyte was the first assault of such size in which this force had participated. Aided by APAs temporarily assigned to SEVENTH Amphibious Force, a total of about 85,000 troops were landed. Preparations were made for a large number of casualties and the following medical plan was evolved:

A minus 3 Day - Two APDs to accompany and afford medical services to the minesweepers which were engaged in clearing channels to the landing beaches.

A Day - Eight Surgical teams in LSTs. Five surgical specialty teams (Orthopedics, Anesthesia, Urology, Chest Surgery, and Ophthalmology). Seventeen LSTs with one medical officer. Eighteen APAs, each with 3-5 medical officers aboard. The total bed capacity of A-Day shipping was 3105 stretcher and 7025 ambulatory.

A Plus 1 Day - A hospital ship to be present from 0600 to 1800.

A Plus 2 Day - Seven LSTs with surgical teams. Twenty-four LSTs with one medical officer. Seven APAs; total bed capacity being 1785 stretcher cases and 4300 ambulatory.

A Plus 3 Day - One hospital ship.

A Plus 4 Day - Six LSTs with surgical teams. Sixteen LSTs with one medical officer. Total bed capacity 525 stretcher and 1400 ambulatory. The LST 464, to remain in Leyte Gulf with a fresh supply of whole blood.

      A Plus 5 Day -   One hospital ship

      A Plus 7 Day -   One hospital ship

The hospital ships assigned to this operation were the Army-staffed MERCY, COMFORT, TASMAN and MAETSUYCKER. In addition, the Navy hospital ships SOLACE, RELIEF, and BOUNTIFUL were held at Ulithi to be called forward if necessary.

    Initial ground forces casualties were light, and at the end of the second day they totalled only 83 killed and 145 wounded. The terrific naval gunfire, plus the rockets and aerial bombs had driven most of the Japanese off the beaches, but as the fighting moved inland Army casualties mounted.

    Japanese aircraft attacks on naval shipping were heavy and the suiciders were encountered for the first time. On the first day there were 9 killed and 40 wounded in ships anchored in Leyte Gulf. Because of this vicious air action, all amphibious ships were moved out of the Gulf as rapidly as possible after unloading. Hospital ships were not permitted to enter the Gulf when scheduled, and even later they were not allowed to remain longer than two to three hours at mid-day. Due to the bad weather, Army hospitals could not be set up as rapidly as planned, and with other ships forced to depart, the LST 464 was the most important medical facility afloat for several days. A total of 6267 casualties were evacuated from the beaches prior to the end of the fighting and a large percentage passed through the LST 464.

    Several lessons were learned at Leyte. Means were needed to furnish medical assistance quickly to ships struck by bombs or suicide planes. The desirability of leaving LSTs with surgical teams at the beach after unloading was emphasized. One or two LSTs with surgical teams were needed in reserve to send to beaches overwhelmed with casualties, or left without medical facilities due to unexpected shifts in schedules or unloading sites.

(i) <u>MAPIA-ASIA ISLAND GROUP - 15 November - 19 November 1944</u>

    In November minor landings were made in the Mapia-Asia Islands. Only one battalion of troops was involved and they were transported in LCIs. The Army furnished medical officers for the landings. Resistance was slight and there were only 19 casualties, which were sent to Morotai.

(j) **MINDORO - 15 December 1944**

There were 16,000 troops landed on the enemy-held island of MINDORO and 14 LSTs with surgical teams were assigned for medical service. Few casualties were sustained at the landing, but the ships engaged in the operation were subjected to suicide plane attacks and suffered many casualties. Two LSTs were sunk, a destroyer was damaged and several PT boats were hit. A total of 553 casualties among Army and Navy personnel were evacuated from this landing area, the majority being taken to hospitals at Biak and Hollandia.

(k) **LINGAYEN GULF - 9 January 1945**

This was the largest single operation in a series designed for the seizure of LUZON, and consisted of a major amphibious assault from bases in Leyte and New Guinea, the latter being 2150 miles away. This meant that ships in convoy would be in danger of enemy air, surface and submarine attack for the greater part of that distance while enroute to the landing beaches. Intelligence indicated strong enemy resistance and heavy casualties were anticipated. The following preparations were made:

S-Day-- Blue Beach--Two 7thPhib Beach Parties; two from APAs.
Six LSTs with surgical teams.
Eleven LSTs with one medical officer.
Nine APAs with 3-5 medical officers.
One APH with 8 medical officers.
One LSV with 2 medical officers.

White Beaches 1 & 2
Two 7th Phib Beach Parties; one APA Beach Party
Three LSTs with surgical teams.
Four LSTs with one medical officer.
Five APAs with 3-5 Medical officers.

White Beach 3
Two APA beach parties.
Two LSTs with surgical teams.
One APA with 4 medical officers.

S Plus 2 Day Blue Beach	Two APAs with 4 medical officers each.
White Beaches 1 & 2	Two LSTs with surgical teams. One APA with 4 medical officers. One APH with 8 medical officers.
S Plus 4 Day Blue Beach	Seven LSTs with one medical officer.
White Beaches 1 & 2	One LST with surgical team. Eleven LSTs with one medical officer.

Six of the surgical team LSTs with augmented personnel, were designated to remain beached for casualty care after unloading, for as long as they were needed. Beach Party medical sections had orders to place aboard the surgical team LSTs only those cases in need of surgery and to send the other wounded direct to APAs. This was to prevent crowding the LSTs with minor cases, thus leaving them free to care for casualties requiring actual surgery. Since the APAs were scheduled for early departure from the area, it was deemed advisable to evacuate as many wounded as possible in them.

The APHs with about 8 medical officers aboard, and with a bed capacity of over 1,000 were held in the transport area as evacuation ships. As they loaded to capacity with litter cases, there were sailed immediately to reduce their exposure to air attack. There were no hospital ships available at Lingayen. In fact, none were permitted in waters of the Sulu and South China seas until the middle of February.

As rescue ships for this operation, three PCE(R)s were given additional medical personnel and supplies, and assigned to rescue duty only. They were fast and maneuverable and were able to go alongside stricken ships to render medical aid and to take off survivors. One was kept at anchor near the flagship, within easy visual signalling distance, so that it could be dispatched on a mission without delay. The others were placed at strategic places in the anchorage areas. One LST with surgical team embarked was also held in reserve near the flagship. Its mission was to replace or supplement any LST on the beach in need of relief or assistance.

Fortunately, opposition was light, except on White Beach 2, and the landing forces advanced inland rapidly with few casualties. By the end of the sixth day only 727 wounded had been evacuated to the rear. Had casualties been heavy, evacuation facilities would have been strained, because, with the hospitals at Leyte Gulf full of sick and wounded, it would have been necessary to transport those from Lingayen as far as Hollandia and Manus and this would have interfered with the schedules for the resupply echelons of large ships.

With favorable weather and surf conditions throughout the initial phases of the landing, the cargo was moved ashore rapidly and the Army quickly erected its Field and Evacuation hospitals.

In this operation there was no delay in moving casualties from the beach into ships fitted to care for them. With the facilities available, it is believed they could have been evacuated just as expeditiously even if the number had been much greater. The PCE(R)s were invaluable and were alongside ships stricken without delay.

Whole blood for this operation was obtained both from the LST 464 and from the Whole Blood Distribution Center at Guam. All ships departing the transport area were directed to deliver their unused supplies of blood to the beach parties for further transfer to the Army.

(1) <u>BATAAN-CORREGIDOR</u> - 15 February 1945

This operation entailed the forcing of Mariveles Bay and the capture of Corregidor. Troops making the landing were composed of one paratroop regiment, an infantry regimental combat team, plus a battalion.

Three LSTs with surgical teams were assigned for care of casualties.

Casualties were heavy. The first wave of paratroops suffered 178 casualties due to the drop. Three were killed and 175 had fractures and dislocations when an adverse wind carried them onto unfavorable terrain. During the first night, 4 LCSs and 1 LSM struck mines or were hit by suicide boats, and sunk or beached in Mariveles Bay. Two destroyers also were mined but withdrew under their own power. Two YMSs were hit by gunfire from Corregidor and suffered casualties.

In addition to the many burn casualties on the LCSs, there were heavy casualties among the Army troops which encountered unexpected opposition on Corregidor. Within three days the surgical LSTs had over 600 seriously wounded aboard. The lightly wounded were retained on Corregidor under Army care. The hospital ship HOPE arrived in Subic Bay and took the patients from the LSTs, which eased the situation. The HOPE was the first hospital ship allowed on the Western side of the Philippines and her arrival was most opportune.

With a plethora of fractures, dislocations, and burns, the surgical teams almost ran out of supplies; but plaster, blood and plasma were flown in from Leyte before the shortage became acute.

(m) CONSOLIDATING OPERATIONS IN PHILIPPINES - February - April 1945

Operations to secure the remainder of the Philipping group were carried out in rapid succession. The number of troops involved in the landings at any time ranged from a division to a battalion. Due to the Japanese custom of retiring inland when the assault craft were sighted, casualties were very few on any of the landing beaches. At least one surgical team was furnished for each of these operations, but only occasionally was surgical care needed at the beach.

(n) BORNEO OPERATIONS - 29 April to 1 July 1945

The SEVENTH Amphibious Force transported, protected, and landed an Australian Infantry Brigade at TARAKAN on 1 May, two Infantry Brigades at BRUNEI BAY on 10 June, and a Division at BALIKPAPAN on 1 July 1945.

Surgical teams were furnished for all these operations. There were two Australian hospital ships on call at Morotai, but they were not needed during the initial phases. Light opposition was encountered at each landing beach by the ground forces. The U.S. Naval minesweepers which worked for several days prior to the landing in each area were subjected to enemy shelling and several were damaged by mines. At TARAKAN, 14 naval personnel were wounded; at BRUNEI BAY, 7 killed and 38 wounded; at BALIKPAPAN, 7 killed and 43 wounded. At BALIKPAPAN 10 mental cases were evacuated.

Australian casualties were 31 wounded the first 48 hours at TARAKAN; 20 killed and 46 wounded the first three days at BRUNEI BAY; 75 killed and 293 wounded the first six days at BALIKPAPAN.

With the completion of the landings in BORNEO, the Philippine campaign was considered to be at an end as far as amphibious assaults were concerned. Ships of the SEVENTH Amphibious Force were thereafter engaged in rolling up the Army bases in the Australia-New Guinea Area.

Medical planning for the proposed attack on Japan was started immediately but hostilities ceased shortly after the plan was completed. A different plan was needed for the occupation of Korea and North China. Even though opposed landings were not anticipated, it was deemed advisable to be prepared. The plans stressed precautions by naval personnel, particularly ashore, to avoid contracting any of the diseases endemic in the occupied ports.

3. DENTAL FACILITIES

With hundreds of small craft in the SEVENTH Amphibious Force on missions that kept them at sea the greater part of the time, it was important that special provisions be made for dental attention for their crews. Accordingly, ten mobile dental units were organized and placed aboard LSTs and LCIs. These units each consisted of a dental officer and dental technician with a portable dental machine. They moved from one ship to another taking care of the dental work needed. Their services were invaluable. Facilities for prosthesis were available in certain large ships of the Service Force, SEVENTH Fleet, such as the USS SAN CLEMENTE and the USS DOBBIN.

4. AMPHIBIOUS TRAINING CENTER

An Amphibious Training Center was established at Milne Bay, New Guinea, in January 1943 and functioned until October 1944, with the primary purpose of training troops in the methods used in amphibious assaults. An experienced medical officer was attached to the staff and conducted classes for medical officers. All medical officers arriving for duty with SEVENTH Amphibious Force were sent to the Training Center for about ten days, unless their services were urgently needed elsewhere.

Here they received instruction in the methods used by this force for care and evacuation of casualties, and they were also briefed in reports and returns, sanitation of ships, and prevention of diseases prevalent in the area.

5. THE LST 464

Necessity was the mother of invention in the case of the LST 464. With the establishment of the base at Milne Bay and the beginning of operations in the New Guinea-Bismarck Archipelago area, it became apparent that a floating hospital unit was urgently needed. There were no Geneva-protected hospital ships in the force. Consequently, an LST, bow number 464, was converted into a hospital. By the use of beaverboard and screen wire, the tank deck was partitioned into offices, operating room, laboratory, X-ray room, isolation ward and storeroom.

Its function was threefold: To provide medical facilities for personnel of small craft lacking medical officers; to receive and care for casualties brought from the landing beaches; and to furnish medical service to the personnel engaged in constructing advance bases when base dispensaries or hospitals were not in operation.

Initially, the LST 464 was staffed with a surgeon, an internist, a dermatologist, urologist, an EENT man, and a Hospital Corps Officer, with about 40 corpsmen. Later, an anesthetist and a psychiatrist were added to the staff for permanent duty. Additional surgeons were placed aboard for temporary duty when needed. The total bed capacity was 175, although the limited messing and laundering facilities of this type of ship made a rapid turnover of patients desirable.

In the early operations such as LAE, FINSCHHAFEN, ARAWE, and CAPE GLOUCESTER, the LST 464 was stationed at advance bases, usually Cape Sudest, Morobe or Buna, in order to receive casualties from the amphibious craft and later transport them to hospitals in Milne Bay. After Humboldt Bay was seized, the 464 proceeded there to act as station hospital ship for the Construction Battalion and other personnel engaged in building the base. She remained in Humboldt Bay, to furnish supplies and whole blood to surgical team ships departing on operations, and continued to make her facilities available to small craft.

When the attack on LEYTE was made the 464 was brought

forward on the fourth day, primarily to furnish blood to other ships and surgical teams, but also to care for casualties if necessary. In the latter capacity she unexpectedly assumed a stellar role. Because of the intense enemy air attacks, the hospital ships were not permitted to enter the gulf as scheduled, and other ships were moved out as fast as they unloaded. The weather delayed completion of the Army hospital facilities, and the 464 became the main facility for the care of casualties in the area. She was armed and, since she did not bear the distinctive markings of a hospital ship, she was frequently under air attack. Her staff worked to the point of exhaustion until most of them were relieved because of fatigue. After several days hospital ships were able to enter the gulf, but remained only a few hours. Their chief service was taking off patients from the 464, which continued to carry on in the gulf. This situation remained unchanged for several weeks.

With the completion of the LEYTE Operation, the 464 remained in Leyte Gulf to act as station hospital ship for small craft until late in March 1945 when she was sent to Subic Bay for similar service. In September she furnished medical services to naval personnel in the beach party and boat pool at Jinsen, Korea, for about three weeks and then she was sent to Taku, China, and Tsingtao for like duty. With the advent of cold weather in November, she was released from duty with SEVENTH Amphibious Force and ordered to report to Administrative Commander, Amphibious Forces Pacific, for disposition.

Prior to its departure, Commander SEVENTH Amphibious Force had the pleasure of awarding, in the name of the President, the Navy Unit Citation to the USS LST 464.

Rear Admiral ALBERT G. NOBLE, U.S. Navy (right), Chief of Staff, Seventh Amphibious Force and later second Commander, Amphibious Group Eight with Commodore RAY TARBUCK, U.S. Navy (left), his successor as Chief of Staff on the occasion of his detachment.

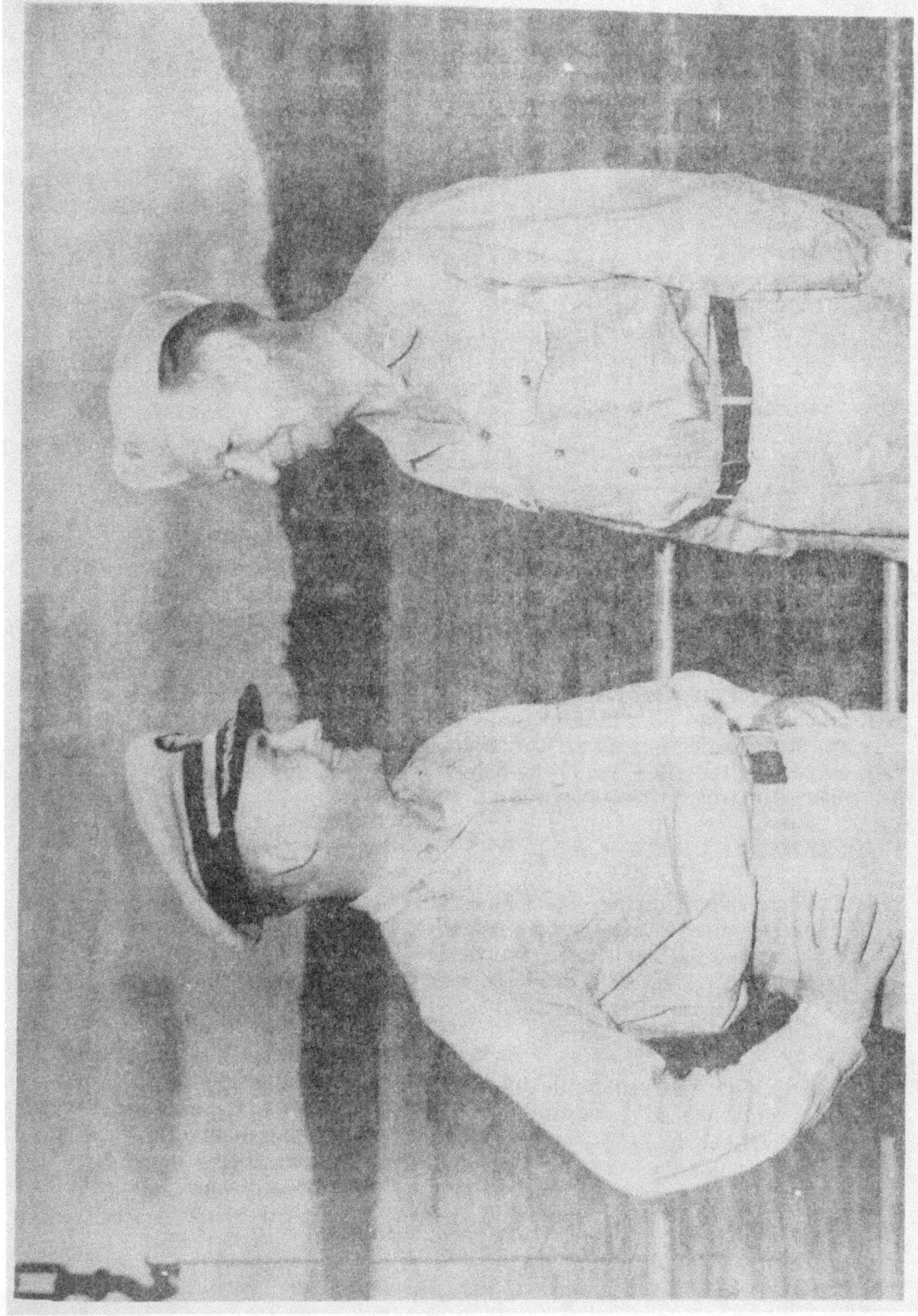

PART II (f)

AIR SUPPORT OPERATIONS

GENERAL

In most cases air support for the SEVENTH Amphibious Force was furnished by land based aircraft of the U.S. Army Air Forces. Only when the success of the operation otherwise would have been hazarded was carrier based air support used. Carrier planes furnished air cover at HOLLANDIA, MOROTAI, and BALIKPAPAN where the assaults were distant from our own bases and dangerously close to those of the enemy, and in the PHILIPPINE Operations from LEYTE to LINGAYEN where the whole strength of our air forces was used.

The potential enemy air strength in numerous bases in the Southwest Pacific always constituted an extreme threat to amphibious operations. Success in landing of troops and continuation of supply, sometimes for a long period, was contingent upon neutralization of enemy air bases and continuous cover for convoys from first light to dark. It was often difficult and sometimes impossible in earlier operations for shore based air forces to provide an adequate air umbrella and at the same time carry on other committments. The distances from their own air bases to the target area were so great that supporting aircraft could stay on station for only short periods. When air cover was limited, lines of supply were endangered until the surrounding enemy air bases could be neutralized. Early seizure of the airstrips in the objective area materially aided this neutralization.

PLANNING AIR SUPPORT

From the beginning, Commander SEVENTH Amphibious Force utilized one naval aviator on his staff for air planning, as air advisor, and liaison with participating units of the Far East Air Forces and Allied Air Force and with Carrier units of the Pacific Fleet. A flag aviation unit augmented the Force to provide expeditious transportation.

In earlier operations, it was often difficult to get air force representatives to cooperate in forming an air plan to the satisfaction of all services. Frequently progress in planning was stalemated because the air force planner did not have authority to speak for his superior. Air plans were particularly vague on such points as: (1) Command of aircraft in the objective area, (2) Details of air support of naval units.

In execution, air plans were not adhered to. Often strike leaders used calls not listed in the plans, and air schedules were not strictly maintained. In later campaigns full air support requested was usually supplied, and air plans better adhered to.

Air Forces had limited equipment and their requirements for strategic missions were heavy. The Commander SEVENTH Amphibious Force, and his group commanders endeavored to give due consideration to these factors when requesting tactical air support.

Land base air was never a satisfactory substitute for carrier based air in the support of either the naval or ground phases of amphibious operations.

PHOTO RECONNAISSANCE

Photographic reconnaissance was extremely meager during earlier operations. Even as late as September 1943, the sole unit in the Southwest Pacific Area, indoctrinated and equipped to make photographs useful for amphibious planning, was the Eighth Photo Squadron of the FIFTH Air Force. Its committments in other fields of photographic reconnaissance were so heavy, and its dependence upon busy operational units for fighter cover so restricting, that it could furnish only a fraction of the pictures needed for timely planning. Actually only one airplane was mounted with equipment essential for beach photographs at that time. For planning the FINSCHHAFEN Operation, only one set of obliques was available to the SEVENTH Amphibious Force.

In later operations more photo-reconnaissance was available. However, the low obliques needed for amphibious planning usually were not obtainable in time for profitable use. Land based air in the Southwest Pacific Area had no system equal to the carrier based air strike for obtaining the close-in photo reconnaissance so necessary for planning amphibious operations.

AIR COORDINATION IN AMPHIBIOUS OPERATIONS

Air Support teams, air controllers and fighter direction teams were placed aboard the headquarters ships for each amphibious operation. Their personnel were usually provided by the service furnishing the majority of the air support. In the earlier operations these were predominately Army personnel. The air control personnel controlled air strikes from the ships until they moved ashore which was usually early in the operation. Army fighter director teams were maintained aboard destroyers especially equipped for this work. Time and again they did yeoman service in the direction of fighters which eventually broke up air attacks directed at convoys.

Commencing with the MOROTAI Operation, Navy Support Air Control units were furnished from Amphibious Forces Pacific Fleet. This personnel effected control of Navy aircraft supporting amphibious operations according to the Support Air Doctrine promulgated by Commander Amphibious Forces Pacific. They also effected such control of Army aircraft as was necessary.. This was usually only checking in of aircraft before a pre-arranged strike. A number of Navy fighter director teams were made available to Commander SEVENTH Amphibious Force who assigned them to various destoyers equipped for fighter direction. In addition a number of Army fighter director officers were also made available and were assigned so that each fighter director ship was prepared to control either Army or Navy aircraft. These Army fighter director officers were furnished by the FIFTH Air Force. When the THIRTEENTH Air Force also was given responsibility in the PHILIPPINES, fighter director officers from that force were assigned to destroyers for training.

FIGHTER DIRECTOR DESTROYER USED TO EXTEND THE LIMIT OF LAND BASED FIGHTER PROTECTION

During the LAE and FINSCHHAFEN campaigns the main threat of enemy air was from their large bases at KAVIANG and RABAUL. Enemy air strikes from those bases usually came across VITIAZ STRAIT. To counter such attacks the destroyer REID with Army fighter direction personnel aboard was stationed in the STRAIT. The result was that on several occasions a surprised enemy was caught and destroyed by land based aircraft as far as 120 miles from his objective.

SUMMARY OF AIR SUPPORT OF AMPHIBIOUS OPERATIONS IN THE SOUTHWEST PACIFIC

<u>EARLY NEW GUINEA OPERATIONS</u>: Aircraft of the FIFTH Air Force

effectively supported these operations and all subsequent Amphibious Operations in the Southwest Pacific Areas. The air support in these earlier operations was marked by excellent fighter protection when the enemy air strength was still great. This was particularly true at LAE, FINSCHHAFEN and again at CAPE GLOUCESTER. At Cape Gloucester, the enemy air reaction was considerably reduced by the carrier strikes on RABAUL, made a few days before. A comment should be made on the effect of incorrect evaluation of air observations on the operations against the ADMIRALTY ISLANDS. Air reconnaissance reports indicated there were few Japanese on LOS NEGROS ISLAND. On that assumption, the plan was for a reconnaissance in force by ground troops. However, two days before the landing, scouts reported that the island was "lousy with Japs". It was then too late to change the plan and the success of the operation was in jeopardy until reinforcements could be brought forward several days later.

TANAHERAH BAY-HUMBOLDT BAY-AITAPE: Eight escort carriers with their screen, commanded by Rear Admiral R. DAVISON, participated in these simultaneous operations, under operational control of Commander SEVENTH Amphibious Force. These ships were temporarily transferred from the Pacific Fleet for the operation. They were assisted by fast carrier strikes on airfields in the SARMI-WADKE Area on D-1 Day and the SENTANI Airfield at HOLLANDIA on D Day. Thirteen enemy aircraft were shot down and 88 destroyed on the ground in these attacks.

FROM WADKE TO MOROTAI: Because carriers were occupied at the time in the MARIANAS Campaign, air cover for WADKE-TOEM, BIAK, NOEMFOOR and SANSAPOR operations was entirely land based. Fighters came from such a distance to the east that in order to return for landing at their bases in daylight, they left the objective area long before dark. This was cause for considerable concern, but fortunately, the enemy failed to take advantage of the opportunity to strike and there was little enemy air activity. However, the condition served to illustrate a disadvantage of land based air support for amphibious operations.

MOROTAI OPERATION: An Escort Carrier Group (4 CVEs under the command of Rear Admiral T. L. SPRAGUE, and 2 CVEs with Rear Admiral C.A.F. SPRAGUE), was employed in the MOROTAI Operation under operational control of Commander SEVENTH

Amphibious Force. A Fast Carrier Group (CarDivs 22 and 25) also participated and furnished fighter sweeps when it became evident that attack aircraft from the FIFTH Air Force could not be moved up to the objective area in time. At first, Commander-in-Chief, Pacific Fleet, was not inclined to risk fast carriers so close to enemy air bases. However, the Army Air Force had so thoroughly neutralized the enemy air bases on HALMAHERA, CELEBES, and MINDANAO that they did not constitute serious threats, and use of the group of fast carriers was approved for direct support of the MOROTAI Operation on D and D-1 days.

LEYTE TO LINGAYEN: The Air operations in this campaign transcend the limit of supporting amphibious operations to such an extent that they will not be considered here.

CONSOLIDATING OPERATIONS THROUGHOUT THE PHILIPPINES: February - June 1945: These operations were supported effectively by land based aircraft of the FIFTH and THIRTEENTH Air Force. Two outstanding examples of excellent air support for amphibious operations occurred during this period. The first was the capture of CORREGIDOR by combined airborne-amphibious landing. The amphibious landing might even be considered as having been in support of the air operation, an interesting reversal of normal practice. The second was the air support of the LEGASPI landing. Sufficient cruisers and destroyers were not available, due to other committments, to furnish naval gunfire normally required for such an operation. Instead, low level bombing and strafing attacks by aircraft of the FIFTH Air Force neutralized the landing area to such good effect that the troops went ashore in the conventional manner for a successful amphibious landing -- standing up.

BORNEO OPERATIONS: The TARAKAN and BRUNEI BAY operations were supported by RAAF and the THIRTEENTH Air Force based at TAWI-TAWI in the SULU Archipelago and at PALAWAN. Japanese air activity was light and, although covering aircraft were based at a great distance from the objective area, air protection was adequate. The plan for air cover in the BALIKPAPAN operation posed a more serious problem. BALIKPAPAN landings were scheduled for 1 July, with minesweeping and air strikes two weeks earlier. It had been planned to use the air strip at TARAKAN, 300 miles to the north, as a base for covering fighters, but the air strip was not ready for operation by the time minesweeping off BALIKPAPAN was to commence. The nearest alternative base was at TAWI-TAWI, 420 miles from BALIKPAPAN. Operations from such a distance would substantially reduce the time that fighters could remain over the target area, and leave the the minesweepers and their covering forces without air support during part of the daylight hours. To improve this situation, the Attack Force Commander (Commander Amphibious Group EIGHT) requested two CVEs to support the operations from D-1 to D+2 days. Commander in Chief, Pacific Fleet, supplied three such carriers under command of Rear Admiral W. D. SAMPLE, USN. They were assigned for fighter cover only, but on F+2 day, they made the last strike by escort carriers against the Japanese in this war, to the evident appreciation of the Australian ground troops.

PART II (g)

ADMINISTRATIVE COMMAND SEVENTH AMPHIBIOUS FORCE

CHRONOLOGICAL ACCOUNT

By October of 1944, the SEVENTH Amphibious Force had grown to consist of two (2) AGC's, one (1) Transport Division, one (1) APc Flotilla, three (3) LST Flotillas, three (3) LCI Flotillas and six (6) LCT Flotillas. Two (2) Amphibious Group Commanders with their staffs were attached. In addition to the above vessels, the following were due to report to the Force in the near future: two (2) LST Flotillas, two (2) LSM Flotillas, three (3) LCI Flotillas, one (1) LCS Flotilla and one (1) LCT Flotilla. The administration and logistics of this rapidly expanding force, which was operating in an area where base facilities and services often left much to be desired, required an ever increasing number of administrative personnel on the Staff of the Force Commander, with the result that working space and quarters on the Force Flagship became increasingly crowded. Further, and more important, combat operations soon to be carried out would require the presence of the Force Flagship in forward areas for extended periods. It was necessary that the Force Commander and his Staff be relieved during these periods of administrative details, most of which could be more expeditiously handled in an area farther to the rear.

Accordingly, Commander SEVENTH Amphibious Force requested establishment of a separate Administrative Command on 29 September 1944. On 2 October 1944 Commander SEVENTH Fleet approved this request, and on 7 October 1944, the Administrative Commander SEVENTH Amphibious Force was established under the command of Captain Harold J. NELSON, USN. On this date, Commander SEVENTH Amphibious Force promulgated a new Force Organization, which established the functions of the Administrative Command SEVENTH Amphibious Force.

USS HENRY T. ALLEN (APA 15) previously had been made available to Commander SEVENTH Amphibious Force by Commander SEVENTH Fleet for an administrative flagship. The mobility acquired by basing the Administrative Command afloat was deemed desirable and later operations proved the soundness of the plan. HENRY T. ALLEN, although in poor material condition, carried out her mission as Administrative

Flagship in a satisfactory manner. Prior to being designated, she was given a short availability in Brisbane, Australia, for minor alterations to better suit her for duty as a flagship. Further alterations were later effected by forces afloat, but none were of a permanent nature. In January 1945, she was redesignated by the Chief of Naval Operations as "AG 90"

In addition to the forces afloat previously mentioned, the shorebased activities of the SEVENTH Amphibious Force were placed under the administrative cognizance of the Administrative Commander. These included Supply Representatives at Sydney and Brisbane, Australia; a Naval Beach Party Camp; and an Amphibious Training Center. A Supply Representative previously maintained at Milne Bay, New Guinea, had been recalled prior to the establishment of the Administrative Command. The Beach Party Camp, initially at Hollandia, New Guinea, was assigned a Commanding Officer and Headquarters Unit under Administrative cognizance of the Commander, Administrative Command. This activity housed and trained eleven (11) Naval Beach Parties during the period covered by this report. The Amphibious Training Center, initially at Stringer Bay, New Guinea, provided amphibious training for Army Divisions designated by the Commander-in-Chief, Southwestern Pacific Area. This training was the responsibility of a Training Group Commander. Administration of the Training Center was also the responsiblility of its Commanding Officer to whom the Administrative Command provided logistic support and administrative assistance when requested by him or directed by Commander SEVENTH Amphibious Force.

From 7 October 1944 to 22 December 1944, the Administrative Command was primarily engaged in assisting the Force Commander in readying his Force for future operations. During most of this period both flagships were in company at Hollandia, New Guinea, and the various staff sections functioned much as they had before the organization of the Administrative Command. The Flag Secretary to Commander SEVENTH Amphibious Force, and the Awards Officer were carried in the Administrative Flagship and the Flag Secretary acted as Secretary to the Administrative Commander. Operational functions of the Force were carried out almost entirely by the Force Commander's Staff.

On 4 January 1945, the Supply Representative, Brisbane, Australia reported the disestablishment of his unit and the similar unit at Sydney, Australia. The officers and enlisted personnel from these units were then transferred to the Staff of the Administrative Commander.

On 22 December 1944, the Commander SEVENTH Amphibious Force proceeded in his flagship to conduct the Leyte Operation. From that date until 26 January 1945, the Commander Administrative Command remained in his flagship at Hollandia, New Guinea and performed in general the duties of a Rear Echelon in addition to his normal administrative functions. During this period his Operations Section was supplemented by Officers from the Force Commander's Staff to provide sufficient assistance for conducting rear area operations and coordinating resupply from the main staging area at Hollandia, New Guinea. A separate Task Group designation was assigned to him as SEVENTH Amphibious Force Representative, Hollandia, New Guinea.

On 26 January 1945, Commander Administrative Command proceeded with his flagship to Leyte Gulf, and arrived 29 January 1945. From this date until 8 February 1945, the Force Commander's flagship was also present in Leyte Gulf.

During February and March 1945, the Amphibious Training Center and the Naval Beach Party Camp were moved from Stringer Bay and Hollandia respectively to Subic Bay, where they established new bases and continued their functions. In July 1945 the personnel of nine of the eleven Naval Beach Parties were regrouped to conform with the Beach Party Organization prescribed by the Standard Operating Procedure of Commander Amphibious Forces Pacific.

On 8 February 1945 Commander SEVENTH Amphibious Force preceeded in his flagship to the Subic Bay - Manila area. From this date until the disestablishment of his Command on 15 August 1945, Commander Administrative Command was based afloat in the Leyte Gulf, which was the main staging area during the entire period for the Amphibious operations being conducted in the Philippine and Borneo areas. During this period, the Administrative Command was engaged in providing logistics and administrative support for the vessels and activities of the SEVENTH Amphibious Force.

On 20 May 1945, Captain J. E. CHAPMAN, USN relieved Captain Harold J. NELSON, USN, as Commander Administrative Command SEVENTH Amphibious Force.

On 15 August 1945, pursuant to orders from Commander SEVENTH Amphibious Force, Commander Administrative Command

SEVENTH Amphibious Force, reported with USS H. T. ALLEN to the Commander Amphibious Forces, U.S. Pacific Fleet, for duty and was re-established as Commander Administrative Command, Amphibious Forces, U.S. Pacific Fleet, PHILIPPINES under Commander Administrative Command, Amphibious Forces, U.S. Pacific Fleet.

DESCRIPTION OF DEVELOPMENT AND OPERATION

The establishment of the Administrative Command, SEVENTH Amphibious Force accomplished a separation from the staff of Commander SEVENTH Amphibious Force of the officer and enlisted personnel responsible to the Force Commander for administrative matters. Theretofore, the Staff of the Force Commander was organized into major subdivisions, namely Operations and Administration, each under an Assistant Chief of Staff. The Administrative group consisted of the following staff sections: Maintenance, Personnel, Supply, Medical, Gunnery, Radio Material, Training (Naval Units), Secretarial and Communications. On 7 October 1944, the Assistant Chief of Staff, Administration, became Chief Staff Officer to the Commander Administrative Command, and the foregoing staff sections were transferred almost intact, together with Communications and Secretarial sections, and a small operations section. The nucleous of personnel for the latter three sections was provided from the Force Commander's staff. Additional personnel was obtained later as it was needed.

Upon activation of his command, the Commander Administrative Command, SEVENTH Amphibious Force, was assigned cognizance of the following matters, in accordance with general policies and directives to be issued by Commander SEVENTH Amphibious Force:

- (a) Maintenance and Supply.
- (b) Personnel.
- (c) Health, Sanitation and Evacuation.
- (d) Welfare and Recreation.
- (e) Ships locations.
- (f) Repair availabilities.
- (g) Hydrographic information.
- (h) Boats and boat pools.
- (i) Gunnery training and logistics.
- (j) Training of beach parties, demolition units, rocket craft, fire fighting and other special units.
- (k) Legal matters.
- (l) Mail.

(m) Publication and Basegram Issuing Office.
(n) Inspections.
(o) The following additional matters when the Force Flagship was absent in an operating status:

(1) Staging for current operations.
(2) Operational control of vessels not engaged.
(3) Substitutions in echelons as required.
(4) Specific missions as assigned.

The Administrative Commander was directed to prepare and issue Type and Training Instructions to the Force, and to communicate directly with Commander SEVENTH Fleet, Commander Service Force, SEVENTH Fleet, Army officials, and other appropriate commands and activities, with respect to all matters under his cognizance. The Administrative Commander was directed to refer only matters of policy, major alterations, and major personnel changes to Commander SEVENTH Amphibious Force.

In addition to administering to the needs of those units attached to the SEVENTH Amphibious Force, the Commander, Administrative Command, arranged for repairs and logistics of vessels assigned to the Force for operational purposes. Through liaison with Service Force, SEVENTH Fleet, facilities afloat and ashore, destroyers, destroyer escorts, patrol craft, and minecraft were repaired and supplied whenever the need was apparent.

SUMMARY

The Administrative Command fulfilled a useful purpose in expediting and improving the administration of the units of the SEVENTH Amphibious Force during the period of its existence. Whether or not it is advisable to establish such a separate subordinate command in any future instance will depend upon the size of the Force and surrounding circumstances. Such an organization will lesson to some extent the control of a Force Commander over his Force. It will also occasion delays in some instances in handling matters which must pass through both Commanders before a proper decision can be reached. It requires a complete understanding on the part of the subordinate Commander and his staff of the policies and desires of the Force Commander. On the other hand it frees the Force Commander of many administrative details so that he may concentrate on combat operations, and permits administrative business to proceed without interruption by such operations. The later advantages were deemed to outweigh disadvantages in the case of the SEVENTH Amphibious Force.

USS BLUERIDGE, FORCE FLAGSHIP DECEMBER 43 TO JUNE 45

USS CATOCTIN, SEPT. 45 TO DEC. 45

USS ANCON, JUNE 45 TO SEPT. 45

ANNEX (A)

CHART OF PACIFIC OCEAN AREA SHOWING

OPERATIONS BY THE SEVENTH

AMPHIBIOUS FORCE

ANNEX (A)

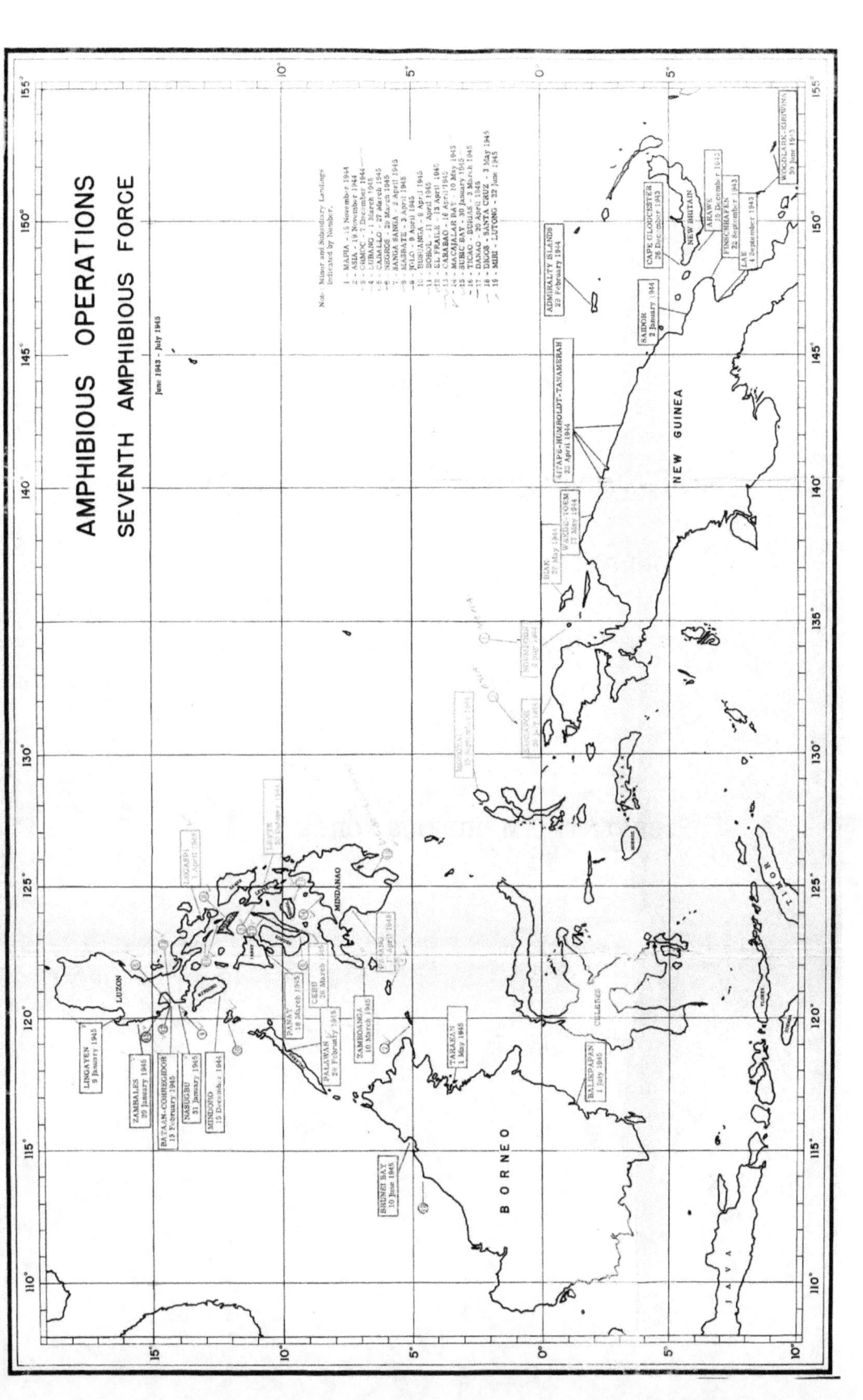

ANNEX (B)

DESIGNATION OF OPERATION PLANS AND

OPERATION ORDERS FOR MAJOR

AMPHIBIOUS OPERATIONS

SEVENTH AMPHIBIOUS FORCE

Annex (B)

OPERATION PLANS AND ORDERS FOR MAJOR AMPHIBIOUS OPERATIONS

Geographical Area	Operation Plan	Landing Date
WOODLARK-KIRIWINA ISLAND	CTF 76 Op. Plan (1-43)	6-30-43
LAE, NEW GUINEA	CTF 76 Op. Plan (2-43)	9-4-43
FINSCHHAFEN, NEW GUINEA	CTF 76 Op. Plan (3-43)	9-22-43
ARAWE, NEW BRITAIN	CTF 76 Op. Plan (3A-43)	12-15-43
CAPE GLOUCESTER, NEW BRITAIN	CTF 76 Op. Plan (3B-43)	12-26-43
SAIDOR, NEW GUINEA	CTF 76 Op. Plan (4-43)	1-2-43
ADMIRALTY ISLANDS	CTF 76 Op. Plan (1-44) and (2-44)	2-29-44
AITAPE-HUMBOLDT-TANAMERAH	CTF 77 Op. Plan (3-44)	4-22-44
WAKDE, NEW GUINEA	CTF 77 Op. Plan (4-44)	5-17-44
BIAK, NEW GUINEA	CTF 77 Op. Plan (5-44)	5-27-44
NOEMFOOR, NEW GUINEA	CTF 77 Op. Plan (6-44)	7-2-44
SANSAPOR, NEW GUINEA	CTF 77 Op. Plan (7-44)	7-30-44
MOROTAI, HALMAHERAS	CTF 77 Op. Plan (8-44)	9-15-44
LEYTE, PHILIPPINE ISLANDS	CTF 78 Op. Plan (101-44) CTG 78.1 At. Plan (1-44)	10-20-44
MAPIA-ASIA ISLANDS	CTF 78 Op. Plan (102-44)	11-15-44
ORMOC, LEYTE	CTG 78.3 ComPhibGrp 9 Attack Order (5-44)	12-7-44
MINDORO, PHILIPPINE ISLANDS	CTG 78.3 ComPhibGrp 9 Operation Order (4-44)	12-15-44
LINGAYEN, LUZON	CTF 78 Op. Plan (103-44) CTG 78.1 At. Plan (2-44)	1-9-45

Annex (B)

Geographical Area	Operation Plan	Landing Date
SUBIC, LUZON	CTF 78 Op. Plan (2-45) CTG 78.3 ComPhibGrp 9 Attack Order (3-45)	1-29-45
NASUGBU, LUZON	CTF 78 Op. Plan (2-45 CTG 78.3 ComPhibGrp 8 Op. Plans (1-45)(2-45)(3-45)	1-31-45
BATAAN-CORREGIDOR, LUZON	CTG 78.3 ComPhibGrp 9 Op. Plan (4-45)	2-15-45
VERDE ISLAND, VISAYAN GROUP	CTG 78.2 Dispatch 230352 February to CTG 78 ComLCIFlot 15 Dispatch 230841 Feb. to ComLCIGroup 72	2-24-45
PUERTA PRINCESSA, PALAWAN ISLAND	CTF 78 Op. Plan (3-45) CTG 78.2 ComPhibGrp 8 Op. Plan (2-45)	2-28-45
LUBANG ISLANDS	CTU 78.9.7 ComLCIFLOTS Op. Order (1-45)	3-1-45
TICAO-BURIAS ISLANDS, VISAYAN GROUP	CTF 78 Op. Plan (4-45) CTG 76.6.5 Mailgram 272346 February 45.	3-3-45
ZAMBOANGA, MINDANAO	CTF 78 Op. Plan (5-45) CTG 78.1 ComPhibGrp 6 Attack Order (A602-45)	3-10-45
ROMBLON-SIMARA, VISAYAN GROUP	CTU 78.9.7 ComLCIFlots 7th Phib Op. Plan (2-45)	3-12-45
ILOILO, PANAY	CTF 78 Op. Plan (6-45) CTG 78.3 ComPhibGrp 9 Op. Plan (5-45)	3-18-45
BUIANACAO-BACO, LUZON	CTU 78.9.7 ComLCIFlots 7thPhib, Op. Plan (3-45)	3-23-45
CEBU CITY, CEBU	CTF 78 Op. Plan (7-45) CTG 78.2 ComPhibGrp 8 Op. Plan (3-45)	3-26-45

Annex (B)

Geographical Area	Operation Plan	Landing Date
CABALLO ISLAND, MANILA BAY	CTF 78 Despatch 251017 Mar. 45 to ComDesDiv 44	3-27-45
NEGROS ISLAND	CTF 78 Op. Plan (6-45) CTG 78.3 ComPhibGrp 9 Op. Plan (5-45)	3-28-45
LEGASPI (BICOL), LUZON	CTF 78 Op. Plan (8-45) CTG 78.4 ComLCIFlot 7 Op. Plan (3-45)	4-1-45
SANGA SANGA, TAWI TAWI, SULU ARCHIPELAGO	CTF 78 Op. Plan (5-45) ComPhibGrp 6 Attack Order A602-Com7thPhibRep Zamboanga Attack Order 1-45 (CTG 76.10)	4-2-45
MASBATE ISLAND, VISAYAN GROUP	CTG 78.3 Op. Plan	4-3-45
JOLO, SULU ARCHIPELAGO	CTF 78 Op. Plan (5-45) ComPhibGrp 6 Attack Order A6-2-45 Com7thPhibForce Rep ZAMBOANGA Attack Order 1-45 (CTG 76.10) and Attack Order 2-45	4-9-45
BOHOL	CTG 78.2 Op. Plan (3-45) ComPhibGrp 9 Op. Plan (10-45)	4-11-45
EL FRAILE, MANILA BAY	CTF 78 Despatch 090555 April 45	4-13-45
CARABAO ISLAND, MANILA BAY	CTF 74 Despatch 121046 April 45	4-16-45
MALABANG (PARANG) MINDANAO	CTF 78 Op Plan (9-45) CTG 78.2 Op. Plan (4-45)	4-17-45
TARAKAN, BORNEO	CTF 78 Op. Plan (10-45) CTG 78.1 ComPhibGrp 6 Attack Order (A604-45)	5-1-45

Annex (B)

Geographical Area	Operation Plan	Landing Date
DAVAO GULF (DIGOS-SANTA CRUZ) MINDANAO	CTG 78.2 ComPhibGrp 8 Op. Plan (5-45)	5-3-45
MACAJALAR BAY (AGUSAN) MINDANAO	CTF 78 Op. Plan (7-45) CTG 78.3 ComPhibGrp 9 Op. Plan (11-45)	5-10-45
BRUNEI BAY, BORNEO	CTF 78 Op. Plan (11-45) CTG 78.1 ComPhibGrp 6 Attack Order (A606-45)	6-10-45
BALIKPAPAN, BORNEO	CTF 78 Op. Plan (12-45) CTG 78.2 ComPhibGrp 8 Op. Plan (6-45)	7-1-45
DAVAO GULF, MINDANAO	CTG 78.2 ComPhibGrp 8 Op. Plan (5-45)	5-3-45
SARANGANI BAY, MINDANAO	CTF 78 Op. Plan (9-45) & Despatches 150026 May & 240309 June CTG 78.1 Op. Plan (A901-45) CTU 76.6.11 Op. Order (1-45)	7-12-45
BALUT ISLAND, MINDANAO	CTG 78.1 ComPhibGrp 9 Op. Plan (A901-45) CTU 76.6.11 Op. Order (2-45)	7-20-45
JINSEN, KOREA	7th Fleet Op. Plan (13-45) CTF 78 Op. Plan (A1702-45)	9-8-45
TIENTSIN, CHINA	7th Fleet Op. Plan (13-45) CTF 78 Op. Plan (A1703-45)	9-30-45
TSINGTAO, CHINA	7th Fleet Op. Plan (13-45) CTF 78 Op. Plan (A1703-45)	10-11-45
CHINESE ARMY LIFT	CTF 78 Op. Plan (A1704-45)	10-30-45

ANNEX (C)

CHARTS OF TASK ORGANIZATION OF FORCES

Assigned for

OPERATIONS IN THE SOUTHWEST PACIFIC AREA by

SEVENTH AMPHIBIOUS FORCE

30 June 1943   -   12 July 1945

(44 CHARTS)

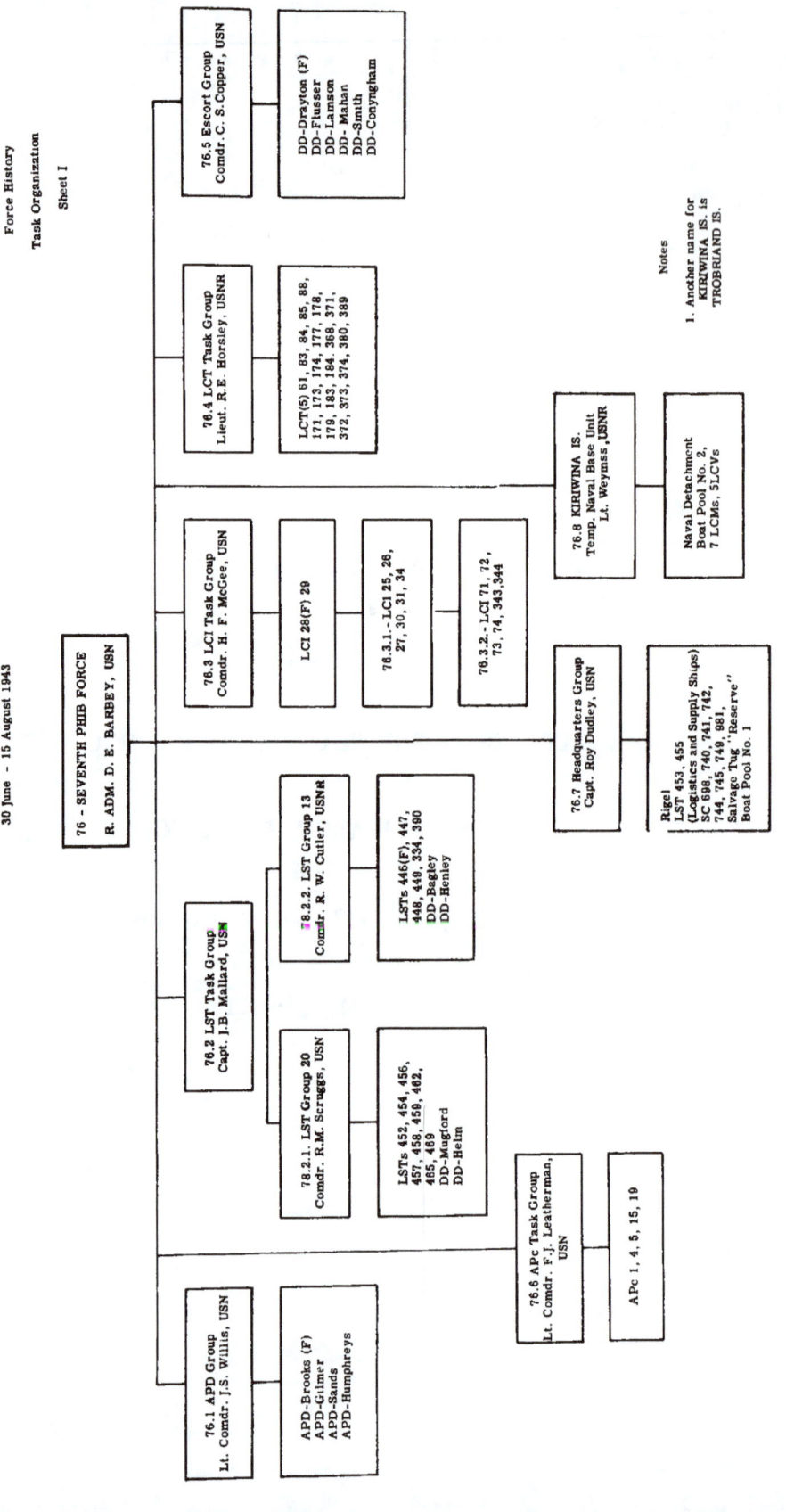

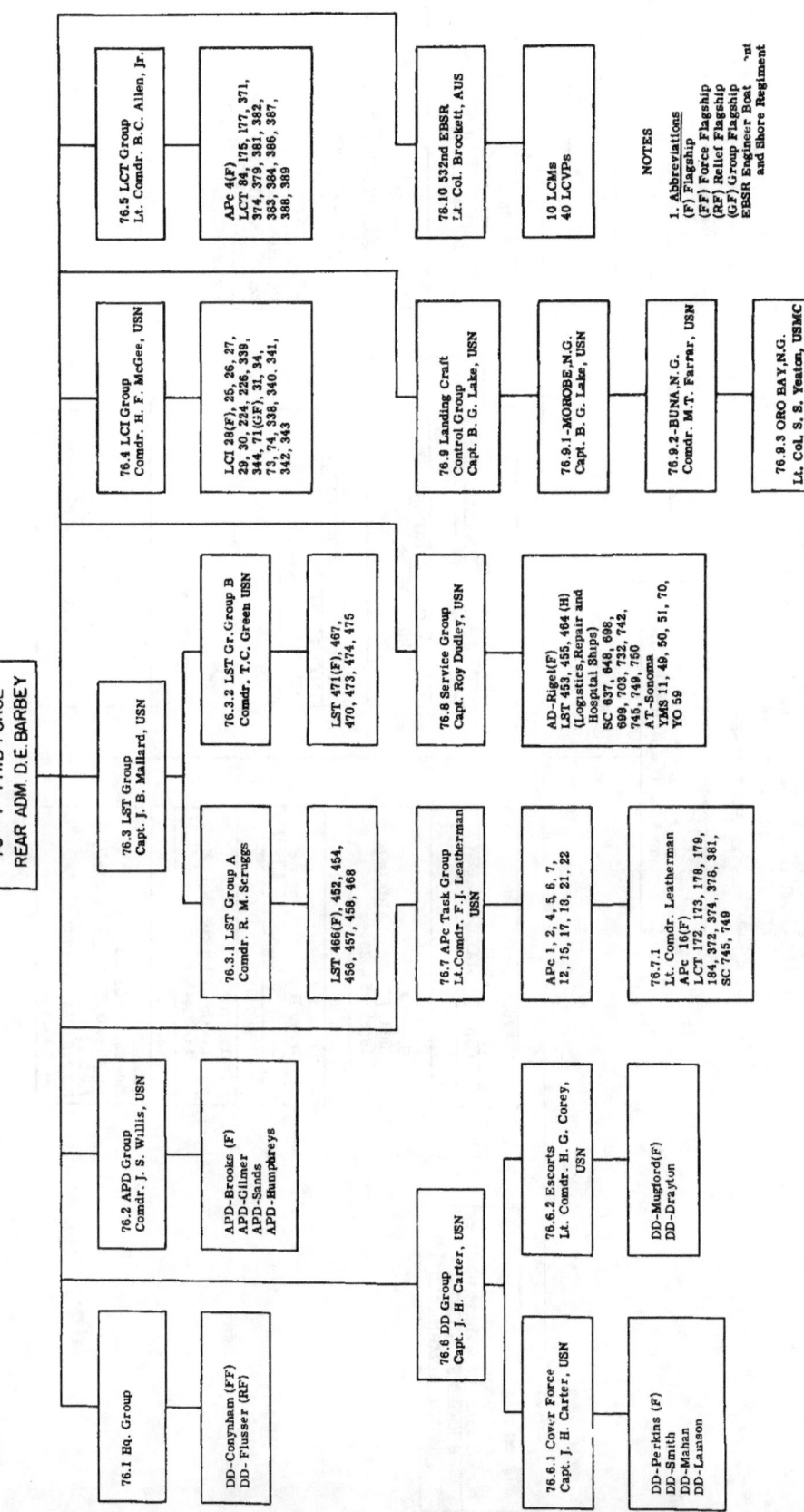

TASK ORGANIZATION
FINSCHHAFEN OPERATION
SCARLET BEACH
22 SEPTEMBER 1943

CTF 76
Seventh Phib Force
Rear Adm. D.E. BARBEY, USN

TG 76.1
Headquarters Group
Rear Adm. D.E. BARBEY, USN

Flagship CONYNGHAM
Relief Flagship HENLEY

TG 76.6
Destroyer Group
Capt. J.H. CARTER, USN

TU 76.6.1
Cover Unit A
Capt. J.H. CARTER, USN
PERKINS(F), SMITH, REID, MAHAN

TU 76.6.2
Bombardment Unit B
Lt. Comdr. P.H. FITZGERALD, USN
LAMSON(F), FLUSSER, MUGFORD, DRAYTON

TG 76.4
LCI Group
Comdr. H.F. McGEE, USN

Lt. G.E. WEYALL, USNR
28(F), 25, 26, 27, 29, 30, 224, 226, 344

Lt. Comdr. J.P. HURNDALL, USNR
71(F), 31, 34, 73, 74, 338, 340, 342, 343

TG 76.10
Shore Battalion
Lt. Col. BROCKETT, USA
2nd Eng. Sp. Brigade
10 LCM
15 LCVP

TG 76.3
LST Group
Capt. J.B. MALLARD, USN

TU 76.3.1
Group A
Capt. J.B. MALLARD, USN
18(F), 168, 204

TU 76.3.2
Group B
Comdr. R.M. SCRUGGS, USN

TU 76.3.3
Lt. (jg) G.I. NELSON, USN
SONOMA

TG 76.7
Sub Chaser Group
Lt. Comdr. F.J. LEATHERMAN, USN
APC 16
SC 648, 698, 699, 703, 734, 736, 742

TG 76.2
APD Group
Comdr. J.S. WILLIS, USN
BROOKS(F), GILMER, SANDS, HUMPHREYS

Seventh Amphibious
Force History
Task Organization
Sheet 3

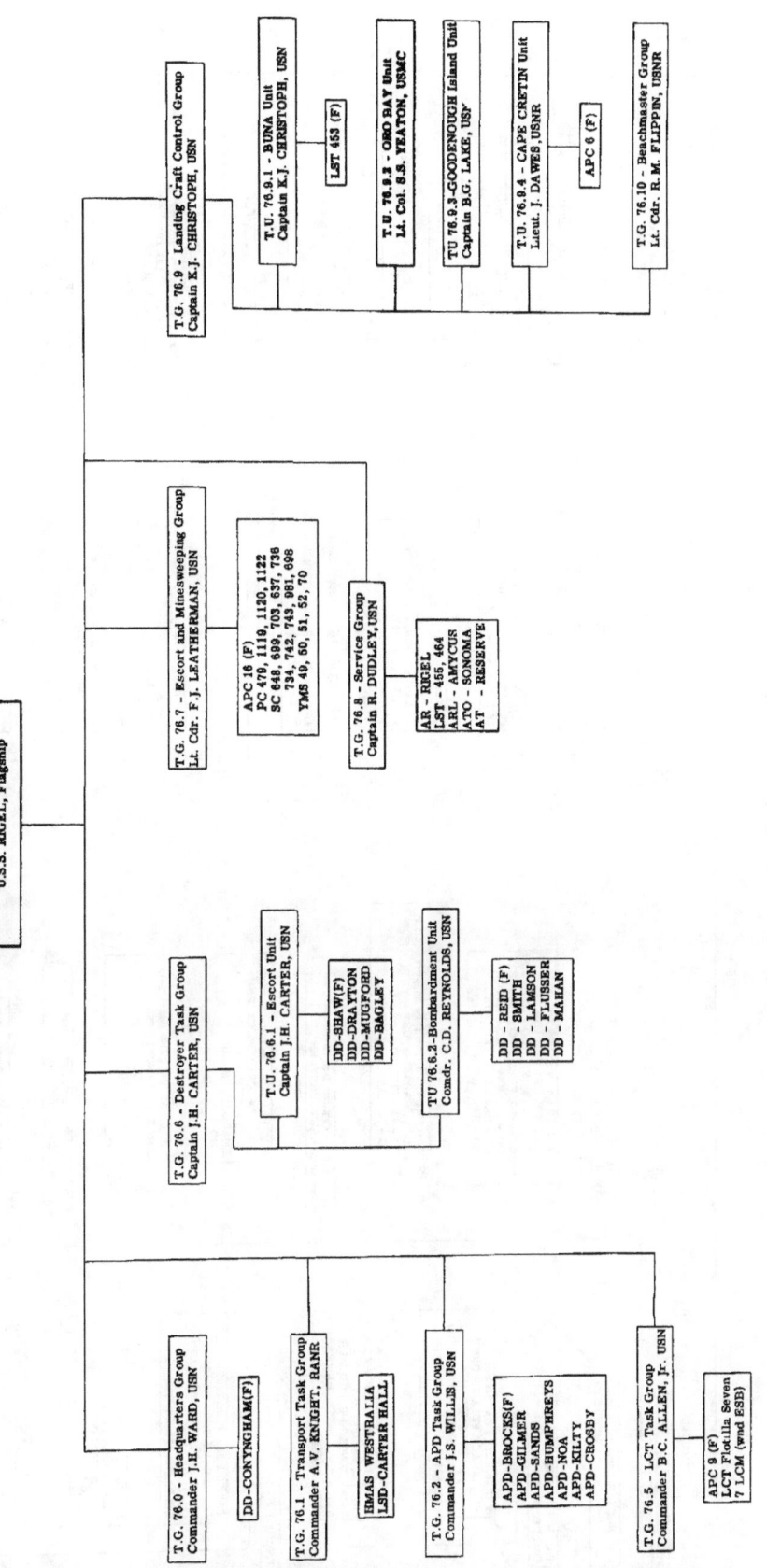

CAPE GLOUCESTER OPERATION ("BACKHANDER")

26 - 28 DECEMBER 1943

Seventh Amphibious
Force History
Task Organization
Sheet 5

T.F. 76
Rear Adm D.E. BARBEY, USN
U.S.S. RIGEL, Flagship

T.G. 76.1 - Eastern Assault Group

- **T.U. 76.1.1 - Headquarters Ship**
  DD - CONYNGHAM

- **T.U. 76.1.2 - APD Task Unit**
  Cdr. J.D. SWEENEY, USN

  - **T.U. 76.1.21 - First Section**
    (BEACH YELLOW ONE)
    Cdr. J.D. SWEENEY, USN
    APD-STRINGHAM APD-CROSBY
    APD-KILTY   APD-DENT
    APD-WARD

  - **T.U. 76.1.22 - Second Section**
    (BEACH YELLOW TWO)
    Cdr. J.B. WILLIS, USN
    APD - SANDS   APD - GILMER
    APD - NOA   APD - HUMPHREYS
    APD - BROOKS (F)

- **T.U. 76.1.3 - LCI Task Unit**

  - **T.U. 76.1.31 - First Section**
    (BEACH YELLOW ONE)
    Lt. Cdr. J.P. HURNDALL, USNR
    LCI 71 (F)
    LCI 72, 74, 338, 30, 226

  - **T.U. 76.1.32 - Second Section**
    (BEACH YELLOW TWO)
    Lt. N.M. TAYLOR
    LCI 343, 337, 344, 73
    LCI 340, 342, 430, 431

  - **T.U. 76.1.33 - Rocket Section**
    Cdr. D.E. DAY, USN
    LCI 31 (Beach YELLOW ONE),
    LCI 34 (Beach YELLOW TWO).

- **T.U. 76.1.4 - Destroyer Unit**
  Capt. J.H. CARTER, USN

  - **T.U. 76.1.41 - Escort Section**
    Capt. J.H. CARTER, USN
    DD - SHAW (F)   DD - DRAYTON
    DD - MUGFORD   DD - BAGLEY
    DD - LAMSON   DD - HUTCHINS
    DD - BEALE   DD - DALY
    DD - BROWNSON

  - **T.U. 76.1.42 - Close Fire Support Section**
    Cdr. J.A. ROBBINS, USN
    DD - FLUSSER (F)
    DD - MAHAN (Relief HQ Ship)

- **T.U. 76.1.5 - Cruiser Bombardment Unit**
  Rear Adm. CRUTCHLEY, RN

  - **T.U. 76.1.51 - Airdrome Section**
    Rear Adm. CRUTCHLEY, RN
    HMAS AUSTRALIA
    HMAS SHROPSHIRE
    4 DD

  - **T.U. 76.1.52 - YELLOW Beach Sect.**
    Capt. H.A. SPANGEL, USN
    CL - NASHVILLE
    CL - PHOENIX
    4 DD

- **T.U. 76.1.6 - Beach YELLOW Harbor Unit**
  Capt. N.D. BRANTLY, USN

- **T.U. 76.1.61 - Control Section**
  Lieut. R.R. BLAKE
  SC 981   SC 742

- **T.U.76.1.62-Minesweeping Section**
  Lieut. F.P. ALLEN Jr.
  YMS 81 1. SS 52 YMS 70

T.G. 76.2 - Eastern Supply Group
Capt. J.B. MALLARD, USN

- **T.U. 76.2.1 - First Supply Section**
  Cdr. C.H. PETERSON, USCG
  LST 465 (F), 18, 66, 67, 68, 204, 202

- **T.U. 76.2.2 - Second Supply Section**
  Capt. R.M. SCRUGGS, USN
  LST 452 (F), 464, 456, 457, 465, 22, 26

- **T.U. 76.2.3 - Third Supply Section**
  Lt. Cdr. D.M. BAKER, USNR
  LST 459 (F), 458, 168, 170, 171,
  PC 1119, 1120, 1122

- **T.U. 76.2.4 - Fourth Supply Section**
  Lt. Cdr. T.C. GREEN, USN
  LST 474 (F), 467, 468, 470, 475,
  SC 703, 734, 738

T.G. 76.3 - Western Assault Group
Cdr. C.D. REYNOLDS, USN

- **T.U. 76.3.1 - Escort and Bombardment Unit**
  Cdr. C.D. REYNOLDS, USN
  DD - REID (F)   DD - SMITH

- **T.U. 76.3.2 - Small Craft Unit**
  Cdr. B.C. ALLEN, Jr., USN
  14 LCM, 12 LCT, 2 LCM (Rocket DUKWS)
  SC 637, SC 699, PC 479

- **T.U. 76.3.3 - LCI Unit**
  Lieut. C.E. WEYLL, USNR
  LCI 25 (F), 26, 27, 29, 224

T.G. 76.4 - Service Group
Capt. R. DUDLEY, USN
AR - RIGEL (F)
LST 455, 464

T.G. 76.5 - Landing Craft Control Group
Capt. K.J. CRISTOPH, USN

- **T.U. 76.5.1 - BUNA Unit**
  Capt. K.J. CHRISTOPH, USN
  ARL - AMYCUS (F)

- **T.U. 76.5.2 - ORO BAY Unit**
  Lt. Col. S.S. KEATON, USMC
  APc 15

- **T.U. 76.5.3 - CAPE CRETIN Unit**
  Capt. B. ANDERSON
  LST 453 (F)
  APc 6

- **T.U. 76.5.4 - CAPE SUDEST Unit**
  Cdr. JOHNSON

T.G. 76.6 - Reserve Group
Cdr. A.V. KNIGHT, BARR
HMAS WESTRALIA (F)
LSD - CARTER HALL
IX - ETAMIN

T.G. 76.7 - Salvage Group
Lieut. G.I. NELSON, USN
ATO - SONOMA
AT - RESERVE

SAIDOR OPERATION ("MICHAELMAS")

2 - 9 JANUARY 1944

T.F. 76 - Rear Adm. D.E. BARBEY, USN
U.S.S. BLUE RIDGE (FF)
Comdr. L. R. McDOWELL, USN

T.G. 76.1 - Assault Group

TU 76.1.1 - Headquarters Ship
DD - CONYNGHAM

T.U. 76.1.2 - APD Task Unit
Cdr. J.D. SWEENEY, USN

- **T.U. 76.1.21** - First Section (BLUE Beach)
  Lt. Cdr. J.S. WILLIS, USN
  APD - BROOKS (F)   APD - GILMER
  APD - NOA

- **T.U. 76.1.22** - Second Section (WHITE Beach)
  Lt. Cdr. F.D. SCHWARTZ, USN
  APD - HUMPHREYS (F)   APD - SANDS

- **T.U. 76.1.23** - Third Section (RED Beach)
  Cdr. J.D. SWEENEY, USN
  APD - STRINGHAM (F)   APD - CROSBY
  APD - KILTY   APD - WARD

T.U. 76.1.3 - LCI Task Unit
Cdr. H.F. McGEE, USN
(LCI 28 (F))

- **T.U. 76.1.31** - First Section (BLUE Beach)
  Lt. N.M. TAYLOR, USNR
  LCI 73 (F)   LCI 338
  LCI 343   LCI 344

- **T.U. 76.1.32** - Second Section (WHITE Beach)
  Lt. C.E. WEYLL, USNR
  LCI 25 (F), 27, 30,
  LCI 26, 224, 225

- **T.U. 76.1.33** - Third Section (RED Beach)
  Lt. Cdr. J.P. HURNDALL, USNR
  LCI 11 (F), 72, 74,
  LCI 342, 340, 226

T.U. 76.1.4 - Destroyer Unit
Capt. J.H. CARTER, USN

- **T.U. 76.1.41** - Escort Section
  Capt. K.M. McMANES, USN
  DD - HUTCHINS (F)   DD - DALY
  DD - DRAYTON   DD - BAGLEY

- **T.U. 76.1.42** - Bombardment Section
  Capt. J.H. CARTER, USN
  DD - BEALE (F)   DD - REID
  DD - SMITH   DD - MAHAN
  DD - FLUSSER   DD - LAMSON

- **T.U. 76.1.43** - Covering Section
  Comdr. E.F.V. DESCHAINEUX, RAN
  DD - WARRAMUNGA (F)   DD - ARUNTA
  DD - HELM   DD - RALPH TALBOT

T.U. 76.1.6 - Control and Rocket Unit
Capt. N.D. BRANTLY, USN
LCI 31, 34   SC 981, 742

T.G. 76.2 - Supply Group
Capt. J.B. MALLARD, USN

- **T.U. 76.2.1** - First Supply Unit
  Capt. R.M. SCRUGGS, USN
  LST 452 (F), 454, 456
  LST 22, 466, 170

- **T.U. 76.2.2** - Second Supply Unit
  Lt. Cdr. T.C. GREEN, USN
  LST 474 (F), 475, 206
  LST 171, 168, 468
  PC 1119, 1120, 1122

T.G. 76.4 - Service Group
Capt. R. DUDLEY, USN
AR - RIGEL (F)
LST 455, 464

T.G. 76.5 - Landing Craft Control Group
Capt. K.J. CHRISTOPH, USN

- **T.U. 76.5.1** - BUNA Unit
  Capt. K.J. CHRISTOPH, USN
  ARL - AMYCUS (F)

- **T.U. 76.5.2** - ORO BAY Unit
  Lt. Col. S.S. YEATON, USMC
  APc 15

- **T.U. 76.5.3** - CAPE CRETIN Unit
  Capt. B. ANDERSON, USN
  LST 453 (F)   APc 6

- **T.U. 76.5.4** - CAPE SUDEST
  Comdr. JOHNSON, USN
  APc 10

T.G. 76.6 - Reserve Group
Comdr. A.V. KNIGHT, RANR
HMAS WESTRALIA (F)
LSD - CARTER HALL
IX - ETAMIN

T.G. 76.7 - Salvage Group
Lieut. G.I. NELSON, USN
ATO - SONOMA (F),
AT-HMAS RESERVE

T.G. 76.8 - Beachmaster Group
Lieut. R.G. CONGDON, USNR
3 officers, 30 enlisted men

ADMIRALTY ISLANDS OPERATION ("BREWER")

29 FEBRUARY, 1944 – 9 MARCH, 1944

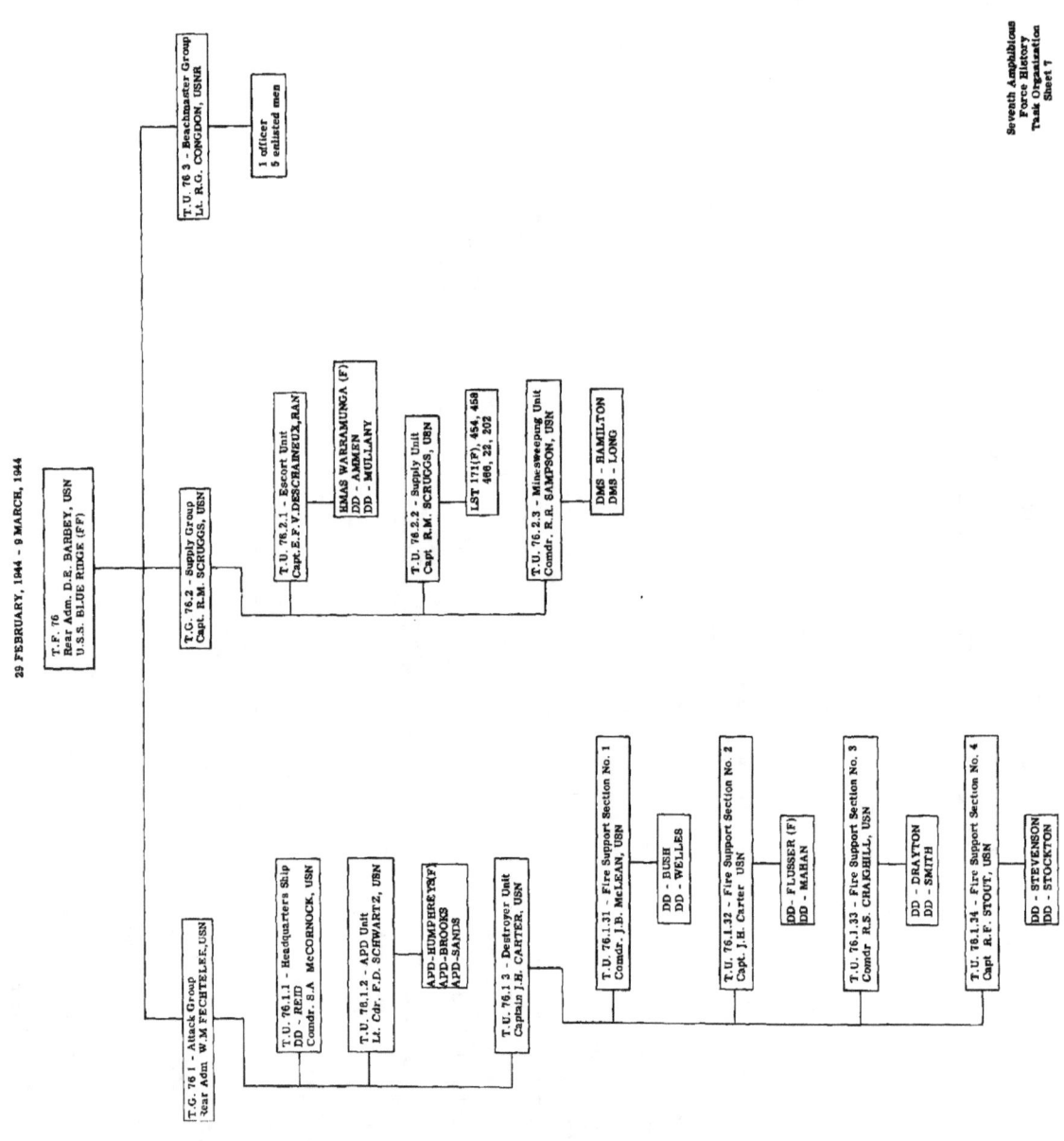

Seventh Amphibious
Force History
Task Organization
Sheet 1

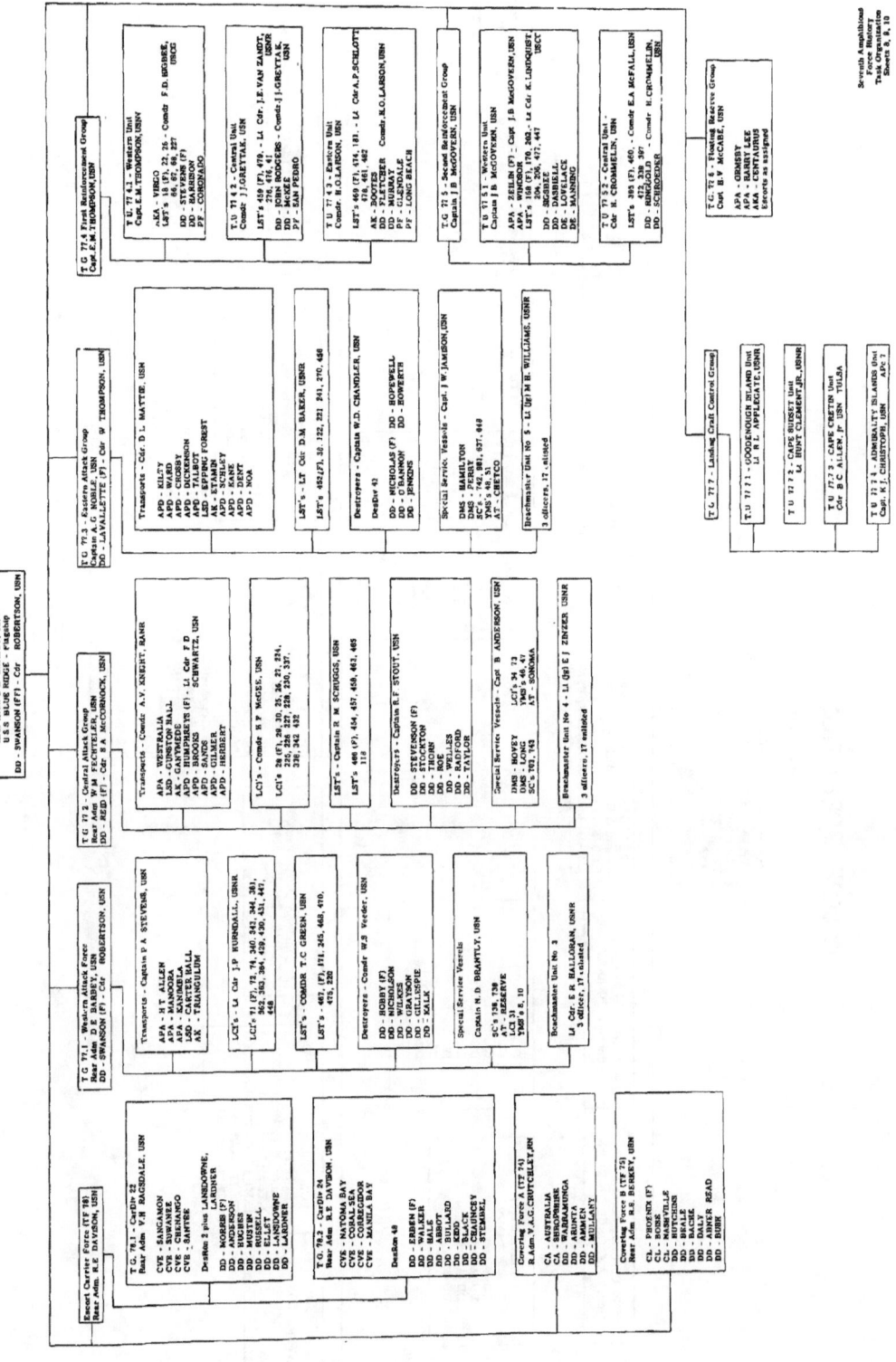

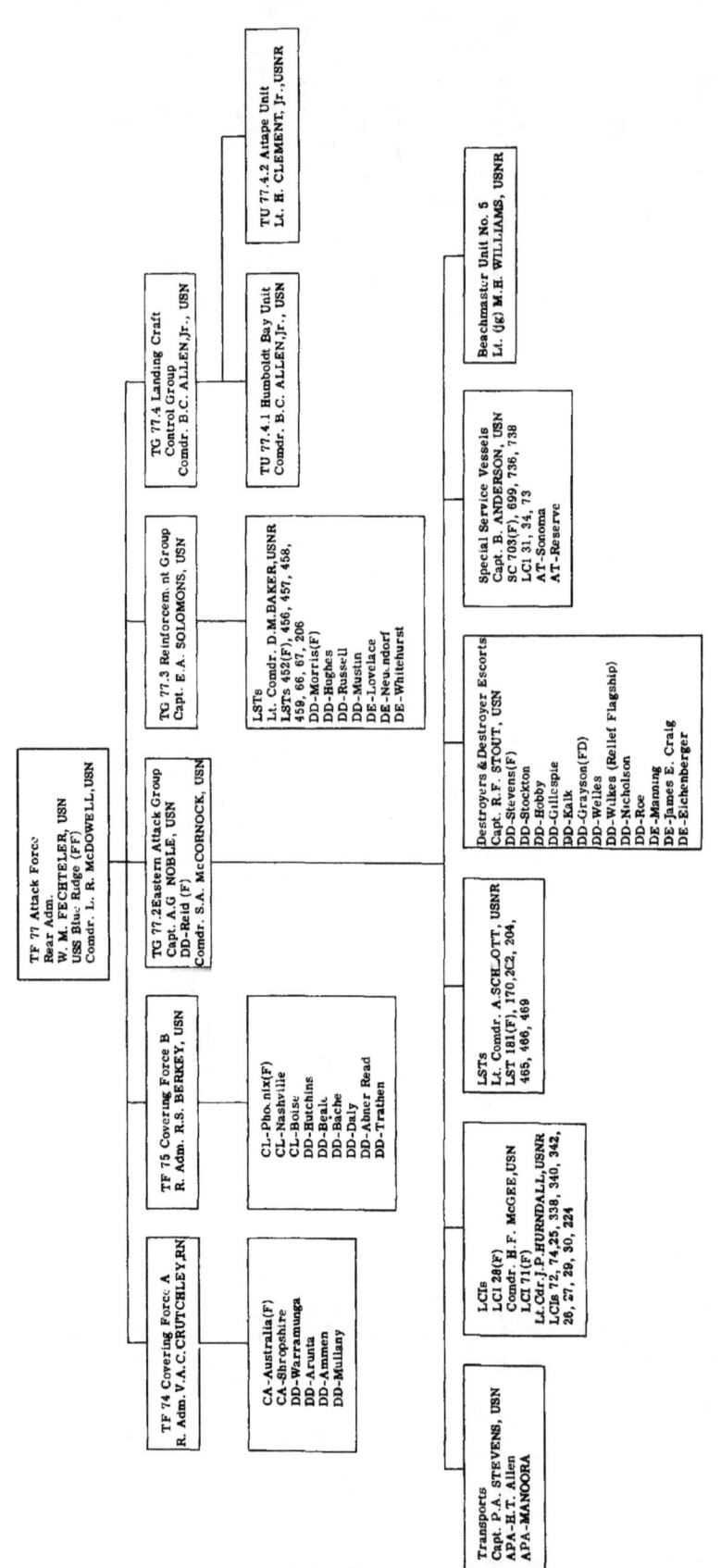

BIAK OPERATION ("HORLICKS")
27 MAY – 11 JUNE 1944

- **T.F. 77 – Attack Force**
  Rear Adm. W.M. FECHTELER, USN
  U.S.S. BLUE RIDGE, Flagship

  - **T.G. 77.1 – Force Flagship**
    Comdr. T.M. FLECK, USN
    - DD – SAMPSON

  - **T.G. 77.2 – Covering Force A**
    (Fire Support Group A)(TF74)
    Rear Adm. CRUTCHLEY, RN
    - CA – SHROPSHIRE
    - CA – AUSTRALIA
    - DD – WARRAMUNGA
    - DD – ARUNTA
    - DD – AMMEN
    - DD – MULLANY

  - **T.G. 77.3 – Covering Force B**(TF 75)
    (Fire Support Group B)
    Rear Adm. R.S. BERKEY, USN
    - CL – PHOENIX
    - CL – NASHVILLE
    - CL – BOISE
    - DD – HUTCHINS
    - DD – BEALE
    - DD – BACHE
    - DD – DALY
    - DD – ABNER READ
    - DD – TRATHEN

  - **T.G. 77.4 – Main Body**
    Rear Adm. W.M. FECHTELER

    - **T.U. 77.4.1 – Fire Support Group C**
      Capt. R.F. STOUT, USN
      - DD – STOCKTON
      - DD – REID
      - DD – HOBBY
      - DD – KALK
      - DD – WELLES
      - DD – GILLESPIE
      - DD – GRAYSON (FD)

    - **T.U. 77.4.11 – Fire Support Unit No. 1**
      - DD – GILLESPIE
      - DD – WELLES

    - **T.U. 77.4.12 – Fire Support Unit No. 2**
      - DD – HOBBY
      - DD – KALK

    - **T.U. 77.4.13 – Fire Support Unit No. 3**
      - DD – STOCKTON
      - DD – REID

    - **T.U. 77.4.14 – Fighter Director Unit**
      - DD – GRAYSON

    - **T.U. 77.4.2 – Fire Support Group D**
      Capt. E.A. SOLOMONS, U.S.N.
      - DD – MORRIS
      - DD – MUSTIN
      - DD – HUGHES
      - DD – RUSSELL

    - **T.U. 77.4.3 – Transport Unit**
      Comdr. D.L. MATTIE, USN
      - APD – KILTY
      - APD – SCHLEY
      - APD – WARD
      - APD – CROSBY
      - APD – HERBERT

    - **T.U. 77.4.4 – LCI Unit**
      Comdr. H.F. McGEE, USN
      - LCI 28 (F) plus 15 LCI's

    - **T.U. 77.4.5 – LST Unit**
      Capt. R.M. SCRUGGS, USN
      - 6 LST's
      - 8 LCT(5)

    - **T.U. 77.4.6 – Special Service Unit**
      Capt. B. ANDERSON, USN

      - **T.U. 77.4.61 – Control Unit**
        Capt. B. ANDERSON, USN
        - SC 703(F), 734, 735
        - 981 Rocket

      - **T.U. 77.4.62 – Rocket Unit**
        Comdr. D.E. DAY, USN
        - LCI 31, 34, 73

      - **T.U. 77.4.63 – Salvage Unit**
        Lieut. G.J. NELSON, USN
        - AT – SONOMA

      - **T.U. 77.4.64 – Demolition Unit**
        Lt.(jg) R.H. FLOWERS, USNR
        - LCI 446
        - Naval Combat Demolition Units Nos. 2 and 3.

  - **T.G. 77.5 – Beach Party**
    Lt. J.B. AVERY, USNR
    - Beach Party No. 4, reinforced.

  - **T.G. 77.6 – Landing Craft Control Group**
    Comdr. B.C. ALLEN, Jr. USN
    - HUMBOLDT BAY LCCO Organization

  - **T.G. 77.7 – First Reinforcement Group**
    Comdr. A.J. GREENACRE, USN

    - **T.U. 77.7.1 – LST Unit**
      - 3 LST

    - **T.U. 77.7.2 – LCI Unit**
      - 6 LCI

    - **T.U. 77.7.3 – Escort Unit**
      - DD – WILKES
      - DD – NICHOLSON
      - DD – SWANSON
      - 2 DE's

  - **T.G. 77.8 – Second Reinforcement Group**
    Comdr. P.R. COFFIN, USN

    - **T.U. 77.8.1 – LST Unit**
      - 7 LST

    - **T.U. 77.8.2 – Escort Unit**
      - DD – ROE
      - DD – WARRINGTON
      - DD – BALCH
      - 2 PF

Seventh Amphibious Force History
Task Organization
Sheet 12

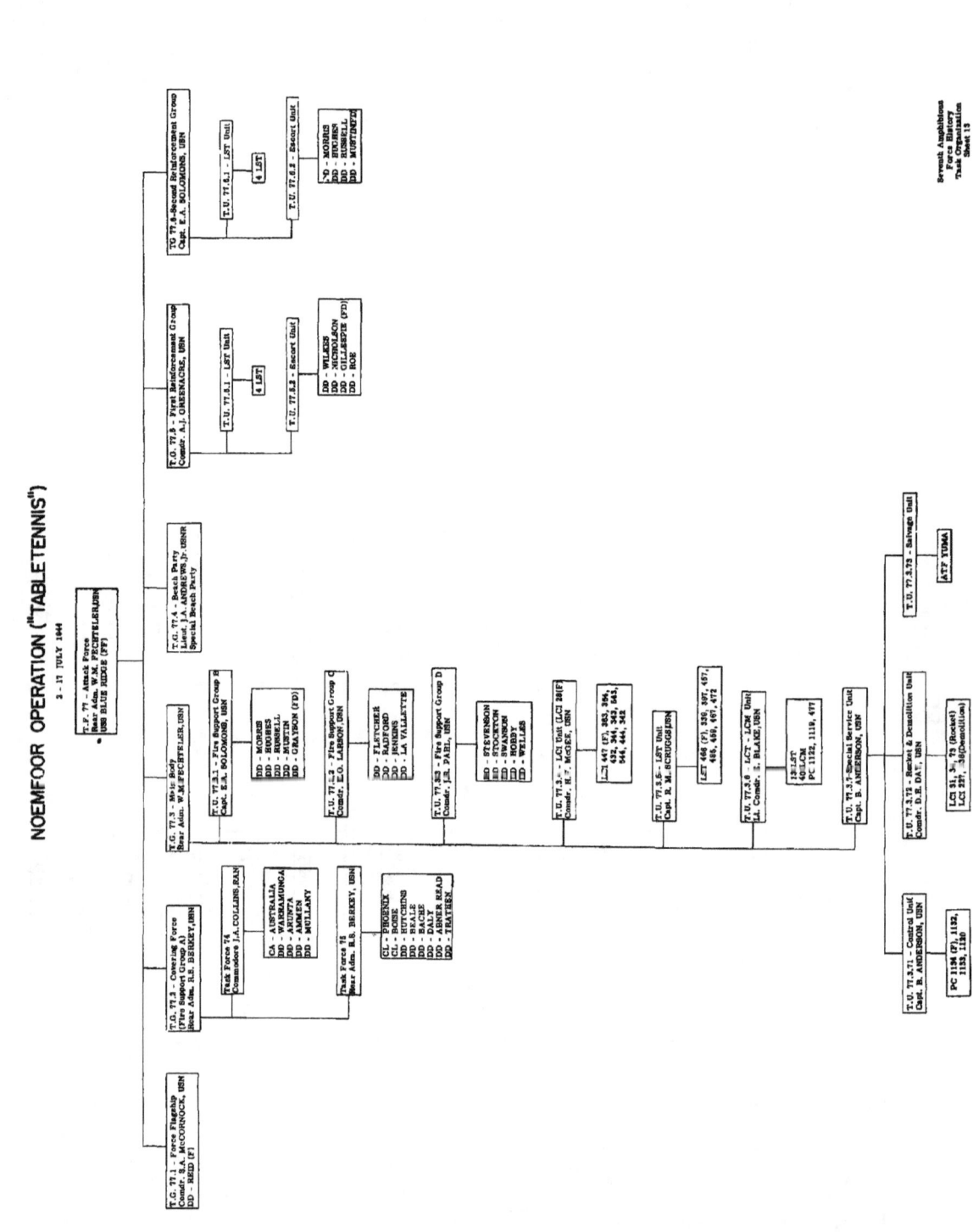

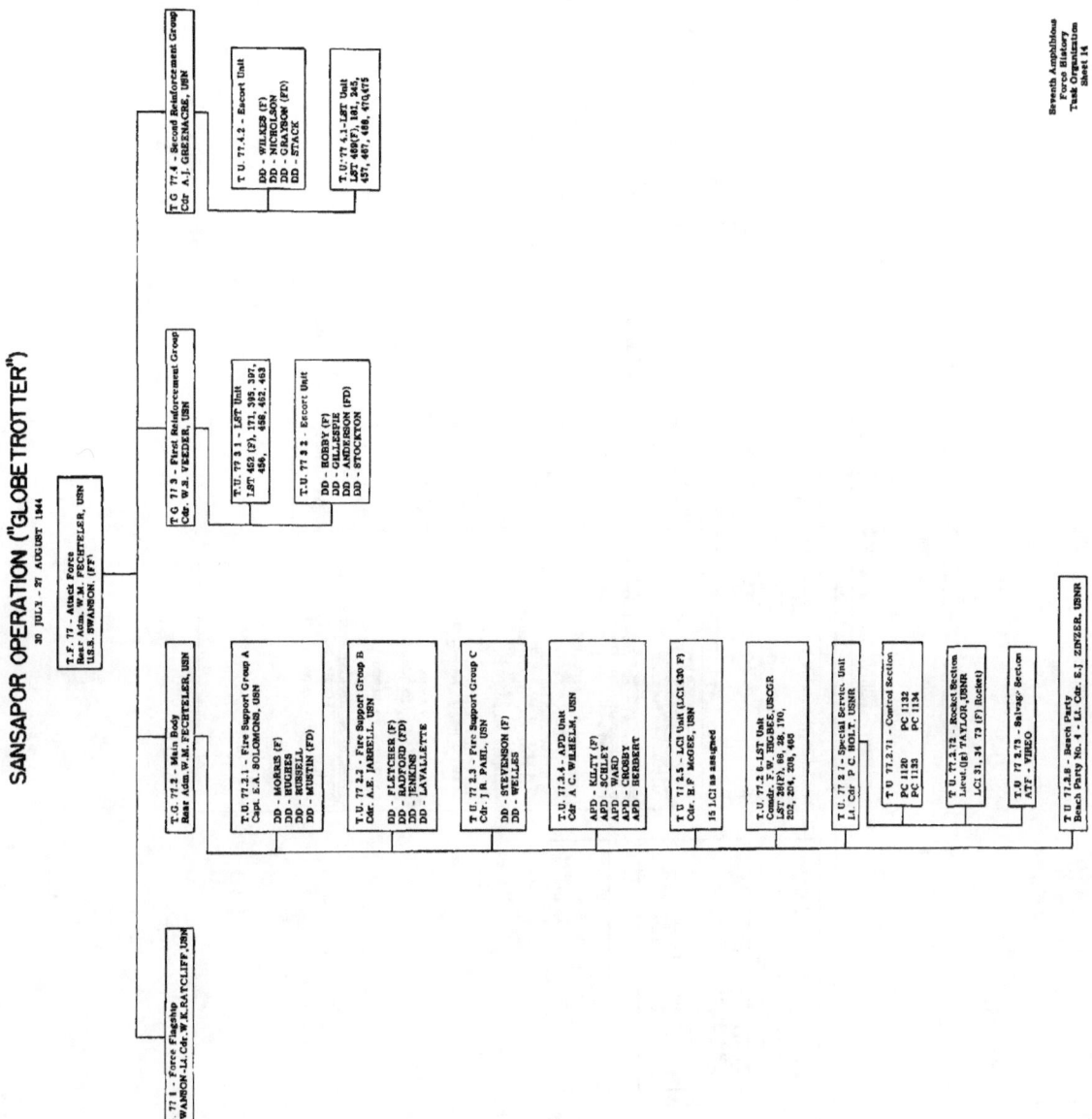

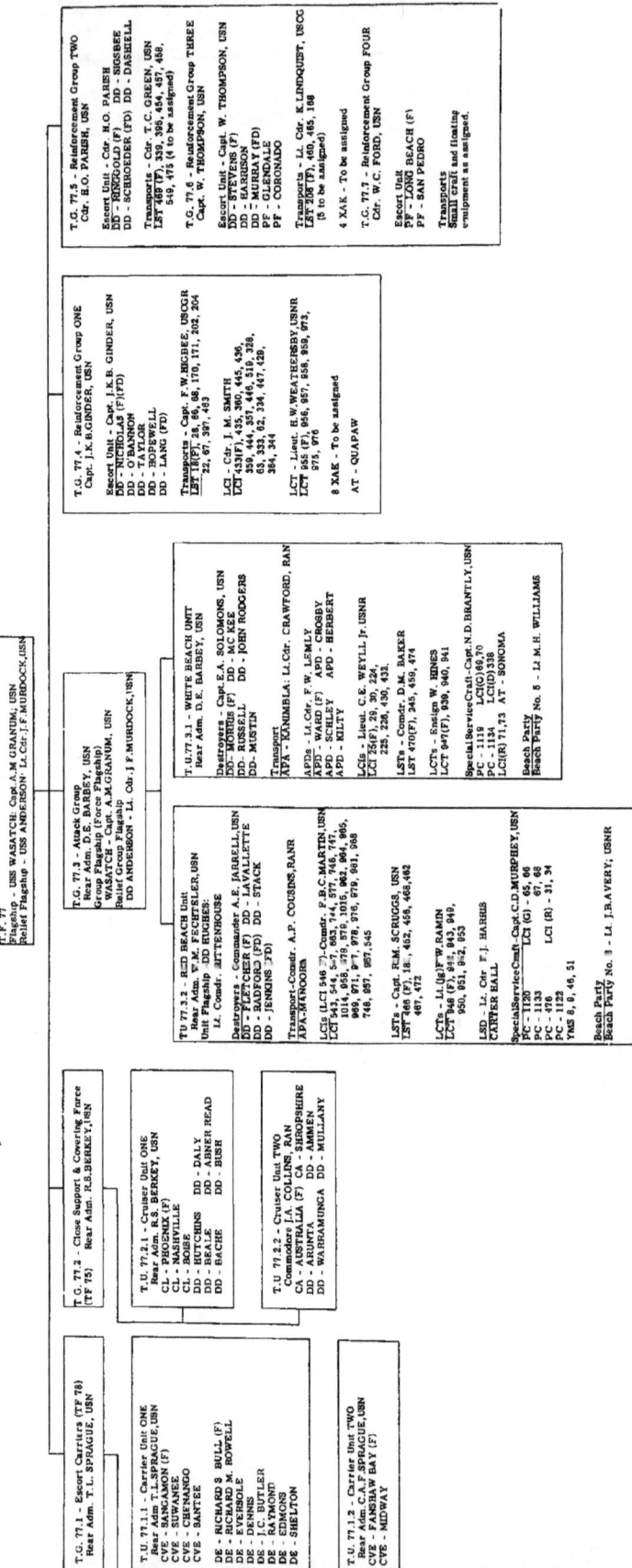

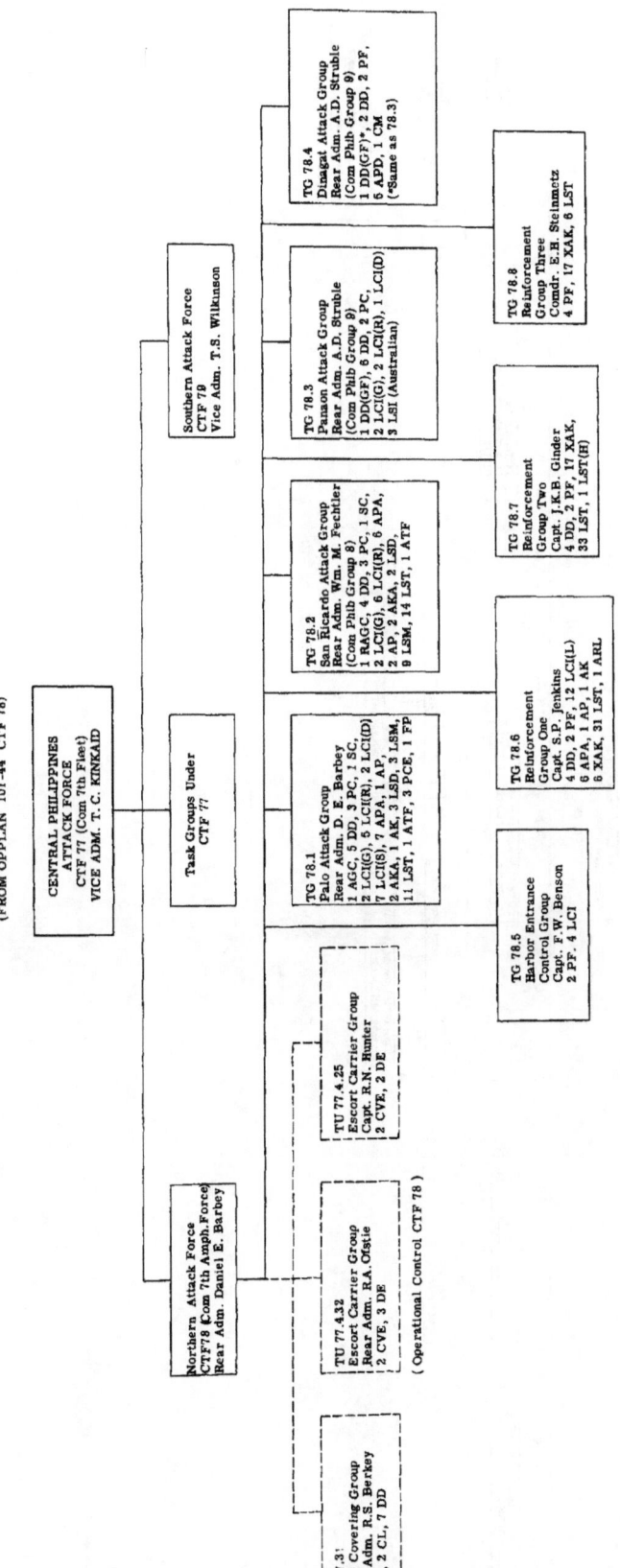

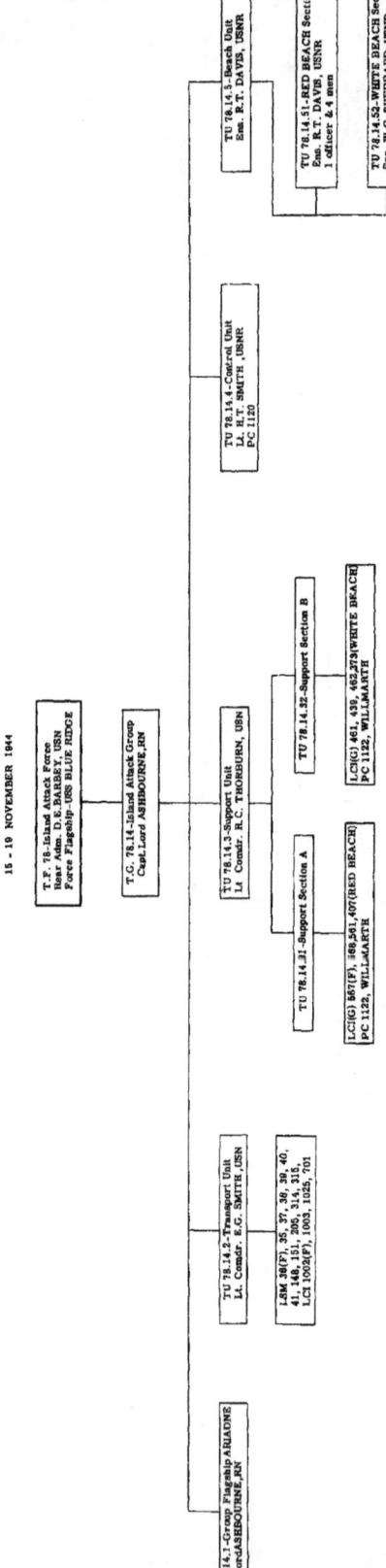

TASK ORGANIZATION
ORMOC OPERATION

7 DECEMBER, 1944

Ref: CTG 78.3 Attack Order No. 5-44

CTF 78
Seventh Amphibious Force
Vice Adm. D.E. BARBEY, USN

CTG 78.3
ORMOC Attack Group
Rear Adm. A.D. STRUBLE, USN

TU 78.3.1
Group Flagship
DD HUGHES

TU 78.3.2
Fast Transport Unit
Comdr. W.S. PARSON, USN

LLOYD (F), WARD,
CROSBY, SCHLEY,
LIDDLE, COFER,
HERBERY, KEPHART

TU 78.3.3
Light Transport Unit
Comdr. W.V. DEUTERMANN, USN

LCI 972 (F), 575, 607, 609,
612, 613, 685, 686, 687, 746,
755, 759, 955, 963, 965, 966,
970, 976, 977, 978, 980, 981,
983, 1021, 1022, 1064

TU 78.3.4
Heavy Transport Unit
Comdr. SHIVLEY, USN

LST 739 (F), 556, 734, 737

TU 78.3.5
Escort Unit
Capt. W.L. FRESEMAN, USN

BARTON (F), Wa
BARTON (F), WALKE,
LAFFEY, O'BRIEN,
SHAW, DRAYTON,
FLUSSER, LAMSON,
SMITH, REID,
CONYNGHAM,
MAHAM

TU 78.3.6
Minesweeping Unit
Comdr. E.D. McEATHRON, USN

SAUNTER (F), PURSUIT,
REQUISITE, SAGE, SALUTE,
SCOUT, SCRIMMAGE, TRIUMPH,
SENTRY, BROOK

TU 78.3.7
Control and Inshore Support
Lt. Comdr. HOLT, USN

SC 731, 736
LCI (R) 230 (F), 34, 237, 238
ATR 31

Seventh Amphibious
Force History
Task Organization
Sheet 18

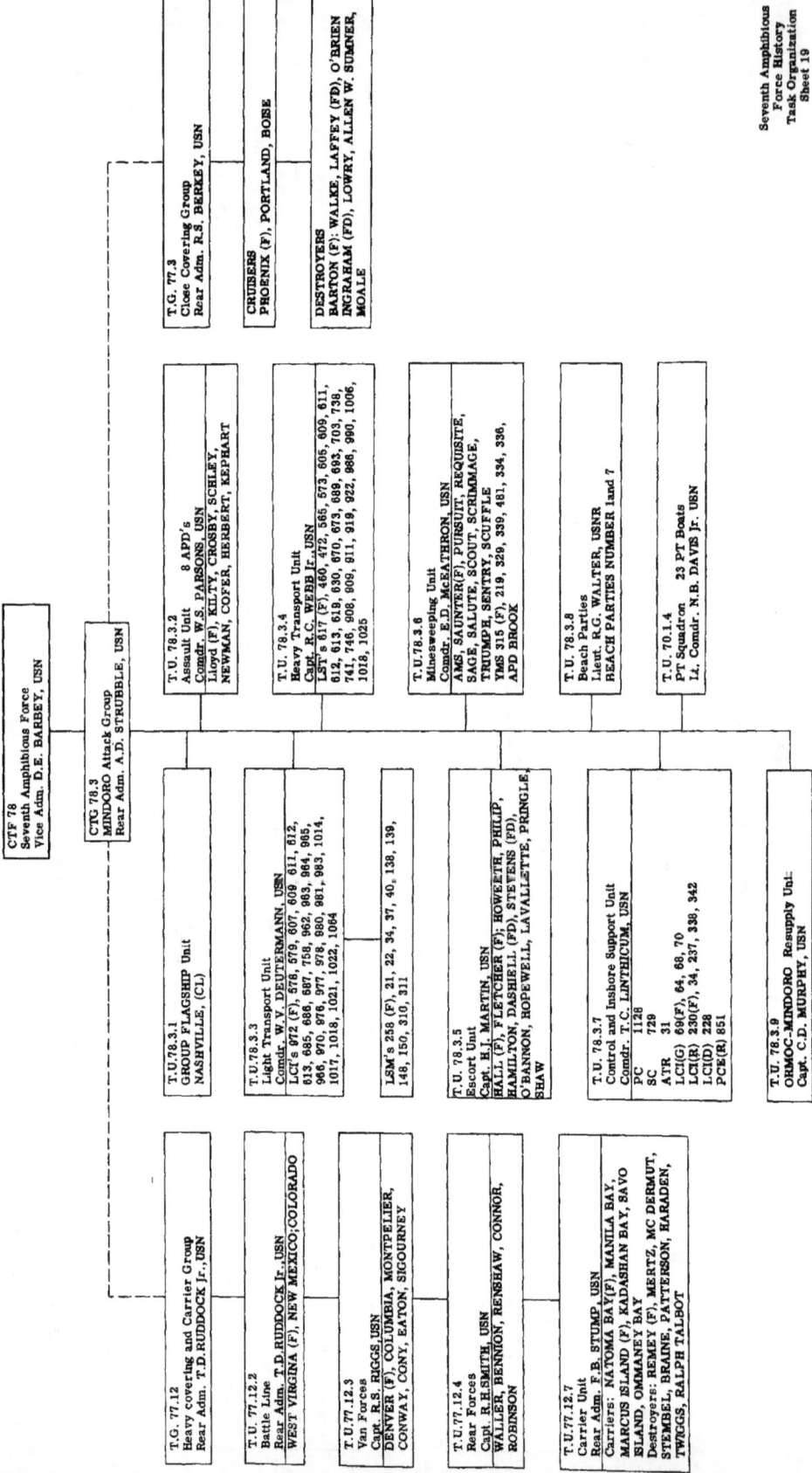

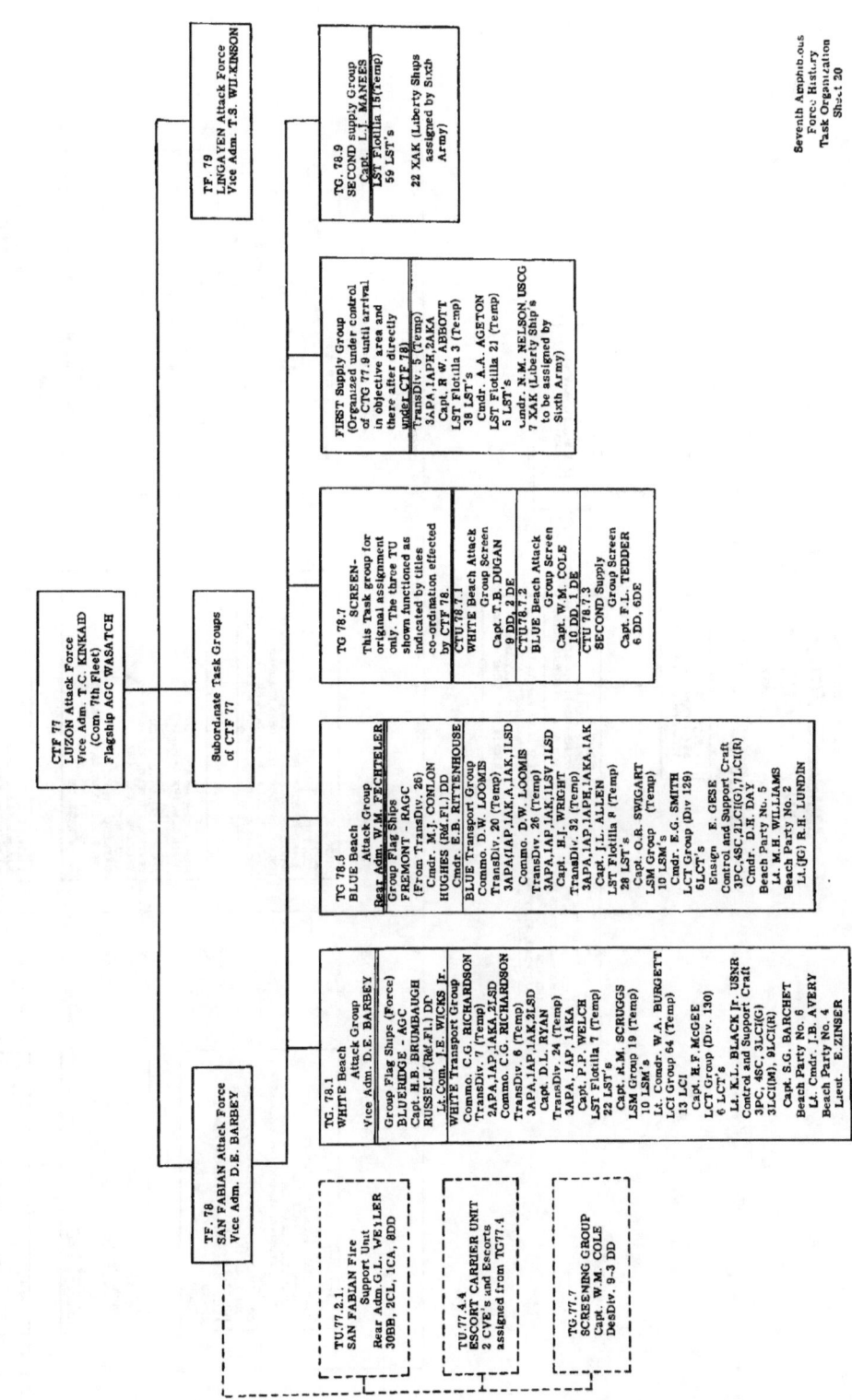

TASK ORGANIZATION
ZAMBALES-GRANDE ISLAND LANDINGS ("MIKE-SEVEN")
29 JANUARY 1945

Ref: Com 7 Phib OP-Plan 2-45, Com Phib Grp 9 OP-Plan 1-45
Com Phib Grp 9 OP-Order 3-45 and CTG 78.3 Action Report 4 Mar.1945

T.F. 78
SEVENTH AMPHIB. FORCE
VICE Adm. D.E. BARBEY, USN

T.G. 78.3
MIKE SEVEN Attack Group
(ZAMBALES Prov.& GRANDE I.)
Rear Adm. A.D. STRUBLE, USN

T.U. 78.3.1 Flagship Unit
MT. McKINLEY - AGC
Capt. W.N. GAMET, USN
WICKES - DD (Relief Flag Ship)

T.U. 71.3.1
FIRE SUPPORT Unit
1 CL, 2 DD
Rear Adm. R.S. RIGGS, USN
CL DENVER
DDs RADFORD, FLETCHER

T.U. 70.1.4
PT UNIT
Lt. H.S.TAYLOR, USNR
VARUNA   AGP
20 PT Boats

T.U.78.3.2
RED BEACH Transport Unit
10APA, 4AP, 5AKA, 1AK, 1LSV(F)
Commo. M.O. CARLSON, USN
HARRIS (SF), LAMAR, SHERIDAN, PIERCE,
DUPAGE, ELMORE, ALPINE, CUSTER, BAXTER,
APPLING   APA
GOLDEN CITY, PRESIDENT POLK, WINGED
ARROW, LA SALLE   AP
MONITOR   LSV
ALCYONE, AQUARIUS, ALSHAIN, ALGOL,
ARNEB   AKA
AURIGA   AK

T.U.78.3.3
BLUE BEACH Transport Unit
3APA, 2AKA, 1AK
Commo. C.G.RICHARDSON, USN
CAVALIER (SF), SARASOTA, HASKELL APA
CAPRICORNUS, CHARA   AKA
MERCURY   AK

T.U 78.3.4
LST Unit
45LST's(Fltd.14), 7LSM, 2XAK
Capt. E.A.SEAY, USN
463, 552, 553, 556, 558, 565, 569, 573,
583, 592, 606, 609, 612, 623, 631, 636, 658,
662, 669, 679, 680, 693, 703, 697, 707, 714,
734, 735, 736, 737, 740, 745, 746, 775, 777,
990, 910, 922, 924, 990, 999, 1008, 1034,
1024, 1025,
LSM 66(F), 63, 64, 67, 86, 288, 269.

T.J.78.3.5
Escort Unit
7BD, 7DE
Capt. B.F. BROWN, USN
SPROSTON, WICKES (FD), YOUNG, PICKLING (F),
ISHERWOOD, LUCE (FD), CHAS. J.BADGER DD's
RILEY (F), LESLIE B. KNOX, McNULTY, METIVIER
GEORGE A. JOHNSON, EUGENE B. ELMORE, DAY DE's

T.J 78.3.6
Minesweeping and Hydrographic Unit
1CAM, 1CM, 1PF, 1APD, 19YMS
Lt. Cdr. J.R. KEEFER, USN
SAUNTER (F), SALUTE, SCOUT, SCRIMMAGE,
SENTRY, SCUFFLE, REQUISITE (F), PURSUIT,
TRIUMPH, SAGE, MONADNOCK AM
RATHBURNE   APD
WHITMAN   DE
YMS 6, 9, 53, 50, 68, 71, 156, 219, 243,
286, 314, 334, 336, 342, 363, 390,
363, 398, 406

T.L.78.3.7
Salvage and Rescue Unit
2ATO, 1ATF, 4LCI
Cmdr. B. HUIE, USN
GRASP (F), KIDATSA   ATO
APACHE, RAIL   ATF
LCI(L), 63, 616, 676, 777

T.U. 78.3.8
Control and Inshore Support Unit
3PC, 4SC, 6LCI(R), 8LCS(L)
Capt. R.E. ARISON, USN
PC 1119, 1122, 1133
SC 521, 867, 995, 1327
LCI(R) 225, 226, 337, 338, 340, 341
LCS(L) 7, 8, 26, 27, 49

T.U. 78.3.9
BEACH PARTY Unit
2 Beach Parties, No's 8 & 9
Lieut. T. NORDYKE, USNR

T.U. 78.3.10
LSGHT Transport Unit   APD
Cmdr. W.S. PARSONS, USN
LLOYD (F), NEWMAN, COFER,
KEPHART

* Note: T.U.78.3.10 Landed troops on
GRANDE Island on E-1 the
Amphibious Operations was
in charge of Commo. CARLSON
in the MONITOR (LSV)

Seventh Amphibious
Force History
Task Organization
Sheet 21

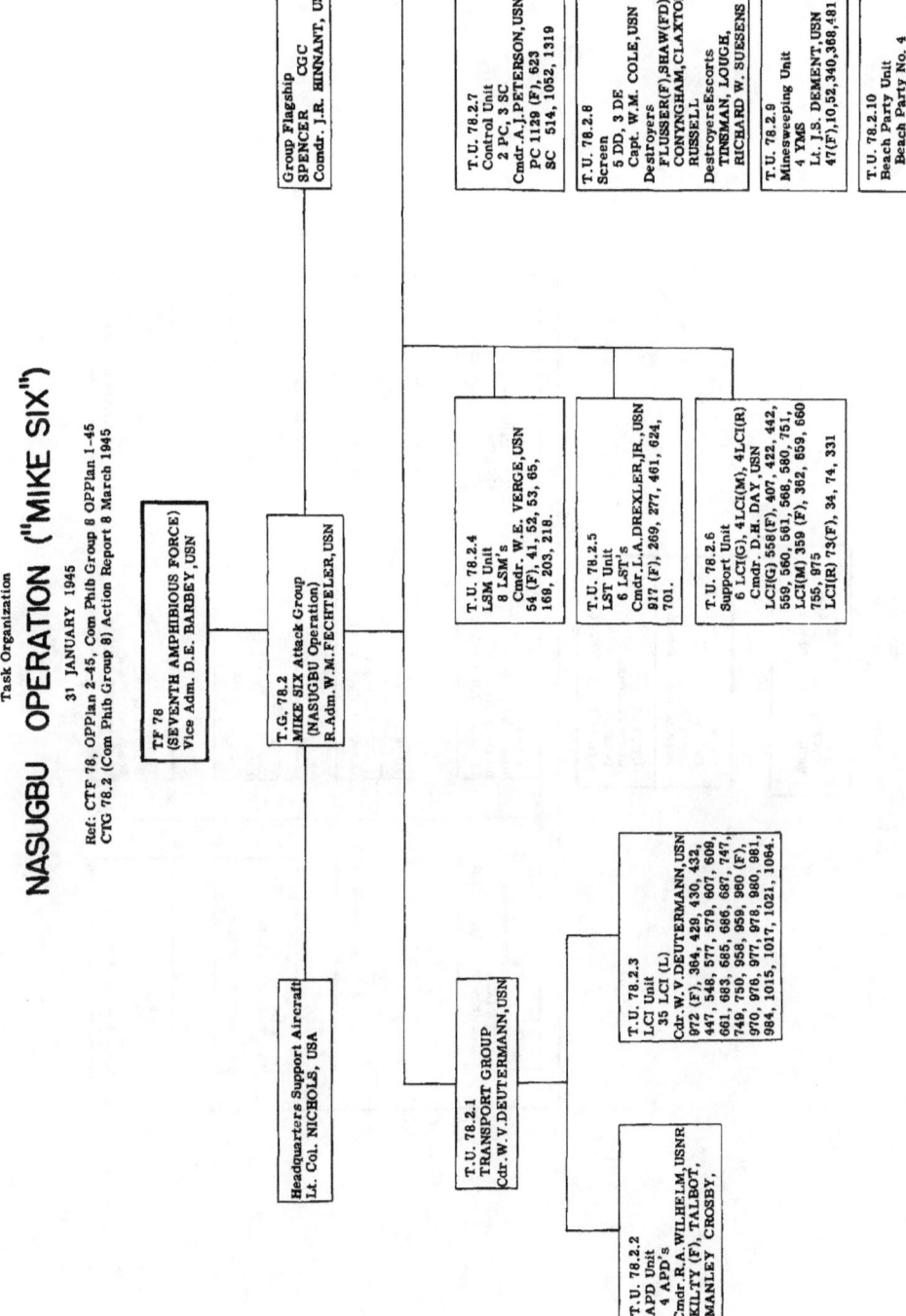

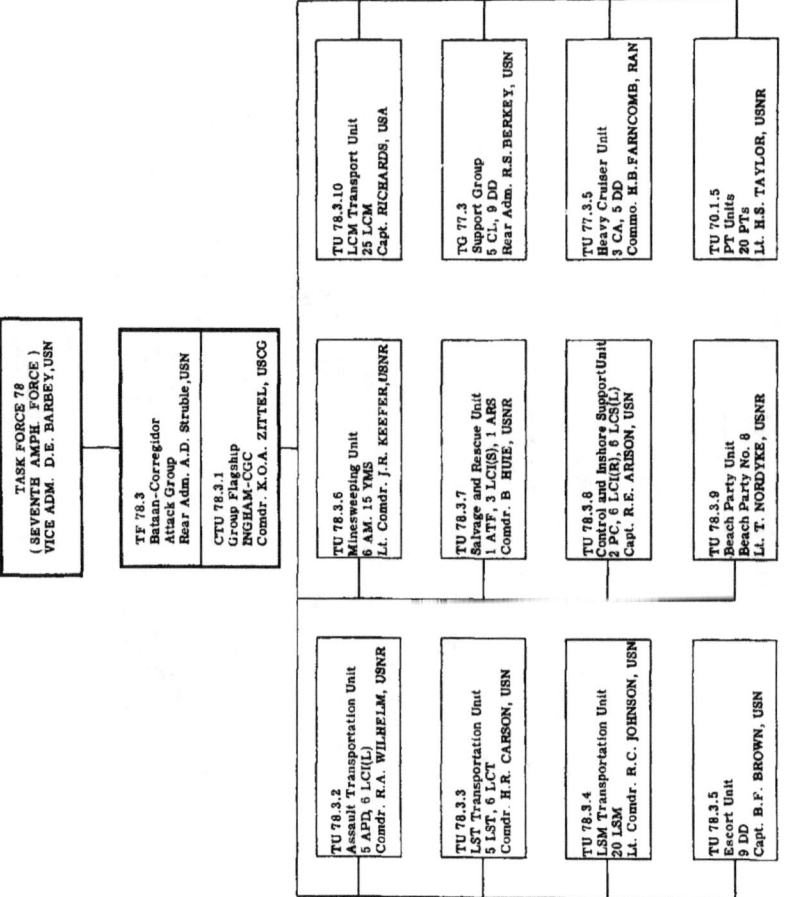

TASK ORGANIZATION
VERDE ISLAND OPERATION
24 FEBRUARY 1945

Ref: Com LCI(L) Flot 24 report of 28 Feb. 45

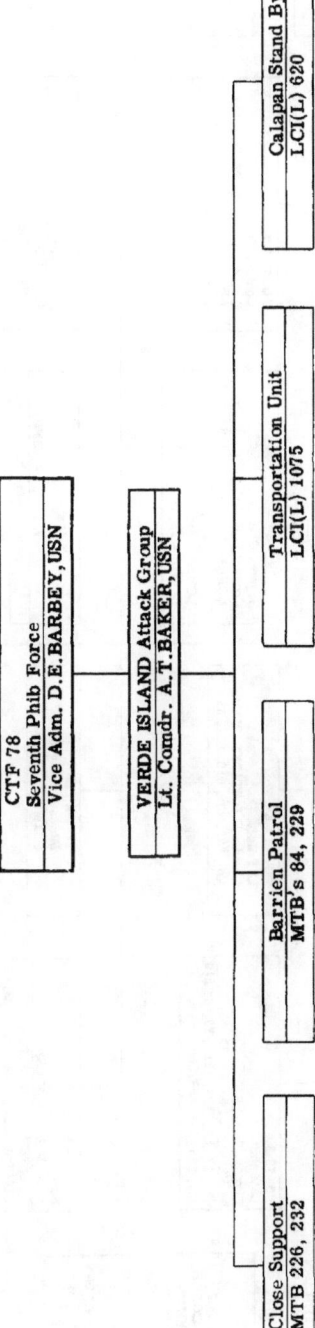

Seventh Amphibious
Force History
Task Organization
Sheet 23.1

| CTF 78 |
| Seventh Phib Force |
| Vice Adm. D.E. BARBEY, USN |

| VERDE ISLAND Attack Group |
| Lt. Comdr. A.T. BAKER, USN |

| Close Support | Barrier Patrol | Transportation Unit | Calapan Stand By |
| MTB 226, 232 | MTB's 84, 229 | LCI(L) 1075 | LCI(L) 620 |

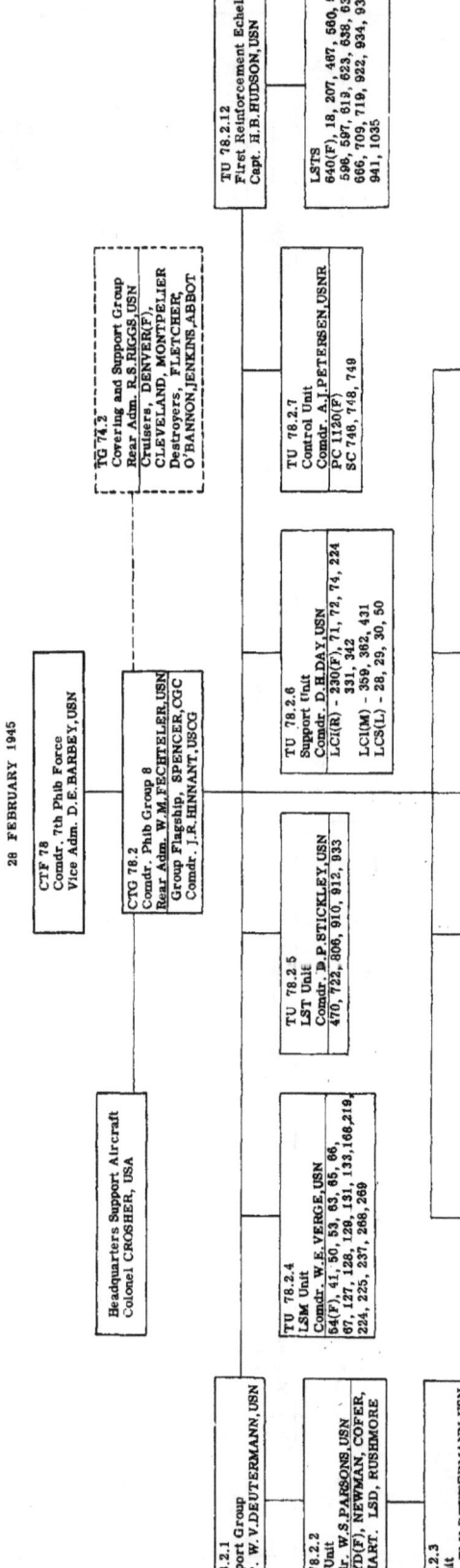

TASK ORGANIZATION

PALAWAN OPERATION ("VICTOR THREE")

28 FEBRUARY 1945

Seventh Amphibious
Force History
Task Organization
Sheet 24

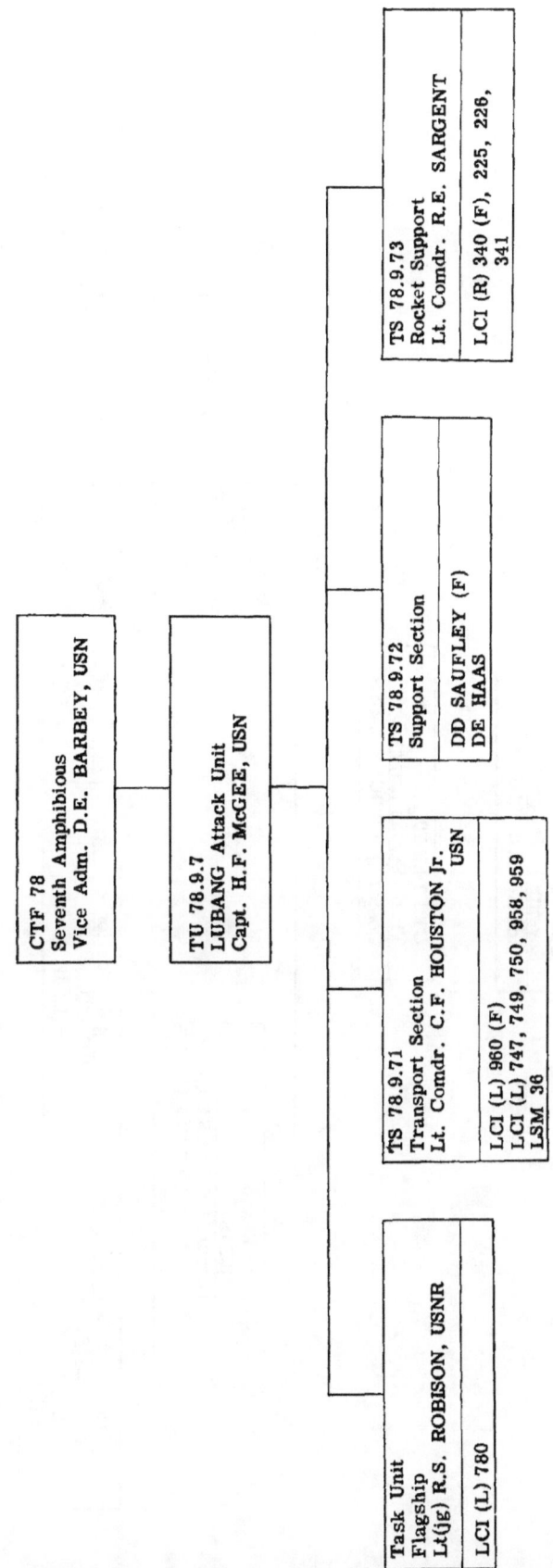

TASK ORGANIZATION
TICAO-BURIAS OPERATION
3 MARCH 1945

Ref: CTU 78.9.10 action report dated 15 March 1945

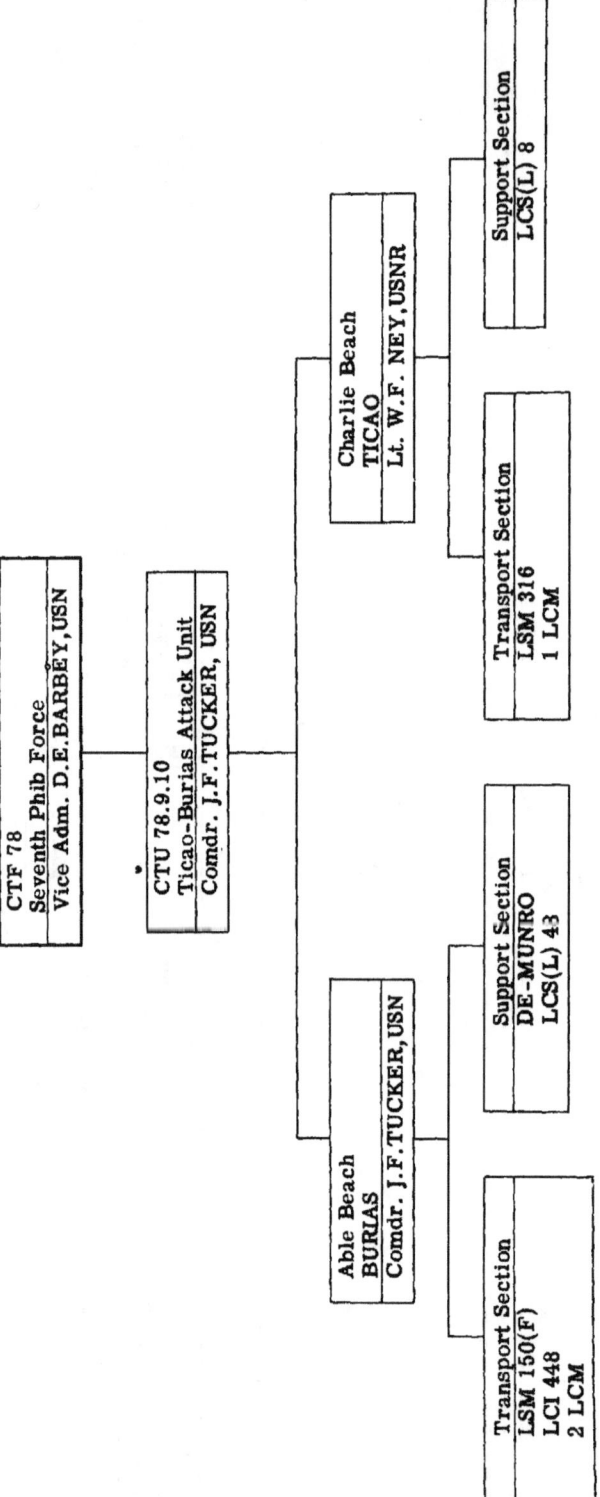

Seventh Amphibious
Force History
Task Organization
Sheet 25.1

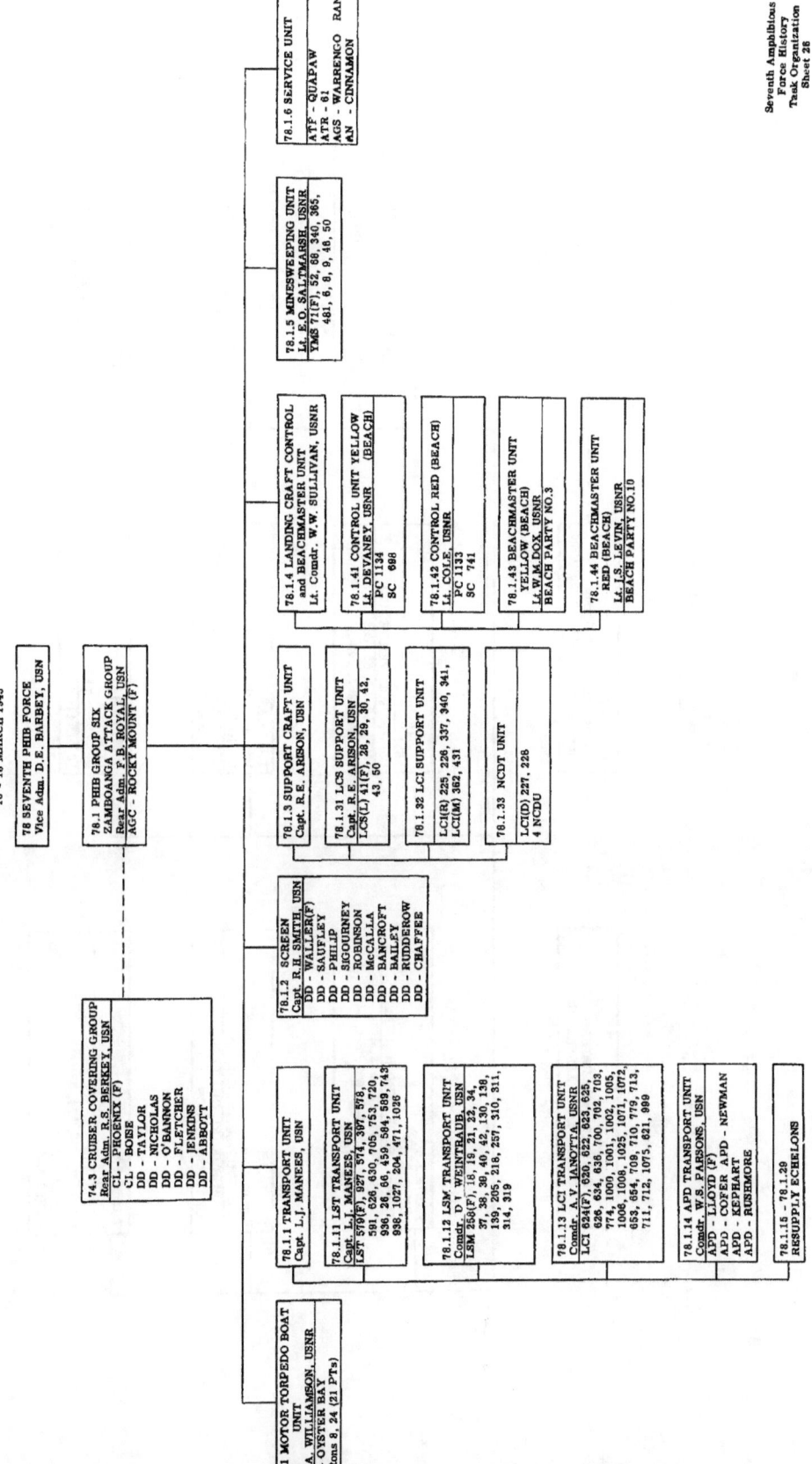

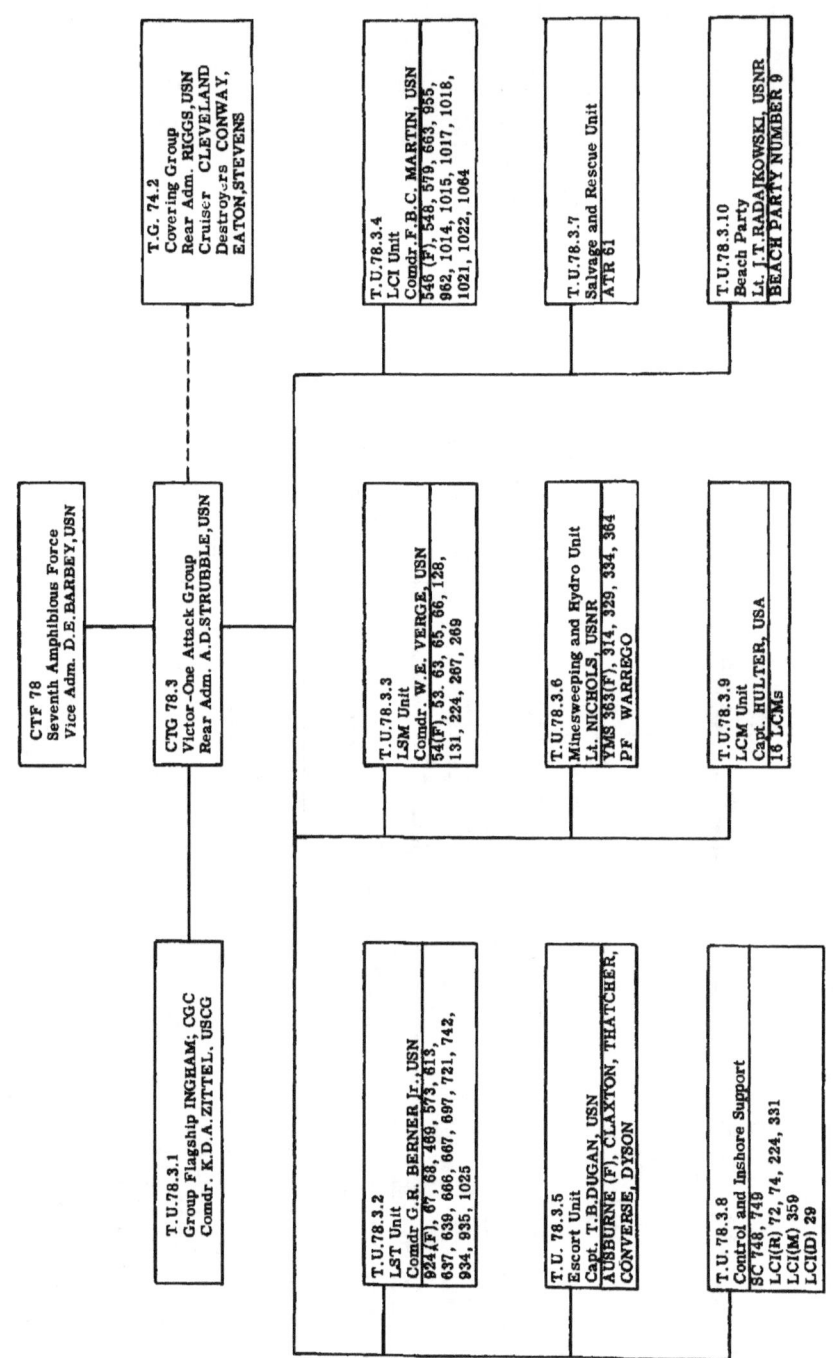

TASK ORGANIZATION
CEBU ("VICTOR TWO")
26 MARCH 1945

- **CTF 78**
  Seventh Amphibious Force
  Vice Adm. D.E. BARBEY, USN

- **CTG 78.2**
  Victor Two Attack Group
  Capt. A.T. SPRAGUE Jr.
  Group Flagship, SPENCER CGC
  Comdr. J.R. HINNANT, USCG

- **Headquarters Support Aircraft**
  Major O'KEEFE, USA

- **T.G. 74.3**
  Comdr. Covering and Support
  Rear Adm. R.S. BERKEY, USN
  Cruisers - PHOENIX, HOBART,
  Destroyers - NICHOLAS,
  O'BANNON, TAYLOR, ABBOT

- **C.T.U. 78.2.2**
  APD Unit
  Comdr. W.S. PARSONS, USN
  LLOYD (F), NEWMAN, KEPHART,
  COFER

- **T.U. 78.2.3**
  LCI Unit
  Comdr. W.V. DEUTERMANN, USN
  972(F), 607, 609, 613, 683, 685,686,
  963, 965, 966(F), 970, 975, 977,978,
  984, 980

- **T.U. 78.2.4**
  LSM Unit
  Lt. Comdr. G.F. BAKER, USN
  168 (F), 35, 50, 150, 151, 219,
  225, 237, 268, 316, 317

- **T.U. 78.2.5**
  LST Unit
  Capt. H.B. HUDSON, USN
  640 (F), 18, 171, 181, 454,
  457, 560, 595, 619, 638,
  709, 777, 922
  LCT's 1296, 830, 747

- **T.U. 78.2.6**
  Support Unit
  Comdr. D.H. DAY, USN
  LCI(R) 230(F), 225, 340, 341, 342
  LCS(L)30(F), 28, 29, 50

- **T.U. 78.2.7**
  Control Unit
  Comdr. A.I. PETERSON, USNR
  PC 1134 (F), 1133

- **T.U. 78.2.8**
  Screen
  Capt. F.D. McCORKLE, USN
  FLUSSER (F), SHAW (FD),
  CONYHAM, DRAYTON, SMITH

- **T.U. 78.2.51**
  LST Tractor Unit
  Comdr. D.P. STICKLEY, USN
  579 (F), 467, 941, 1035

- **T.U. 78.2.9**
  Minesweeping Unit
  Lt. G.L. McNEILL, USNR
  YMS 68(F), 9, 46, 52, 340,
  481, 313, 339

- **T.U. 78.2.10**
  Beach Party
  Lt. M. WILLIAMS, USNR
  Beach Party Number 5

- **T.U. 78.2.11**
  Demolition Party
  LCI(D) 228

- **T.U. 78.2.12**
  Salvage and Service Unit
  ATA 179

Seventh Amphibious
Force History
Task Organization
Sheet 28

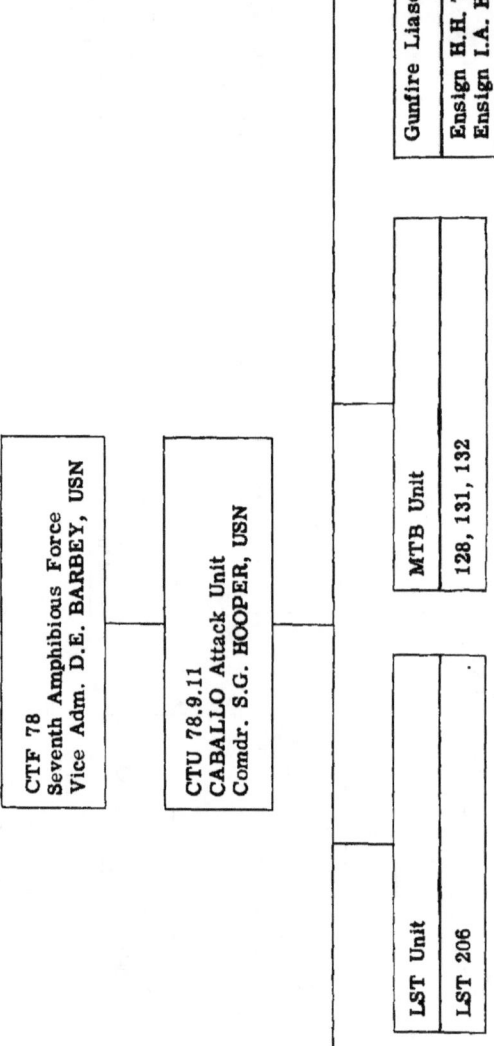

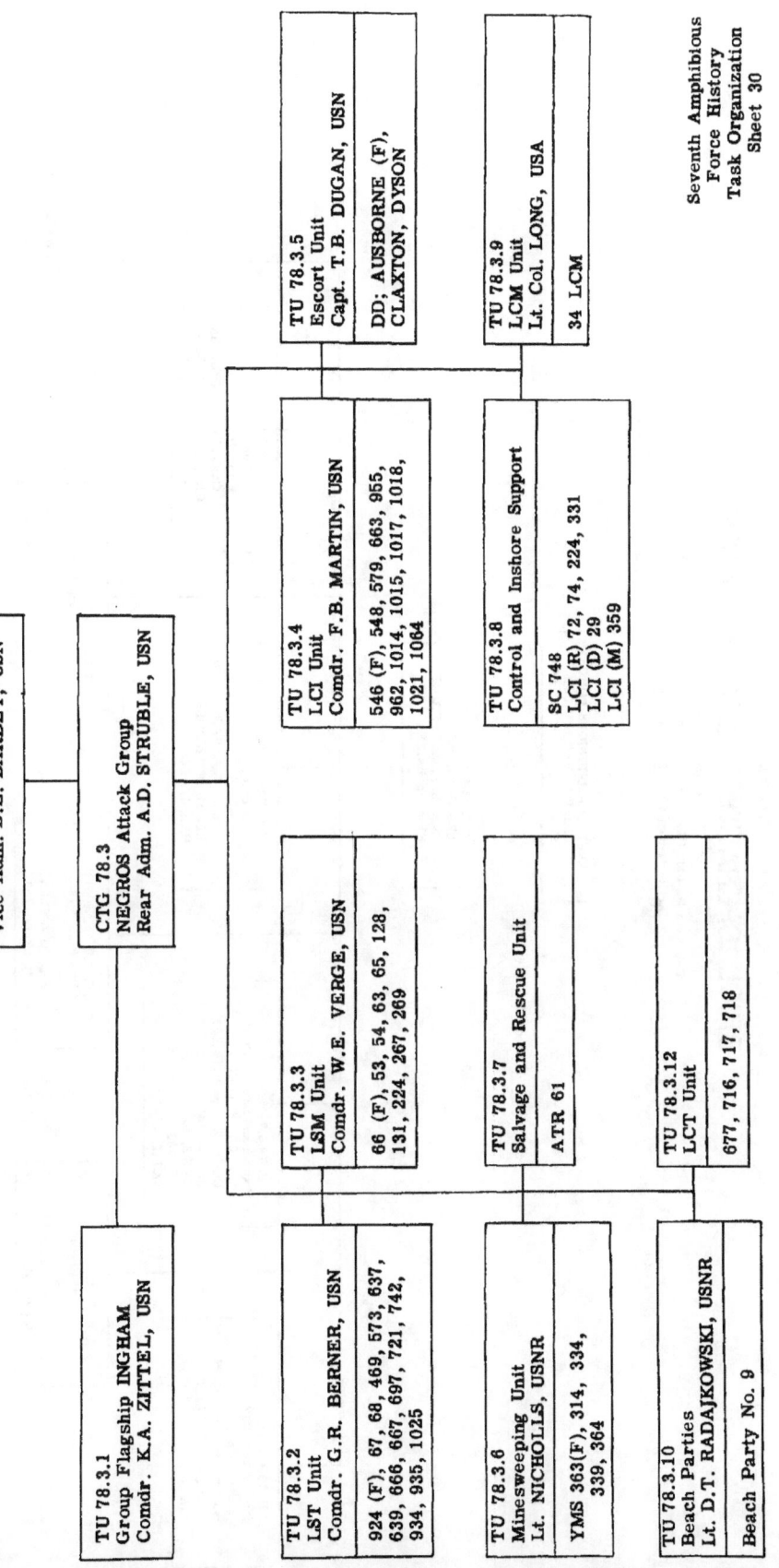

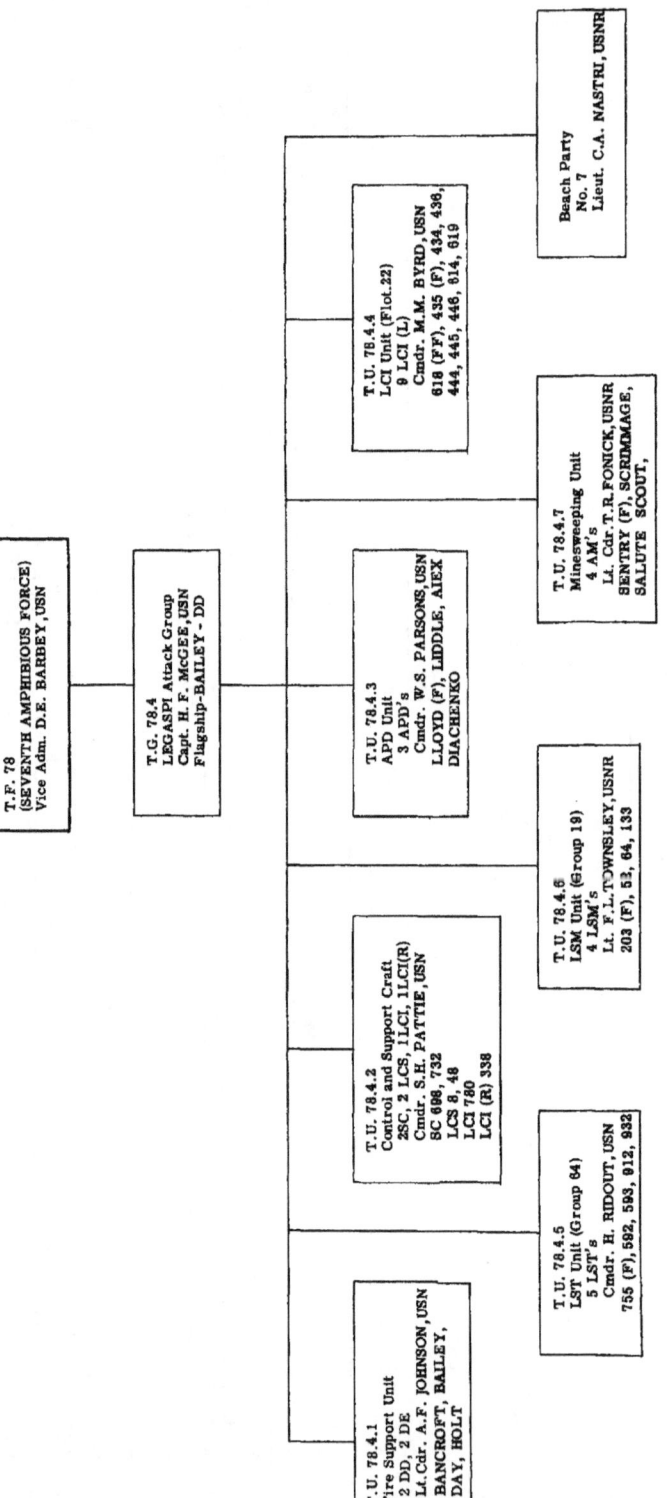

Task Organization

BICOL OPERATION ("LEGASPI LANDING")

1 APRIL 1945

Re: Com 7th Phib OPPlan 8-45, Com LCI Flot 7 OPPlan 3-45
Action Report CTG 78.4 dated 12 May, 1945

T.F. 78
(SEVENTH AMPHIBIOUS FORCE)
Vice Adm. D.E. BARBEY, USN

T.G. 78.4
LEGASPI Attack Group
Capt. H.F. McGEE, USN
Flagship-BAILEY - DD

T.U. 78.4.1
Fire Support Unit
2 DD, 2 DE
Lt. Cdr. A.F. JOHNSON, USN
BANCROFT, BAILEY,
DAY, HOLT

T.U. 78.4.2
Control and Support Craft
2SC, 2 LCS, 1LCI, 1LCI(R)
Cmdr. S.H. PATTIE, USN
SC 698, 732
LCS 8, 48
LCI 780
LCI (R) 338

T.U. 78.4.3
APD Unit
3 APD's
Cmdr. W.S. PARSONS, USN
LLOYD (F), LIDDLE, AIEX DIACHENKO

T.U. 78.4.4
LCI Unit (Flot. 22)
9 LCI (L)
Cmdr. M.M. BYRD, USN
618 (FF), 435 (F), 434, 436, 444, 445, 446, 614, 619

T.U. 78.4.5
LST Unit (Group 64)
5 LST's
Cmdr. H. RIDOUT, USN
755 (F), 582, 593, 912, 932

T.U. 78.4.6
LSM Unit (Group 19)
4 LSM's
Lt. F.L. TOWNSLEY, USNR
203 (F), 53, 64, 133

T.U. 78.4.7
Minesweeping Unit
4 AM's
Lt. Cdr. T.R. FONICK, USNR
SENTRY (F), SCRIMMAGE, SALUTE, SCOUT.

Beach Party No. 7
Lieut. C.A. NASTRI, USNR

Seventh Amphibious
Force History
Task Organization
Sheet 31

TASK ORGANIZATION

SANGA SANGA OPERATION

2 APRIL, 1945

Ref: Com 7th Phib For Rep - Zamboanga Attack Order 1-45

Seventh Amphibious Force History
Task Organization
Sheet 32

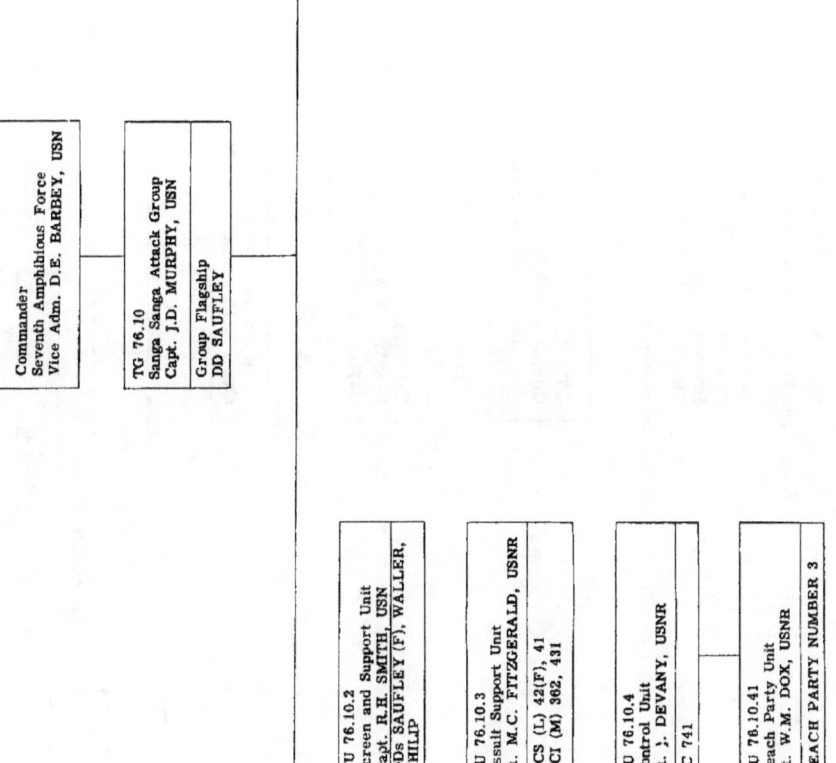

Commander
Seventh Amphibious Force
Vice Adm. D.E. BARBEY, USN

TG 76.10
Sanga Sanga Attack Group
Capt. J.D. MURPHY, USN

Group Flagship
DD SAUFLEY

TU 76.10.2
Screen and Support Unit
Capt. R.H. SMITH, USN
DDs SAUFLEY (F), WALLER, PHILIP

TU 76.10.3
Assault Support Unit
Lt. M.C. FITZGERALD, USNR
LCS (L) 42(F), 41
LCI (M) 362, 431

TU 76.10.4
Control Unit
Lt. J. DEVANY, USNR
SC 741

TU 76.10.41
Beach Party Unit
Lt. W.M. DOX, USNR
BEACH PARTY NUMBER 3

TU 76.10.5
Minesweeping Unit
Lt. E.O. SALTMARSH, USNR
YMS 71(F), 8, 50, 365

TU 76.10.1
Transport Unit
Lt. Comdr. E.E. WEIR, USN

TU 76.10.12
LST-LSM Unit
Lt. Comdr. E.E. WEIR, USN
LST 459
LSM 38, 39, 40, 42, 218, 319

7 LCMs TOWED TO OBJECTIVE

TU 76.10.13
LCI Unit
Lt. Comdr. M.D. COPPERSMITH, USNR
709(F), 653, 710, 711, 779

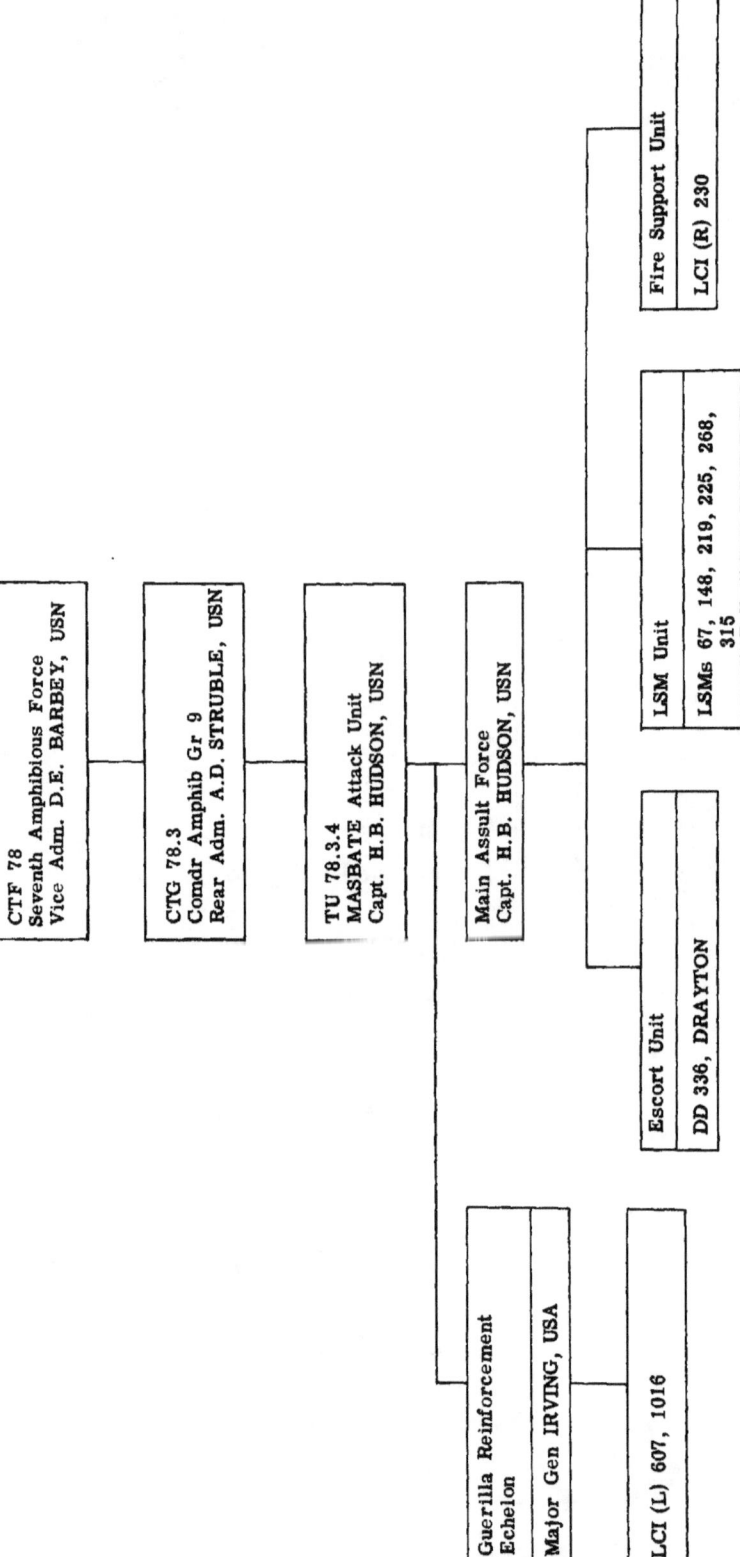

TASK ORGANIZATION
JOLO-BUSUANGA OPERATION
9 APRIL, 1945

Ref: Com 7th Phib For Rep - Zamboanga Attack Order 2-45

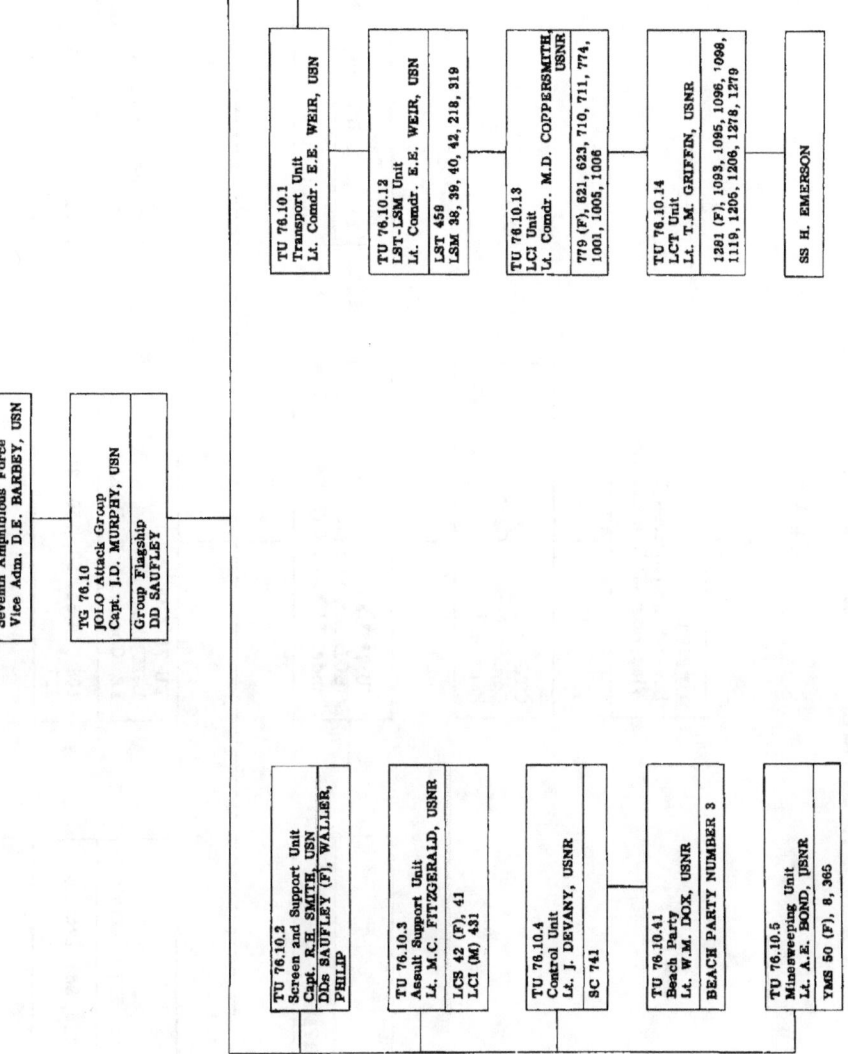

Seventh Amphibious Force History
Task Organization
Sheet 34

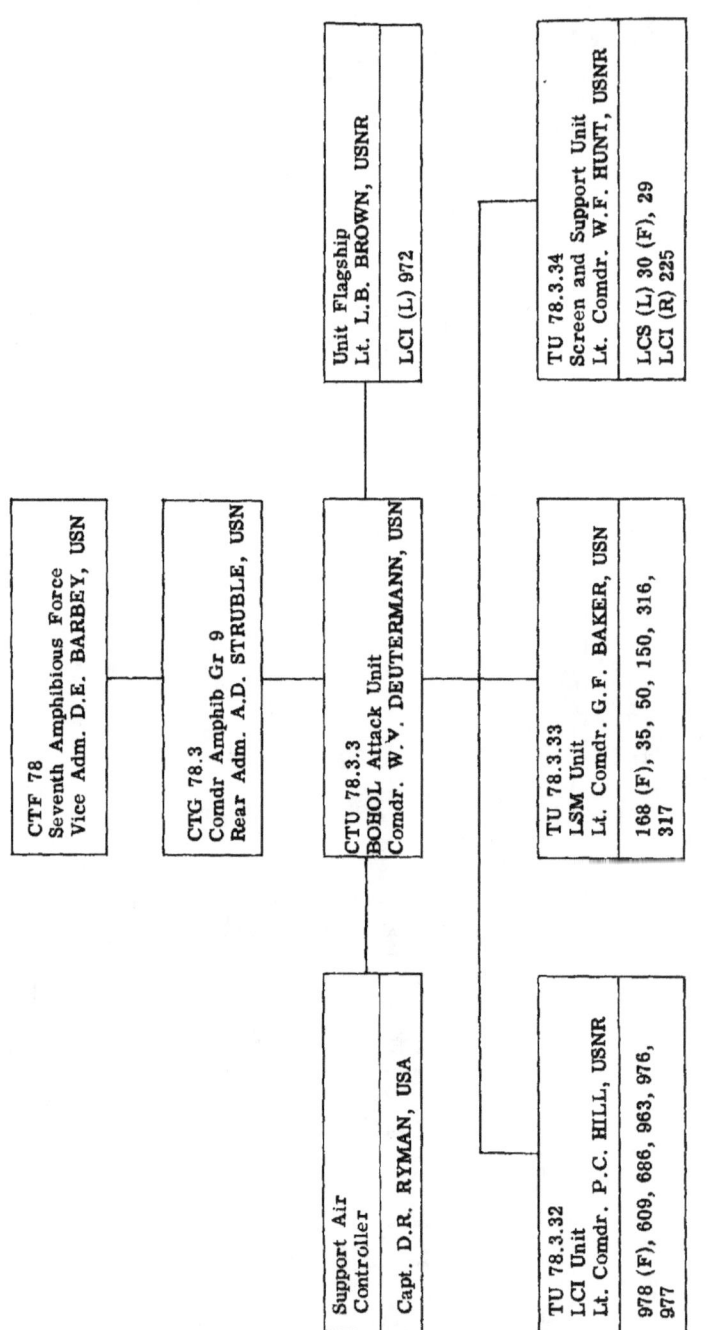

TASK ORGANIZATION
EL FRAILE ("FORT DRUM") OPERATION
13 APRIL 1945

Ref: Hq. 38 Inf. Div. Attack Order 11 APRIL 1945

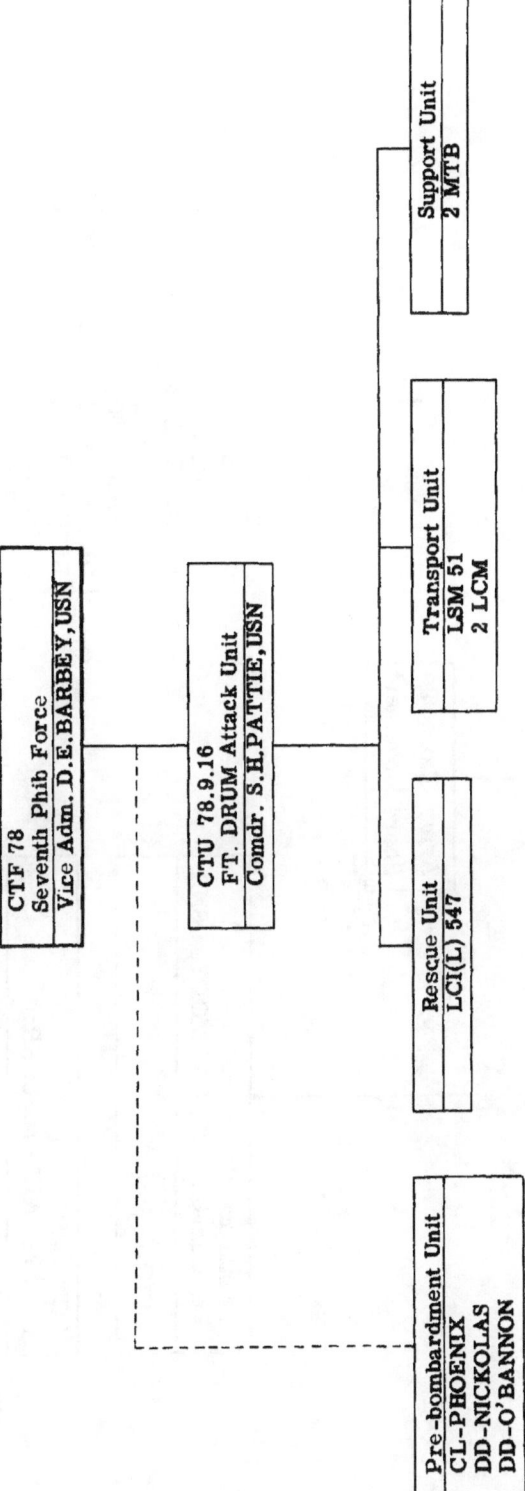

```
┌─────────────────────────┐
│ CTF 78                  │
│ Seventh Phib Force      │
│ Vice Adm. D.E.BARBEY,USN│
└─────────────────────────┘
             │
┌─────────────────────────┐
│ CTU 78.9.16             │
│ FT. DRUM Attack Unit    │
│ Comdr. S.H.PATTIE,USN   │
└─────────────────────────┘
```

Pre-bombardment Unit	Rescue Unit	Transport Unit	Support Unit
CL-PHOENIX	LCI(L) 547	LSM 51	2 MTB
DD-NICKOLAS		2 LCM	
DD-O'BANNON			

Seventh Amphibious
Force History
Task Organization
Sheet 36

TASK ORGANIZATION

CARABAO ISLAND OPERATION

16 APRIL, 1945

Ref: Com Seventh Phib War Diary April 1945

```
CTF 78
Seventh Amphibious Force
Vice Adm. D.E. BARBEY, USN
```

- Army Shore To Shore Movement

Transport Unit *
Lt. Comdr. F.T. CARMODY, USNR
  - LCI(L) 435 (F)

LCT Unit
Lt. J.M. ALLEN, USNR
  - LCT 684 (F), 629, 634, 788, 1256, 1259

TU 74.3.5
Fire Support Unit
Capt. J.H. DUNCAN, USN
  - CL PHOENIX
  - DD NICHOLAS, O'BANNON
  - LCI(R) 331, 224

*Transported artillery from Manila and Subic to vantage points on mainland to be used for fire support.

Seventh Amphibious Force History
Task Organization
Sheet 37

TASK ORGANIZATION
MALABANG-PARANG-COTABATO ("VICTOR FIVE") OPERATION
17 - 18 APRIL 1945
Ref: CTG 78.2 OPPlan 4 - 45

CTF 78
Comdr. Seventh Phib Force
Vice Adm. D.E. BARBEY, USN

CTG 78.2
Victor Five Attack Group
Rear Adm. A.G. NOBLE, USN

TU 78.2.1
Group Flagship Unit
Capt. K.D. RINGLE, USN
Group Flagship WASATCH AGC
Relief Flagship SPENCER CGC

TU 78.2.27
Floating Reserve Unit

- APD Unit
  NEWMAN, LIDDLE
- LST Unit
  775(F), 717
- LSM Unit
  36(F)
- LCI Unit
  690(F), 434, 776, 777, 1033

TU 76.2.26
Red Beach Attack Unit
Capt. G.D. ZURMUEHLEN, USN
Flagship SPENCER CGC 36

- Control Unit
  Lt. H.P. HOPKINS, USNR
  SC 749 (F), 748
- Beach Party
  Lt. W.R. WALKER, USNR
  Beach Party No. 1
- Minesweeping Unit
  YMS 336, 339
- Screen 2 DD
  DYSON(F), McCALLA
- Close Support Unit
  LCI(R) 71(F)
  LCI(G) 21, 22
  PGM 4, 5, 6, 8

- LST Unit
  668(F), 168, 170, 245, 458, 1034,
  463, 470, 473, 636, 680, 722, 806
- LSM Unit
  37, 130
- LCT Unit
  688(F), 382, 383, 740, 820
- TU 76.2.9
  Service & Salvage Unit
  Lt. W.M. HEYWOOD, USNR
  ATR 61
- Demolition Unit
  LCI (D) 227

TU 78.2.25
Green Beach Attack Unit
Rear Adm. A.G. NOBLE, USN
Flagship WASATCH

- TU 78.2.6 Control Unit
  Comdr. A.I. PETERSEN, USN
  PC 1134(F), 1133
- TU 78.2.7 Beach Parties
  Comdr. J.P. GRAFF, USN
  Beach Party No. 11
  Lt. B.W. JONES, USNR
- TU 78.2.10 Minesweeping Unit
  Lt. W.B. BOUTELL, USN
  YMS 315(F), 9, 46, 52, 335
- TU 78.2.11 Screening Unit
  Capt. T.B. DUGAN, USN
  DDs AUSBURNE(F), BRAINE,
  ROBINSON, CLAXTON
- TU 78.2.12 Close Support Unit
  Capt. R.E. ARISON, USN
  LCI (L) 778 (F)
  LCS (L) 28, 43, 50, 67
  LCI (G) 24, 61, 66, 67
  LCI (R) 72, 74, 226, 337, 338,
  340, 341, 342
  PGM 4, 5, 6, 8

- TU 78.2.2 APD Unit
  Comdr. W.S. PARSONS, USN
  LLOYD(F), ALEX DIACHENKO,
  KEPHART
- TU 78.2.3 LCI Unit
  Comdr. M.M. BYRD, USN
  618(F), 436, 518, 519, 614,
  615, 616, 617, 619, 689, 1032
- TU 78.2.4 LSM Unit
  Comdr. D.I. WEINTRAUB, USN
  268(F), 18, 19, 21, 22, 34, 136,
  139, 148, 205, 257, 310, 311
- TU 78.2.5 LST Unit
  Capt. O.R. SWIGART, USN
  614(F), 474, 578, 579, 629,
  631, 699, 705, 707, 719, 927,
  934, 935, 936
  LCT Unit 384, 386, 687, 738, 739,
  772, 861
  PORTUNUS
- Service & Salvage Unit
  ATF 110 QUAPAW
- Demolition Unit
  LCI(D) 228

TG 74.2
Support & Covering Group
Rear Adm. R.S. RIGGS, USN
Cruisers
MONTPELIER(F), DENVER,
CLEVELAND
Destroyers
CONWAY, EATON, STEVENS,
SIGOURNEY, CONY, YOUNG

TU 78.2.16
MOROTAI Staged Unit
Capt. F.J. MEE, USN
LST 632(F), 204, 395, 456, 549,
559, 583, 589, 630, 673, 679, 694,
740, 741, 744, 745, 754, 778, 911,
919, 1016, 1017, 1018
LCI 612(F), 611, 622, 687, 768,
759, 745, 979, 999, 1002, 1003
FLUSSER, SHAW, CONYNGHAM,
JOBB, ALBERT T. HARRIS. 5 DDs

TU 78.2.14
ZAMBOANGA Layover Unit
Comdr. H. RIDOUT, USN
755(F), 466, 592, 593, 618, 631,
757, 910, 912, 933, 953, 937,
942, 992, 1026
SS CHARLES WOLCOTT XAK
SS T.A. JOHNSON XAK

TG 70.1
Motor Torpedo Group
Capt. BOWLING, USN
8 Pt. Boats
PORTUNUS AGP 4

TG 70.5
Hydrographic Unit
Lt. Comdr. G.D. TANCRED, RAN
LACHLAN

Seventh Amphibious
Force History
Task Organization
Sheet 38 - 39

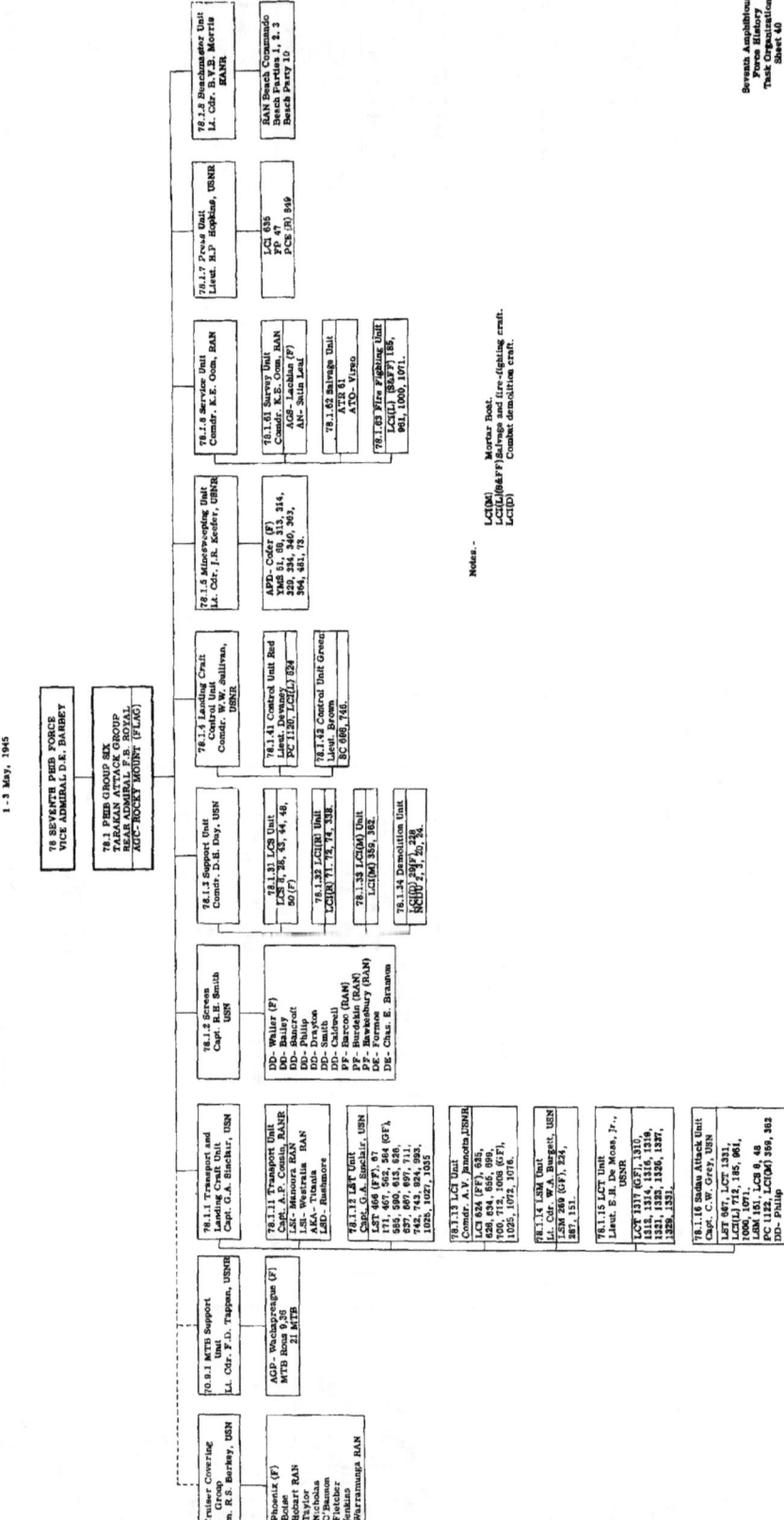

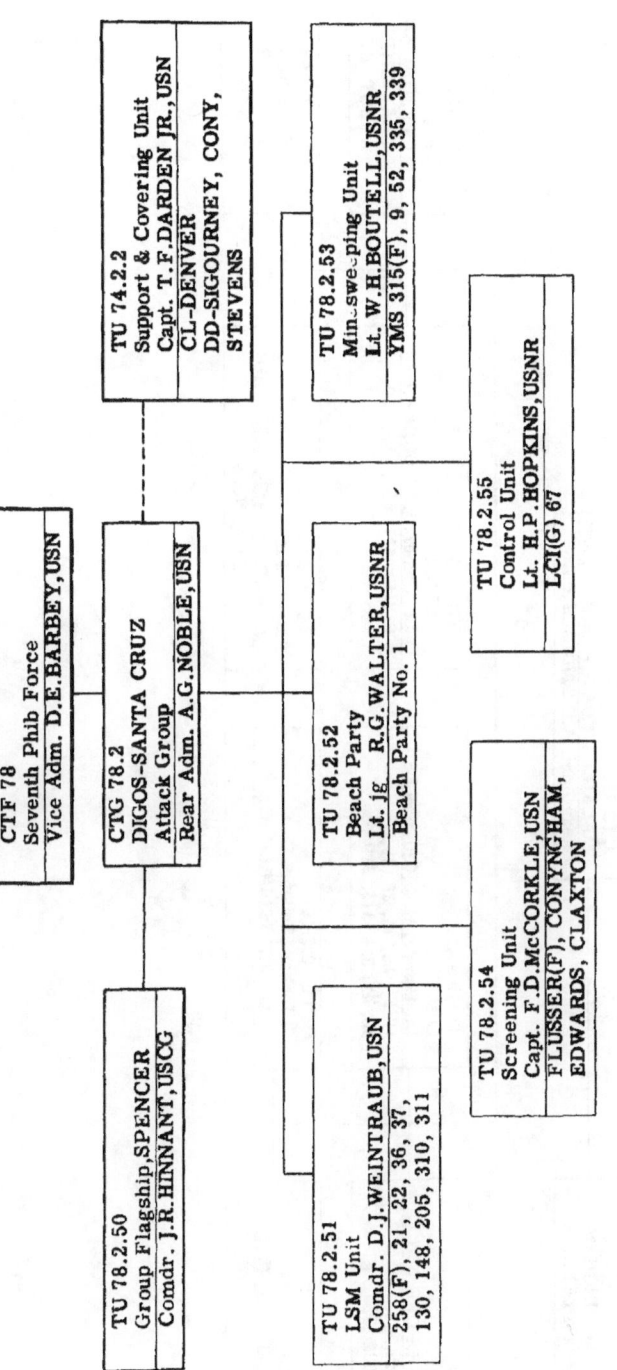

TASK ORGANIZATION

DIGOS-SANTA CRUZ OPERATION

A CONTINUING OPERATION OF V-5
3 MAY 1945

Ref: CTG 78.2 action report dated 18 JUNE 1945

CTF 78
Seventh Phib Force
Vice Adm. D.E.BARBEY, USN

CTG 78.2
DIGOS-SANTA CRUZ
Attack Group
Rear Adm. A.G.NOBLE, USN

TU 74.2.2
Support & Covering Unit
Capt. T.F.DARDEN JR., USN
CL-DENVER
DD-SIGOURNEY, CONY, STEVENS

TU 78.2.50
Group Flagship, SPENCER
Comdr. J.R.HINNANT, USCG

TU 78.2.51
LSM Unit
Comdr. D.J.WEINTRAUB, USN
258(F), 21, 22, 36, 37, 130, 148, 205, 310, 311

TU 78.2.52
Beach Party
Lt. jg R.G.WALTER, USNR
Beach Party No. 1

TU 78.2.53
Minesweeping Unit
Lt. W.H.BOUTELL, USNR
YMS 315(F), 9, 52, 335, 339

TU 78.2.54
Screening Unit
Capt. F.D.McCORKLE, USN
FLUSSER(F), CONYNGHAM, EDWARDS, CLAXTON

TU 78.2.55
Control Unit
Lt. H.P.HOPKINS, USNR
LCI(G) 67

Seventh Amphibious
Force History
Task Organization
Sheet 40.1

TASK ORGANIZATION
MACAJALAR BAY OPERATION
10 MAY 1945

Ref: CTG 78.3 action report dated 31 May 1945

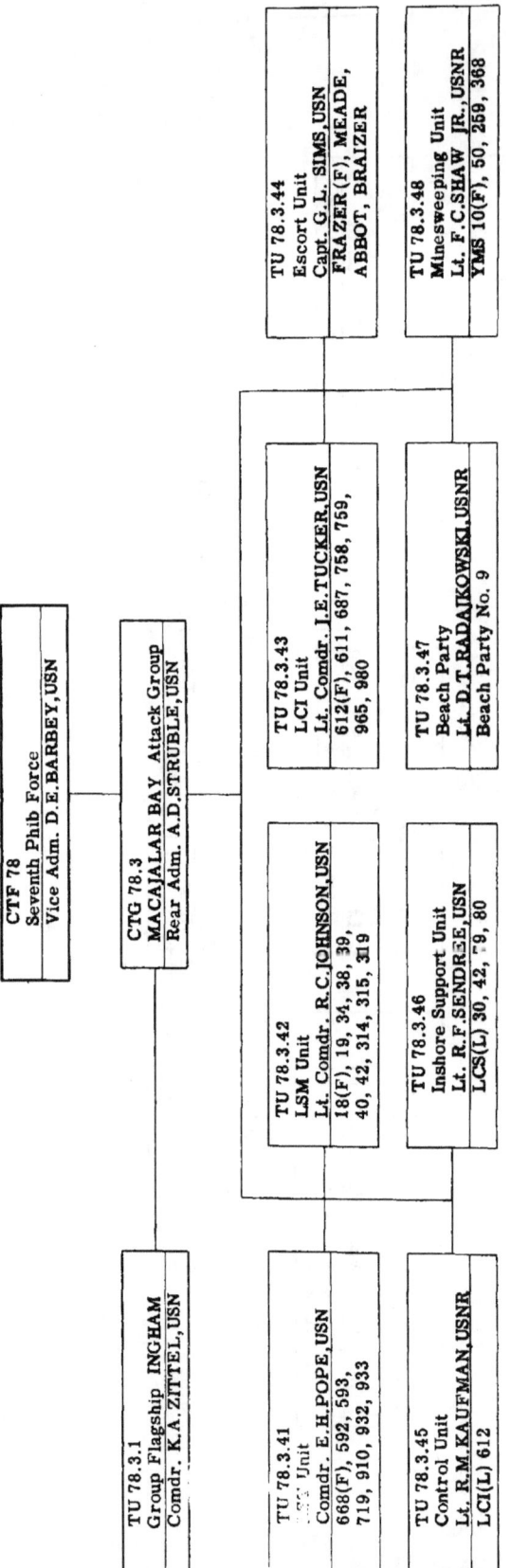

Seventh Amphibious
Force History
Task Organization
Sheet 40.2

TASK ORGANIZATION
BRUNEI OPERATION ("OBOE SIX")
10-17 JUNE, 1945
(From Com 7th Phib Opplan 11-45)

78 SEVENTH PHIB FORCE
VICE ADM. D.E. BARBEY, USN

78.1 Phib Group Six
Brunei Attack Group
Rear Adm. F.B. Royal, USN
AGC-ROCKY MOUNT (F)

74.3 Cruiser Covering Group
Rear Adm. V.A. Berkey, USN
- CL-Phoenix(F)
- CL-Nashville
- CL-Boise
- DD-Robert RAN
- DD-Killen
- DD-A.W. Grant
- DD-Conner
- DD-Charette
- DD-Bell
- DD-Burns
- DD-Arunta RAN

78.1.2 Screen
Capt. E.R. Smith, USN
- DD-Waller
- DD-Saufley
- DD-Philip
- DD-Robinson(F)
- DD-Bancroft
- DD-Bailey
- DD-Edwards
- DD-Caldwell
- DD-Frazier
- DD-McCalla
- DE-D.A. Joy
- DE-C.E. Brannon
- DE-A.T. Harris
- DE-Dufilho
- DE-Day
- PF-Shrewsbury RAN
- PF-Burdekin RAN

78.1.19 Reinforcement Unit
Capt. E. Watts, USN
- LST 626, 613, 667, 742, 743, 951, 980, 1027, 1025, 814(F), 1010, 1066, 763, 944, 877, 981, 662

78.1.20 Reserve Unit
Comdr. W.E. Verge, USN
- LST 573, 566
- LSM 256, 133, 139, 941(F)
- LCI 113, 939, 1075, 1074, 1073

78.1.16 White (Beach)Assault Unit
Capt. L.J. Manees, USN
- DMS-Spencer(F)
- LST 647, 711, 667, 564, 622
- APD-Lloyd
- APD-Kephart
- APD-Alex Dischenko
- APD-D.A. Munro
- LCI 636, 401, 702, 703
- LSM 059, 205, 31(C)25, 138, 61,84

78.1.18 Brown (Beach)Assault Unit
Capt. E.B. Hudson, USN
- LST-Manoora RAN
- LSI-Westralia RAN
- LSD-Carter Hall
- AKA-Titania
- LST 840(F), 560, 891, 896, 816, 668, 709, 818, 941, 806, 912, 386, 975, 465, 942, 637, 1025
- LSM 128, 80, 51, 52, 53, 63, 64, 65
- LCI 744, 745, 746, 749, 956

78.1.17 Green (Beach)Assault Unit
Capt. L.J. Manees, USN
- DMS-Spencer(F)
- LSI-Kanimbla RAN
- LST-547
- LSM 337

78.1.38 White (Beach)Support Unit
Capt. R.E. Arison, USNR
- LCM(R) 45, 46
- LCM(G) 986
- LCI(R) 72(F), 71
- LCI(D) 229
- NCDU 4, 3

78.1.36 Brown (Beach)Support Unit
Lt. Cdr. A.M. Holmes, USNR
- LCM(L) 38, 39, 60
- LCI(R) 1000, 1071
- LCM(G) 22, 64
- LCI(G) 69(F), 70
- LCI(D) 359, 382
- LCI(D) 19
- NCDU 20, 24

78.1.37 Green (Beach)Support Unit
Capt. R.E. Arison, USNR
- LCM(R) 42, 47
- LCI(R) 776(F)
- LCI(G) 65, 66
- LCI(D) 74, 138
- LC(S) 961

78.1.43 Control Unit White (Beach)
Lt. Cdr. F.S.C. Martin, USN
- LC(L) 560(F)
- PC 1122

78.1.42 Control Unit Green (Beach)
Capt. R.E. Arison, USN
- LC(L) 778(F)
- SC 750, 741

78.1.41 Control Unit Brown (Beach)
Lt. Denney
- SC 1132
- SC 988, 732

76.1.1 Motor Torpedo Boat Unit
Lt. Willoughby
- AGP-Willoughby
- MTBRon 13 (12 PTs)

78.1.1 Transport and Landing Craft Unit
Capt. H.B. Hudson, USN

78.1.11 Transport Unit
Capt. A.P. Cousin, RAN
- 3 LSI
- 1 AKA
- 1 LSD
- 6 APD

78.1.12 LST Unit
Capt. H.B. Hudson
- 34 LST

78.1.13 LCI Unit
Capt. W.B. Martin, USN
- LCI 946 (F)
- 31 LCI

78.1.14 LSM Unit
Lt. Cdr. W.R. Vickers, USNR
- 20 LSM

78.1.15 LCT Unit
Lt. E.B. DeMoss Jr., USNR
- LCT 1313, 1314, 1317(GP), 1319, 1351

78.1.3 Support Unit
Capt. R.E. Arison, USN

78.1.4 Landing Craft Control Unit
Lt. J.R. Goodrich
- 2 PC
- 4 SC

78.1.5 Minesweeping Unit
Lt. Cdr. T.R. Fonick, USNR
- AM-Scrimmage(F)
- AM-Salute
- AM-Scout
- AM-Scuffle
- AM-Sentry
- APD-Coder
- YMS 4, 39, 51, 68, 73, 318
- YMS 314, 369, 344, 363, 365

78.1.6 Hydrographic Survey Unit
Lt. Cdr. C.D. Tancred, RAN
- AGS-Lachlan RAN
- AN-Satinleaf
- YMS 160

78.1.8 Beachmaster Unit
Lt. Cdr. McKnapp, RANVR
- RAN Commando Beach Parties 4, 5, 6, 7
- USN Beach Party 10

78.1.7 Salvage and Service Unit

78.1.71 Salvage Unit
- ATF-Pinto
- ATR 61

78.1.72 Firefighting Unit
- LCI(D) 961, 635, 1000, 1071

78.1.73 Service Unit
- AD-Whitcomb
- LST 473

78.1.74 Press Unit
- PCE(R) 849
- PF 47

78.1.31 LCT Unit
Capt. R.E. Arison, USN
- 1 LCI(L)
- 1 LCM(M)

78.1.32 LCI(G) Unit
Lt. Cdr. A.M. Holmes,
- 6 LCI(G)

78.1.33 LCI(R) Unit
Lt. Cdr. R.E. Sargent, USNR
- 3 LCI(R)

78.1.34 LCI(M) Unit
LCM(M) A. Peterson, USNR
- 3 LCM

78.1.35 Demolition Unit
Lt. G. Byrnes
- APD-Blue
- 1 LCI(D)
- 4 NCDD

78.1.91 - 78.1.99
Resupply and Returning Coveys

Seventh Amphibious
Force Historary
Task Organization
Sheet 41

BALIKPAPAN OPERATION ("OBOE TWO")
15 JUNE - 6 JULY 1945

TF 78 SEVENTH PHIB FORCE
VICE ADM. D. E. BARBEY
CL - PHOENIX (FLAG)

78.4 Escort Carrier Group
Rear Adm. W.D. Sample, USN

- CVE-Suwannee(F)
- CVE-Gilbert Islands
- CVE-Block Island
- DD-Helm
- DE-Cloues
- DE-Mitchell
- DE-Kyne
- DE-Lamons
- DE-Donaldson

74 Cruiser Covering Force
Rear Adm. R.S. Berkey, USN

74.2 Cruiser Covering and Support Group
Rear Adm. R.S. Riggs, USN
- CA-Montpelier(F)
- CL-Denver
- CL-Cleveland
- CL-Columbia
- CL-Tromp RNN
- DD-Conway
- DD-Eaton
- DD-Stevens
- DD-Killen
- DD-A.W. Grant
- DD-Arunta RAN

74.1 Cruiser Covering and Support Group
Commo. H.B. Farncomb, RAN
- CL-Shropshire(F) RAN
- DD-Hobart RAN
- DD-Bert
- DD-Metcalf

74.3 Cruiser Covering and Support Group
Rear Adm. R.S. Berkey, USN
- CL-Phoenix(F)
- CL-Nashville
- DD-Bell
- DD-Charrette
- DD-Conner
- DD-Burns

78.2 Phib Group Eight
Balikpapan Attack Group
Rear Adm. A.G. Noble, USN

78.2.1 Group Flagship Unit
Capt. K.D. Ringle, USN
- AGC-Wasatch (F)
- COC-Spencer
- HQ-Support Aircraft

78.2.2 Transport Unit
Capt. A.P. Cousin, RAN
- LSI-Manoora (F) RAN
- LSI-Westralia RAN
- LSI-Kanimbla RAN
- AKA-Titania
- LSD-Carter Hall

78.2.3 Fast Transport Unit
Comdr. W.S. Parsons, USN
- APD-Lloyd(F)
- APD-Newman
- APD-Sephart
- APD-Liddle
- APD-Alex Diachenko

78.2.4 LSM Unit
Capt. D.J. Weintraub, USN
- LCI(FF) 789 (F)

LSM Group Four
Lt. Cmdr. R.C. Johnson, USN
- LSM 18 (GF), 19, 21, 259,
- 268, 28, 310, 311

LSM Group Five
Lt. Cmdr. F.G. Smith, USN
- LSM 486(FF), 66, 171,
- 181, 206, 245, 459, 462,
- 470, 471, 474(GF), 476,
- 673, 714, 725, 910, 911

LSM Group Six (med.)
Lt. Cdr. E.E. Weire, USN
- LSM 432(GF), 38, 39, 40,
- 207, 223, 224

78.2.5 LST Unit
Capt. F.J. Mee, USN
- LST 632(FF), 168,396,
- 397, 452, 454, 487, 639,
- 664, 694, 703, 731, 740,
- 777, 935, 938, 1015,
- 1017, 1018

78.2.36 LST Unit
Capt. G.A. Sinclair, USN
- LST 485(FF), 65, 171,

78.2.6 LCI Unit
Cdr. A.V. Jannotta, USNR
- LCI 634(FF), 422, 625,
- 626, 630, 634, 636, 699, 700,
- 712, 999, 1002(GF),
- 1003, 1005(GF), 1035,
- 1072, 1078

78.2.7 Control Unit
Cdr. A.J. Peterson, USNR
- PC 1134(F), 610
- SC 688, 750, 747

78.2.8 Close Support Unit
Cdr. D. Day, USN
- LCS(L) 30, 8, 27, 28, 29,
- 39G(FF), 41, 42, 43, 46,
- 51, 68(R) 31, 34, 73, 225,
- 229(CF), 231, 237, 338
- LCI (G) 21, 22, 34, 61,
- 65, 67

78.2.9 Minesweeping Unit
Lt. Cdr. T.R. Fonick, USNR
- AM-Sentry (F)
- AM-Scout
- AM-Scuffle

YMS Unit
Lt. Cdr. D.W. Blakeslee, USNR
- APD-Cofer
- LSM 1
- YMS 4,6, 9, 10, 11, 39,
- 46, 47, 49, 50, 51, 52,
- 53, 69, 48, 72, 84, 85,
- 97, 107, 224, 250, 286,
- 313, 314, 315, 334,
- 335, 336, 338, 339,
- 340, 363, 364, 365,
- 366, 367, 368, 369

78.2.10 Beach Party Unit
Cdr. J.P. Graff, USN
- Beach Party No.2

78.2.11 Demolition Unit
Lieut. L.A. States, USNR
- APD-Kline
- APD-Schmitt
- UDT 11, 18

78.2.13 LCT Unit
Lieut. E.J. Buckley, USNR
- LCT Group 73
- LCT 1081, 1289, 1291,
- 1295(F), 1299, 1297,
- 1298, 1300, 1301, 1304,
- 1308, 1309, 1325, 1329

LCT Group 91
Lieut. R.R. Coffin, USNR
- LCT 83, 178, 372, 373,
- 864, 868, 990, 992,
- 1014, 1096, 1198(GF),
- 1237

78.2.14 Salvage and Firefighting Unit
Lt. Cdr. H. Pond, USNR
- ARS - Cable(F)
- LCI(g) 970, 705, 1000, 1071
- ATR 61

78.2.15 Service Unit
Lt. Cdr. E.K. Wallace, USNR
- AO-Chepachet
- ARL-Creon
- LST 67, 171
- AOG-Genesee
- AOG-Saktonches
- AK-Poissett
- IX-Bauahan
- LSM-120
- PS 154, 361
- YP 431
- ATF-Yuma
- YD 95

78.2.16 Representative
Com 7th Phib Force
Capt. C.W. Gray, USN

78.2.17 Hydrographic Unit
Cdr. J.M. Little, RANR
- AGS-Wantago RAN
- YMS-196
- AN-Mango

78.2.1-31 Forward
78.2.1-37

Convoy Units

78.2.1-75
Returning Convoy Units

78.1.16 Press Unit
LCI(L) 635
PF 47

78.2.15 Screen
Capt. F.D. McCorkle, USN
Desron 5
- DD-Drayton
- DD-Flusser(F)
- DD-Conyngham
- DD-Smith

Desdiv 14
Capt. G.L. Sims, USN
- DD-Bailey
- DD-Frazier(F)

Desdiv 22
Capt. R.H. Smith, USN
- DD-Saufley
- DD-Waller
- DD-Robinson(F)
- DD-Sutherland
- PF-Gascoyne

- DE-Chaffee
- DE-R.A. Stewart
- DE-Edmonds
- DE-J.E. Thomas

78.2.16 MTB Unit
Lt. Cdr. F.D. Tappan, USNR
- AGP-Willoughby
- AGP-Varuna
- ATR 36
- MTBRons 10, 27
- (13 PTs)

Seventh Amphibious
Force Mistory
Task Organization
Sheet 42

TASK ORGANIZATION
SARANGANI BAY OPERATION
12 JULY 1945

Ref: CTU 76.6.11 action report dated 31 July 1945

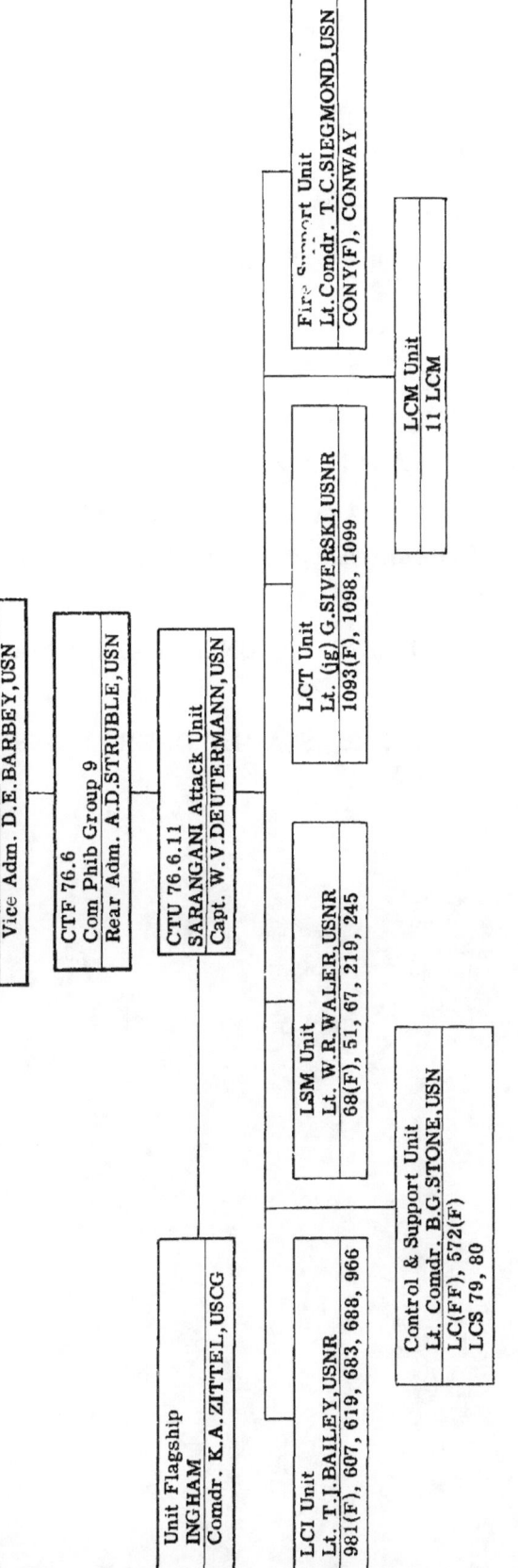

Seventh Amphibious
Force History
Task Organization
Sheet 42.1

- **CTF 78** — Seventh Phib Force — Vice Adm. D.E. BARBEY, USN
- **CTF 76.6** — Com Phib Group 9 — Rear Adm. A.D. STRUBLE, USN
- **CTU 76.6.11** — SARANGANI Attack Unit — Capt. W.V. DEUTERMANN, USN

Unit Flagship INGHAM — Comdr. K.A. ZITTEL, USCG

LCI Unit — Lt. T.J. BAILEY, USNR — 981(F), 607, 619, 683, 688, 966

Control & Support Unit — Lt. Comdr. B.G. STONE, USN — LC(FF), 572(F), LCS 79, 80

LSM Unit — Lt. W.R. WALER, USNR — 68(F), 51, 67, 219, 245

LCT Unit — Lt. (jg) G. SIVERSKI, USNR — 1093(F), 1098, 1099

Fire Support Unit — Lt. Comdr. T.C. SIEGMOND, USN — CONY(F), CONWAY

LCM Unit — 11 LCM

ANNEX (D)

LIST OF NAVAL COMMANDERS, LANDING FORCE COMMANDERS

AND MAJOR LANDING UNITS PARTICIPATING

IN MAJOR ASSAULT OPERATIONS

ANNEX (D)

LIST OF NAVAL COMMANDERS, LANDING FORCE

COMMANDERS AND MAJOR LANDING FORCE UNITS

KEY: (a) Naval Commander for Operation.
     (b) Landing Force Commander.
     (c) Major Landing Force Unit or Units.

WOODLARK

(a) Rear Admiral BARBEY, USN.
(b) Brigadier General CUNNINGHAM, USA.
(c) 112th Cavalry Regimental Combat Team (Reinforced)

LAE

(a) Rear Admiral BARBEY, USN.
(b) Major General WOOTEN, A.I.F.
(c) 9th Australian Infantry Division, A.I.F.
    (Australian Imperial Forces)

FINSCHHAFEN

(a) Rear Admiral BARBEY, USN.
(b) Major General WOOTEN, A.I.F.
(c) 9th Australian Infantry Division, A.I.F.

ARAWE

(a) Rear Admiral BARBEY, USN.
(b) Brigadier General CUNNINGHAM, USA.
(c) 112th Cavalry Regimental Combat Team (Reinforced).

CAPE GLOUCESTER

(a) Rear Admiral BARBEY, USN.
(b) Major General RUPERTUS, USMC.
(c) FIRST Marine Division (Reinforced).

SAIDOR

(a) Rear Admiral BARBEY, USN.
(b) Brigadier General CLARENCE MARTIN, USA.
(c) 126th Infantry Regimental Combat Team (Reinforced)
    (32nd Division)

ANNEX (D)

ADMIRALTY ISLANDS

    (a) Rear Admiral FECHTELER, USN.
    (b) Brigadier General CHASE, USA.
    (c) FIRST Brigade (Reinforced), 1st Cavalry Division.

AITAPE

    (a) Captain A. G. NOBLE, USN.
    (b) Brigadier General J. A. DOE, USA.
    (c) 163rd Regimental Combat Team (Reinforced) (41st Division)

HUMBOLDT BAY

    (a) Rear Admiral FECHTELER, USN.
    (b) Major General FULLER, USA.
    (c) 41st Infantry Division (less 163rd Regimental Combat Team) (Reinforced).

TANAMERAH BAY

    (a) Rear Admiral BARBEY, USN.
    (b) Major General IRVING, USA.
    (c) 24th Infantry (Reinforced) (less 1 Regimental Combat Team)

WADKE

    (a) Captain A. G. NOBLE, USN.
    (b) Brigadier General J. A. DOE, USA.
    (c) 163rd Infantry Regimental Combat Team (Reinforced) (41st Infantry Division).

BIAK

    (a) Rear Admiral FECHTELER, USN.
    (b) Major General FULLER, USA.
    (c) 41st Infantry Division (less 163rd Regimental Combat Team) (Reinforced).

ANNEX (D)

NOEMFOOR

    (a) Rear Admiral FECHTELER, USN.
    (b) Brigadier General PATRICK, USA.
    (c) 158th Infantry Regimental Combat Team (Reinforced)

SANSAPOR

    (a) Rear Admiral FECHTELER, USN.
    (b) Major General SIEBERT, USA.
    (c) 6th Infantry Division (Reinforced).

MOROTAI

    (a) Rear Admiral BARBEY, USN.
    (b) Major General HALL, USA.
    (c) XI Corps

        (1) Rear Admiral FECHTELER, USN.
        (2) Major General PERSONS, USA.
        (3) 31st Infantry Division (Reinforced), 126th Infantry Regimental Combat Team of 32nd Division

LEYTE

    (a) Vice Admiral KINCAID, USN.
    (b) Lieutenant General KREUGER, USA.
    (c) SIXTH U.S. Army.

1. NORTHERN ATTACK FORCE

    (a) Rear Admiral BARBEY, USN.
    (b) Major General SIEBERT, USA.
    (c) X Corps

  A. PALO ATTACK GROUP
    (a) Rear Admiral BARBEY, USN.
    (b) Major General IRVING, USA.
    (c) 24th Infantry Division (less 21st Regimental Combat Team) (Reinforced)

ANNEX (D)

    B. RICARDO ATTACK GROUP

        (a) Rear Admiral FECHTELER, USN.
        (b) Major General MUDGE, USA.
        (c) 1st Cavalry Division.

    C. PANAON ATTACK GROUP

        (a) Rear Admiral STRUBLE, USN.
        (b)
        (c) 21st Infantry Regimental Combat Team of 24th Infantry Division.

    D. DINAGAT ATTACK GROUP

        (a) Rear Admiral STRUBLE, USN.
        (b) Lieutenant Colonel MUSSIE, AUS.
        (c) 6th Ranger Battalion.

2. SOUTHERN ATTACK FORCE

    (a) Vice Admiral WILKINSON, USN.
    (b) Major General HODGE, USA.
    (c) XXIV Corps.

    A. ABLE ATTACK GROUP

        (a) Rear Admiral CONNOLLY, USN.
        (b) Major General A. V. ARNOLD, USA.
        (c) 7th Infantry Division.

    B. BAKER ATTACK GROUP

        (a) Rear Admiral ROYAL, USN.
        (b) Major General BRADLEY, USA.
        (c) 96th Infantry Division.

MAPIA-ASIA

    (a) Captain LORD ASHBOURNE, RN.
    (b)
    (c) Elements of the EIGHTH Army.

ANNEX (D)

ORMOC

    (a) Rear Admiral STRUBLE, USN.
    (b) Major General BRUCE, USA.
    (c) 77th Infantry Division (less 1 Regimental Combat Team) (Reinforced).

MINDORO

    (a) Rear Admiral STRUBLE, USN.
    (b) Brigadier General DUNKEL, USA.
    (c) 19th Regimental Combat Team from 24th U.S. Infantry Division. 503rd Parachute Regiment.

LINGAYEN

    (a) Vice Admiral KINCAID, USN.
    (b) Lieutenant General KREUGER, USA.
    (c) SIXTH U.S. Army.

1. LINGAYEN ATTACK FORCE

    (a) Vice Admiral WILKINSON, USN.
    (b) Major General GRISWOLD, USA.
    (c) XIV Corps.

    A. ABLE ATTACK GROUP

        (a) Rear Admiral KILAND, USN.
        (b) Major General BEIGHTLER, USA.
        (c) 37th Infantry Division

    B. BAKER ATTACK GROUP

        (a) Rear Admiral ROYAL, USN.
        (b) Major General RAPP BRUSH, USA.
        (c) 40th Infantry Division.

2. SAN FABIAN ATTACK FORCE

    (a) Vice Admiral BARBEY, USN.
    (b) Major General SWIFT, USA.
    (c) I Corps.

ANNEX (D)

    A. WHITE BEACH ATTACK GROUP

        (a) Vice Admiral BARBEY, USN.
        (b) Major General WING, USA.
        (c) 43rd Infantry Division.

    B. BLUE BEACH ATTACK GROUP

        (a) Rear Admiral FECHTELER, USN.
        (b) Major General PATRICK, USA.
        (c) 6th Infantry Division.

3. RESERVE GROUP

    (a) Rear Admiral CONNOLLY, USN.
    (b) Major General MULLINS, USA - Brigadier General McNIDER, AUS.
    (c) 25th Infantry Division - 158th Regimental Combat Team.

ZAMBALES

    (a) Rear Admiral STRUBLE, USN.
    (b) Major General HALL, USA - Brigadier General CHASE, USA.
    (c) XI Corps Troops - 38th U.S. Infantry Division.
        134th Regimental Combat Team of 24th Infantry Division.

NASUGBU

    (a) Rear Admiral FECHTELER, USN.
    (b) Major General SWING, USA.
    (c) 11th Airborne Division (less Parachute Regimental Combat Team).

BATAAN-CORREGIDOR

    (a) Rear Admiral STRUBLE, USN.
    (b) Brigadier General CHASE, USA - Colonel JONES, AUS.
    (c) 38th Infantry Division - 503rd Parachute Regiment.

PALAWAN

    (a) Rear Admiral FECHTELER, USN.
    (b) Major General J. A. DOE, USA.
    (c) 186th Regimental Combat Team of 41st Infantry Division.

ANNEX (D)

LUBANG

    (a) Captain H. F. McGEE, USN.
    (b)
    (c) 1st Battalion, 21st Infantry of 24th Division.

ZAMBOANGA

    (a) Rear Admiral ROYAL, USN.
    (b) Major General J. A. DOE, USA.
    (c) 41st Infantry Division.

PANAY

    (a) Rear Admiral STRUBLE, USN.
    (b) Major General RAPP BRUSH, USA.
    (c) 40th Infantry Division (less 1 Regimental Combat Team).

CEBU

    (a) Captain A. T. SPRAGUE, USN.
    (b) Major General W. A. ARNOLD, USA.
    (c) Americal Division (less 164th Regimental Combat Team).

CABALLO

    (a) Rear Admiral STRUBLE, USN.
    (b) Brigadier General CHASE, USA.
    (c) Elements of 38th Division.

NEGROS

    (a) Captain A. T. SPRAGUE, USN.
    (b) Major General W. A. ARNOLD, USA.
    (c) Americal Division (less 164th Regimental Combat Team).

LEGASPI

    (a) Captain H. F. McGEE, USN.
    (b) Bridadier General McNIDER, AUS.
    (c) 158th Regimental Combat Team (Reinforced)

ANNEX (D)

SANGA SANGA

    (a) Captain J. D. MURPHY, USN.
    (b) Colonel MORONEY, AUS.
    (c) One Battalion Landing Team of 163rd Regimental Combat Team of 41st Infantry Division.

MASBATE

    (a) Captain H. B. HUDSON, USN.
    (b) Colonel STRATTA, AUS.
    (c) 108th Regimental Combat Team of 40th Infantry Division.

JOLO

    (a) Captain J. D. MURPHY, USN.
    (b) Colonel MORONEY, AUS.
    (c) Elements of 41st Infantry Division.

BUSANGAS

    (a) Commander L. R. NEVILLE, USN.
    (b)
    (c) Elements of the 186th Regimental Combat Team of 41st Infantry Division.

BOHOL

    (a) Captain W. V. DEUTERMANN, USN.
    (b)
    (c) 1 Battalion Landing Team of 164th Regimental Combat Team of Americal Division.

EL FRAILLE

    (a) Commander S. H. PATTIE, USN.
    (b) Lieutenant Colonel LOBIT, AUS.
    (c) 1st Battalion of 151st Regimental Combat Team of 38th Division.

PARANG, MINDANAO

    (a) Rear Admiral NOBLE, USN.
    (b) Lieutenant General SIEBERT, USA.
    (c) X Corps (24th and 31st Infantry Divisions)

ANNEX (D)

MACAJALAR

    (a) Rear Admiral STRUBLE, USN.
    (b)
    (c) 108th Regimental Combat Team of 40th Infantry Division.

TARAKAN

    (a) Rear Admiral ROYAL, USN.
    (b) Brigadier General WHITEHEAD, A.I.F.
    (c) 26th Australian Infantry Brigade Group (Reinforced) A.I.F.

BRUNEI BAY

    (a) Rear Admiral ROYAL, USN.
    (b) Major General G. F. WOOTEN, A.I.F.
    (c) 9th Australian Division (less 26th Brigade), A.I.F.

BALIKPAPAN

    (a) Rear Admiral NOBLE, USN.
    (b) Major General MILFORD, A.I.F.
    (c) 7th Australian Division, A.I.F. (plus Corps Artillery).

KOREAN OCCUPATION

    (a) Vice Admiral BARBEY, USN.
    (b) Lieutenant General HODGE, USA.
    (c) XXIV Corps.

    A. INITIAL LIFT

        (a) Commodore T. H. BRITTAIN, USN.
        (b) Major General A. V. ARNOLD, USA.
        (c) 7th Infantry Division.

    B. INITIAL FOLLOW-UP

        (a) Commodore J. H. PALMER, USN.
        (b) Brigadier General D. J. MEYERS, USA.
        (c) 40th Infantry Division.

ANNEX (D)

C. FINAL FOLLOW-UP

    (a) Commodore J. H. PALMER, USN.
    (b) Major General C. E. HURDIS, USA.
    (c) 6th Infantry Division.

CHINA OCCUPATION

    (a) Vice Admiral BARBEY, USN.
    (b) Major General K. E. ROCKEY, USMC.
    (c) III Marine Amphibious Corps.

1. TIENTSIN, CHINA

    (a) Commodore T. H. BRITTAIN, USN.
    (b) Major General De W. PECK, USMC.
    (c) 1st Marine Division.

2. TSINGTAO, CHINA

    (a) Commodore E. T. SHORT, USN.
    (b) Major General L. C. SHEPHERD, USMC.
    (c) SIXTH Marine Division.

ANNEX (E)

TABLE AND CHART SHOWING TROOPS AND CARGO TRANSPORTED IN MAJOR ASSAULT OPERATIONS

SEVENTH AMPHIBIOUS FORCE

ANNEX (E)

ANNEX (E)

Troops and Tonnage Carried by
SEVENTH AMPHIBIOUS FORCE
in Amphibious Assault Landings
30 June 1943 - 1 July 1945

Amphibious Shipping Lifts

Operation	Assault		Follow-Up		Total	
	Pers	Tons of Equip. & Supplies	Pers	Tons of Equip. & Supplies	Pers.	Tons of Equip. & Supplies
WOODLARK ISLAND	2,600	2,400	9,500	32,700	12,100	35,100
KIRIWINA ISLAND	2,500	1,400	2,200	6,400	4,700	7,800
LAE	7,800	3,300	8,700	8,900	16,500	12,200
FINSCHHAFEN	5,300	3,000	5,000	5,000	10,300	8,000
ARAWE	2,200	2,200	2,600	6,000	4,800	8,200
CAPE GLOUCESTER	12,500	8,700	11,500	14,300	24,000	23,000
SAIDOR	7,200	3,000			7,200	3,000
ADMIRALTY ISLANDS	1,000		8,300	14,500	9,300	14,500
AITAPE	6,300	4,700	10,100	12,800	16,400	17,500
HUMBOLDT BAY	8,400	4,800	13,400	18,800	21,800	23,600
TANAMERAH BAY	10,400	4,500	21,500	17,500	31,900	22,000
TOEM-WADKE	7,800	4,400	18,000	18,000	25,800	22,400
BIAK	7,500	5,600	21,000	20,300	28,500	25,900

ANNEX (E)

Troops and Tonnage Carried by SEVENTH AMPHIBIOUS FORCE in Amphibious Assault Landings
30 June 1943 - 1 July 1945

Amphibious Shipping Lifts

Operation	Assault Pers.	Assault :Tons of :Equip. & :Supplies	Follow-Up Pers.	Follow-Up :Tons of :Equip. & :Supplies	Total Pers.	Total :Tons of :Equip. & :Supplies
NOEMFOOR	7,100	5,900	13,400	18,500	20,500	24,400
SANSAPOR	7,300	4,800	20,900	40,300	28,200	45,100
MOROTAI	17,000	9,000	39,800	96,800	56,800	105,800
LEYTE	39,800	38,400	44,400	48,000	84,200	86,400
ORMOC	3,800	3,600	3,000	9,000	6,800	12,600
MINDORO	16,600	27,600	5,100	16,800	21,700	44,400
LINGAYEN	43,500	41,300	91,200	108,800	134,700	150,100
LUZON REINFORCEMENT			90,600	78,500	90,600	78,500
SUBIC BAY	44,400	53,400			44,400	53,400
NASUGBU	8,000	4,200			8,000	4,200
CORREGIDOR	4,300	6,400			4,300	6,400
PALAWAN	8,500	12,300	7,700	13,200	16,200	25,500
ZAMBOANGA	14,500	11,500	5,900	15,100	20,400	26,600
SULU ARCHIPELAGO	6,600	4,700	900	1,800	7,500	6,500

ANNEX (E)

Troops and Tonnage Carried by
SEVENTH AMPHIBIOUS FORCE
in Amphibious Assault Landings
30 June 1943 - 1 July 1945

Amphibious Shipping Lifts

Operation	Assault Pers.	Assault Tons of Equip. & Supplies	Follow-Up Pers.	Follow-Up Tons of Equip. & Supplies	Total Pers.	Total Tons of Equip. & Supplies
PANAY	9,800	10,500	3,400	7,100	13,200	17,600
CEBU	10,800	11,200	3,800	9,400	14,600	20,600
BOHOL-NEGROS	5,600	3,300			5,600	3,300
PARANG-MINDANAO	24,500	27,300	34,800	49,600	59,300	76,900
DAVAO-MINDANAO			4,100	8,000	4,100	8,000
MACAJALAR BAY, MINDANAO	4,100	3,600	1,500	3,000	5,600	6,600
LEGASPI	4,500	1,700	1,600	2,000	6,100	3,700
Minor Philippine Oper.	6,000	6,000			6,000	6,000
TARAKAN	13,500	15,200	4,600	7,700	18,100	22,900
BRUNEI BAY	25,400	26,200	8,100	23,300	33,500	49,500
BALIKPAPAN	25,000	26,800	8,600	26,800	33,600	53,600
TOTALS	432,100	402,900	525,200	758,900	957,300	1161,800

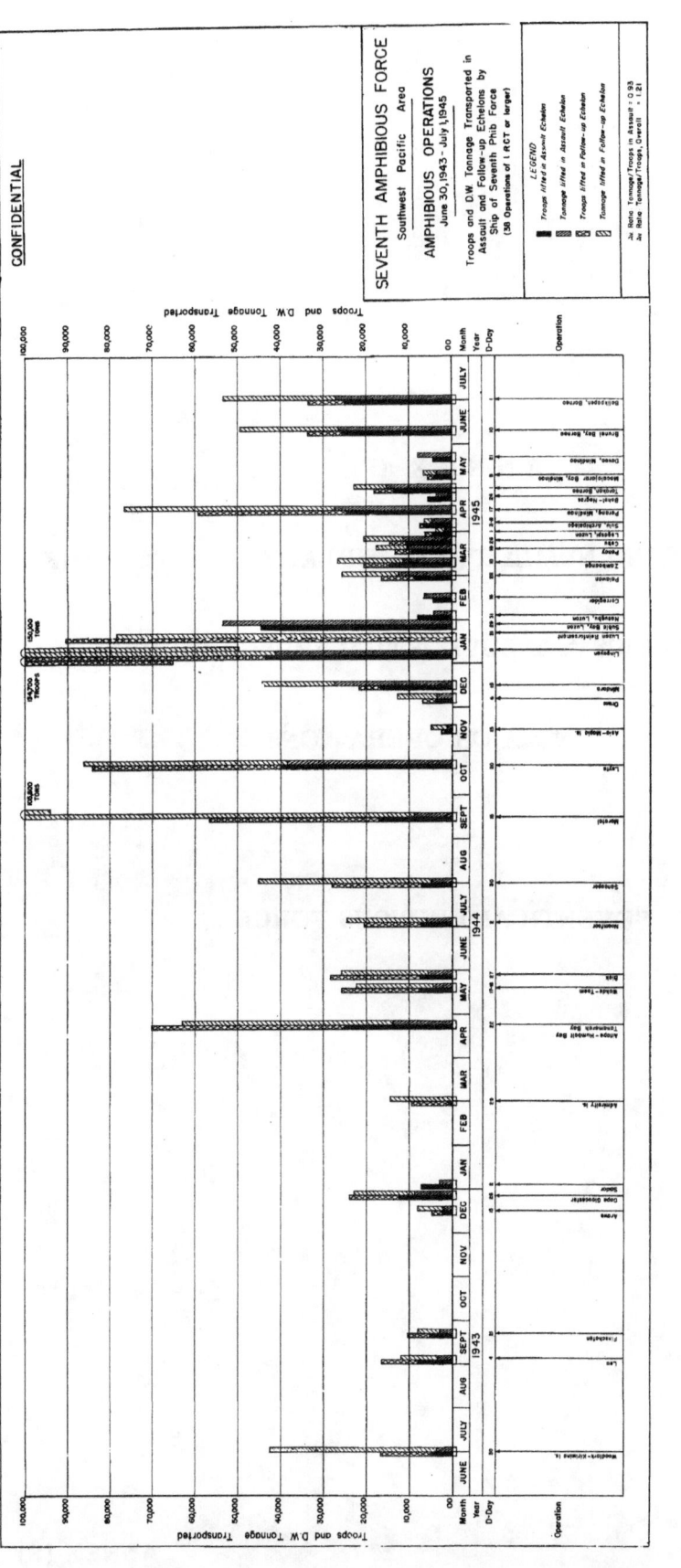

ANNEX (F)

CHART SHOWING NUMBER AND DISPLACEMENT TONNAGE

OF AMPHIBIOUS AND SUPPORTING SHIPS EMPLOYED

IN MAJOR OPERATIONS

SEVENTH AMPHIBIOUS FORCE

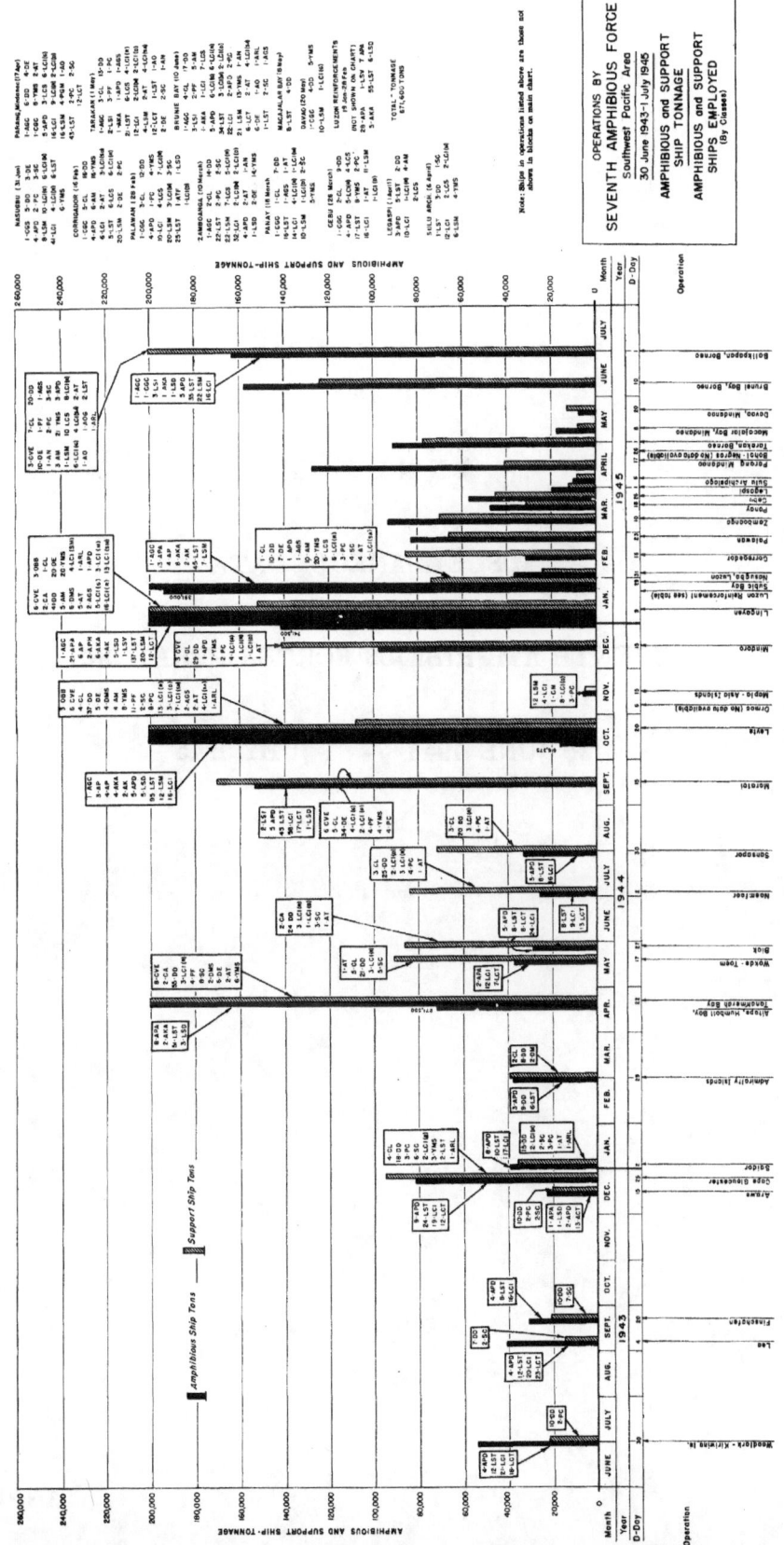

ANNEX (G)

MISCELLANEOUS DATA

SEVENTH AMPHIBIOUS FORCE OPERATIONS

30 JUNE 1943 - 1 JULY 1945

ANNEX (G)

ANNEX (G)

MISCELLANEOUS DATA

SEVENTH AMPHIBIOUS FORCE OPERATIONS
30 JUNE 1943 - 1 JULY 1945

Operations	Times H-Hour : Sunrise	Carrier Air Support Available	Staging Area	Distance from Staging Area
WOODLARK	2100(K) : 0630(K)	No	Milne Bay	150
KIRIWINA	0630(K) : 0611(K)	No	Townsville, Australia.	710
LAE	0630(K) : 0612(K)	No	Buna Milne Bay	150 320
FINSCHHAFEN	0445(K) : 0558(K)	No	Lae Buna	60 140
ARAWE	0630(L) : 0646(L)	No	Goodenough Is.	245
GLOUCESTER	0715(L) : 0653(L)	No	Buna Goodenough Is. Milne Bay	210 270 385
SAIDOR	0650(K) : 0605(K)	No	Goodenough Is.	340
ADMIRALTY ISLANDS	0815(L) : 0820(L)	No	Buna	430
AITAPE	0645(K) : 0626(K)	Yes	Finschhafen	430*
HUMBOLDT BAY	0700(K) : 0634(K)	Yes	Finschhafen	520*
TANAHMERAH BAY	0700(K) : 0636(K)	Yes	Goodenough Is.	820*
TOEM-WADKE	0800(K) : 0640(K)	No	Aitape	225
BIAK	0715(K) : 0651(K)	No	Humboldt Bay	300

*Direct. A devious route was used by assault echelons.

G-1

ANNEX (G)

MISCELLANEOUS DATA

SEVENTH AMPHIBIOUS FORCE OPERATIONS
30 JUNE 1943 — 1 JULY 1945

Operations	Times H-Hour : Sunrise	Carrier Air Support Available	Staging Area	Distance from Staging Area
NOEMFOOR	0800(K) : 0703(K)	No	Toem	265
SANSAPOR	0700(K) : 0715(K)	No	Toem	440
MOROTAI	0830(I) : 0622(I)	Yes	Aitape Toem	905 690
LEYTE	1000(I) : 0630(I)	Yes	Hollandia Manus Finschhafen	1240 1565 2075
ORMOC	:	Yes	Leyte	160
MINDORO	: 0709(I)	Yes	Leyte	480
LINGAYEN	0930(I) : 0730(I)	Yes	Aitape Sansapor	2135 1835
LUZON REINFORCEMENT	— : —	Yes	Leyte Morotai Biak	810 1380 1770
ZAMBALES SUBIC BAY	0830(I) : 0730(I)	Yes	Leyte	640
NASUGBU	0815(I) : 0728(I)	No	Leyte	560
CORREGIDOR	0900(I) : 0721(I)	No	Subic Bay	25
PALAWAN	0845(I) : 0719(I)	No	Mindoro	285
ZAMBOANGA	0915(I) : 0701(I)	No	Mindoro	335

ANNEX (G)

MISCELLANEOUS DATA

SEVENTH AMPHIBIOUS FORCE OPERATIONS
30 JUNE 1943 - 1 JULY 1945

Operations	Times H-Hour	Sunrise	Carrier Air Support Available	Staging Area	Distance from Staging Area
SULU ARCHIPELAGO	0800(I)	0649(I)	No	Zamboanga	175
PANAY	0830(I)	0655(I)	No	Lingayen	525
CEBU	0830(I)	0646(I)	No	Leyte	235
PARANG MINDANAO	0800(I)	0635(I)	No	Mindoro Morotai	490 470
DAVAO		0622(I)	No	Parang	270
MACAJALAR BAY, MINDANAO		0623(I)	No	Ormoc	150
LEGASPI	1000(I)	0642(I)	No	Subic Bay	360
TARAKAN	0815(I)	0700(I)	No	Morotai	650
BRUNEI BAY	0915(I)	0705(I)	No	Morotai	950
BALIKPAPAN	0900(I)	0715(I)	Yes	Morotai	800

G-3

ANNEX (H)

LIST OF CODE NAMES USED TO DESIGNATE OPERATIONS

GEOGRAPHICAL LOCATIONS AND TASK FORCES

IN THE SOUTHWEST PACIFIC AREA

SEVENTH AMPHIBIOUS FORCE
OPERATIONS

ANNEX (H)

CODE NAMES

Used in Southwest Pacific Area

NAME OF OPERATION	OPERATION CODE	GEOGRAPHICAL CODE NAME
WOODLARK	CHRONICLE	MANTLE SHELF
KIRIWINA	CHRONICLE	
LAE	POSTERN	BINOCULARS
FINSCHHAFEN		DIMINISH
ARAWE	BY PRODUCT	DIRECTOR
CAPE GLOUCESTER	BACKHANDER	BACKHANDER
SAIDOR	MICHAELMAS	MICHAELMAS
ADMIRALTY ISLANDS	DEXTERITY	BREWER
AITAPE	RECKLESS	PERSECUTION
HUMBOLDT	RECKLESS	LETTERPRESS
TANAMERAH	RECKLESS	NOISELESS
WADKE	STRAIGHT LINE	STICKATNOUGHT
BIAK	HORLICKS	HORLICKS
NOEMFOOR	TABLETENNIS	TABLETENNIS
SANSAPOR	GLOBETROTTER	
MOROTAI	INTERLUDE	
LEYTE	MUSKETEER - KING TWO	ACCUMULATION
MAPIA-ASIA	ISLAND	
ORMOC		

H-1

ANNEX (H)

NAME OF OPERATION	OPERATION CODE	GEOGRAPHICAL CODE NAME
MINDORO	MUSKETEER - LOVE THREE	NOTE: In later stages of SWPA Campaign the practice of using code name to indicate geographical location fell into disuse.
LINGAYEN	MUSKETEER - MIKE ONE	
ZAMBALES	MIKE SEVEN	
BATAAN-COOREGIDOR		
PALAWAN	VICTOR THREE	
LUBANG		
ZAMBOANGA	VICTOR FOUR	
CEBU	VICTOR TWO	
CABALLO ISLAND		
NEGROS ISLAND		
LEGASPI		
SULU ARCH		
PANAY	VICTOR ONE	
VISAYAN ISLANDS		
BOHOL ISLAND		
EL FRAILE		
CARABAO		
PARANG	VICTOR FIVE	
TARAKAN	OBOE ONE	
BRUNEI BAY	OBOE SIX	

H-2

ANNEX (H)

NAME OF OPERATION	OPERATION CODE	GEOGRAPHICAL CODE NAME
BALIKPAPAN	OBOE TWO	
JINSEN, KOREA	CAMPUS	
TIENTSIN	BELEAGER	

ADDITIONAL GEOGRAPHICAL CODE NAMES

PLACE	GEOGRAPHICAL CODE NAME
ADMIRALTY ISLAND	BREWER
AITAPE	PERSECUTION
BRISBANE	AMATORY
CAIRNS	LARDY DARDY
CAPE CRETIN	SHAGGY
DAVAO	BLAZE UP
DOROMENA	BEGONIA
FINSCHHAFEN	RED HERRING
GASMATA	LAZARETTO
GOODENOUGH ISLAND	AMOEBA-MICROCOSM
GUADALCANAL	MAIN YARD - CACTUS
HALMAHERA ISLAND	FEARSOME
HOLLANDIA	BEWITCH-RECKLESS
HUMBOLDT BAY	LETTERPRESS
KIRIWINA	BIRTHDAY
KAIBOLA	ORATOR

H-3

ANNEX (H)

PLACE	GEOGRAPHICAL CODE NAME
LAE	SCHOOL BOY
LOS NEGROS	UNDER DOG
MADANG	EQUILIBRIUM
MANADO, CELEBES	KITCHEN MAID
MANUS	TEACUP - MERCANTILE
MILNE BAY	PEMMICAN-BENEVOLENT
NEW BRITAIN	ARABIC
MUNDA	JACONET
NEW CALEDONIA	CHECKSTRAP - POPPY
NEW GEORGIA	APERIANT
NEW GUINEA ISLANDS	CENTRAL
NEW IRELAND ISLANDS	CARDIAC
NEW ZEALAND	SPOONER
NOUMEA	LECTERN - WHITE POPPY
ORO BAY	CELLULOID
PERTH	BRAVES
PORT DARWIN	ASTER
PORT MORESBEY	SCARAMOUCHE-CARAMEL
RABAUL	MEMSAHIB
RENDOVA ISLAND	DOWISER
RUSSEL ISLANDS	EMERITUS

ANNEX (H)

PLACE	GEOGRAPHICAL CODE NAME
SAIDOR	MICHAELMAS
SALAMAUA	DOUBLET
SARMI (NEW GUINEA)	NOSERING
SEA ADLER HARBOR	BICARBONATE
SOLOMON ISLANDS	ARTHRITIS
TALAUD ISLAND	GOSSIP MONGER
TANAMERAH	MAWSEED
TOWNSVILLE	CALLOUS
TRUK	LUGSAIL
TULAGI	ANACONDA - RING BOLT
VELLA LAVELLA	DOGEARED
VITIAZ POINT	BOILING POINT
WEWAK	PIPSQUEAK
WOENDI	STINKER

ORGANIZATIONAL CODE NAMES

NAME	CODE NAME
503rd Parachute Infantry Regiment	UNCAGE
NEW BRITAIN Force (6th Army)	ESCALATOR
NEW BRITAIN Force (non-secret)	ALAMO
NEW GUINEA Force	NATIVE

ANNEX (H)

NAME	CODE NAME
7TH AUSTRALIAN Infantry Division	OUTLOOK
South Pacific Forces in SWPA	IRON GREY

These code names were principally in use during the NEW GUINEA phase of the war in the Southwest Pacific Area.

There were some operations which had no code names, principally because they were done on despatch orders or because they were part of an overall operations such as NEGROS which was part of Victor Two. After the war moved to the PHILIPPINE Area the use of Geographical code names fell into disuse except for use as shipping designators.

www.ingramcontent.com/pod-product-compliance
Lightning Source LLC
Chambersburg PA
CBHW082120230426
43671CB00015B/2756